VOCABULARIANS

VOCABULARIANS
Integrated Word Study in the Middle Grades

Stenhouse PUBLISHERS
www.stenhouse.com

Portland, Maine

Brenda J. **Overturf** with Leslie H. **Montgomery** and Margot Holmes **Smith**

Stenhouse Publishers
www.stenhouse.com

Every effort has been made to contact copyright holders and students for permission to reproduce borrowed material. We regret any oversights that may have occurred and will be pleased to rectify them in subsequent reprints of the work.

Credits
Figure 3.3: Text from *The Big Wave* by Pearl S. Buck. Copyright © 1947 by the Curtis Publishing Company; Copyright © 1948, 1976 by Pearl S. Buck. Used by permission of HarperCollins Publishers.
Appendix B: "Concept of Definition Map" by Robert M. Schwartz and Taffy E. Raphael. From "Concept of Definition: A Key to Improving Students' Vocabulary," *The Reading Teacher*, Vol. 39, No. 2. Copyright © 1985. Published by International Literacy Association.
Appendix C: "Semantic Feature Analysis" by Patricia L. Anders and Candace S. Bos. From "Semantic Feature Analysis: An Interactive Strategy for Vocabulary Development and Text Comprehension," *Journal of Reading*, Vol. 29, No. 7. Copyright © 1986. Published by International Literacy Association.
Appendix D: Adapted Frayer Model based on "A Schema for Testing the Level of Cognitive Mastery" (working paper) by D. Frayer, W. C. Frederick, and H. J. Klausmeier. Copyright © 1969, Wisconsin Research and Development Center for Cognitive Learning.

Library of Congress Cataloging-in-Publication Data
Overturf, Brenda J.
   Vocabularians : integrated word study in the middle grades / Brenda J. Overturf ; with Leslie H. Montgomery and Margot Holmes Smith.
   pages cm
Includes bibliographical references and index.
ISBN 978-1-62531-016-3 (pbk. : alk. paper) -- ISBN 978-1-62531-047-7 (ebook) 1. Vocabulary--Study and teacher (Middle school) I. Title
LB1631.O87 2015
372.6'1--dc23
                                                                    2014048052

Cover design, interior design, and typesetting by Brigitte Coffman

Manufactured in the United States of America

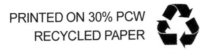

PRINTED ON 30% PCW
RECYCLED PAPER

21 20 19 18 17 16 15   9 8 7 6 5 4 3 2 1

For the possibilities that young adolescents represent

Contents

Acknowledgments • viii

Introduction • 1

Chapter 1: Why Focus on Vocabulary Development? • 9

Chapter 2: Organizing for Middle Grades Vocabulary Development • 31

Chapter 3: Words and Context • 53

Chapter 4: Developing Morphological Awareness • 71

Chapter 5: A Deeper Dive into Words and Phrases • 89

Chapter 6: Creative Practice for Vocabulary Prowess • 117

Chapter 7: Assessing Vocabulary Learning • 141

Epilogue • 163

Appendix A: Crystal Ball Words • 173

Appendix B: Concept of Definition Map • 174

Appendix C: Semantic Feature Analysis • 175

Appendix D: Adapted Frayer Model • 176

Appendix E: Vocabulary Journal Organizer • 177

References • 179

Index • 199

Acknowledgments

Many people make a book a reality. Of course, Leslie Montgomery and Margot Holmes Smith, my coauthors on *Word Nerds: Teaching All Students to Learn and Love Vocabulary,* are at the top of the list for this one. Their perceptions about vocabulary development in the classroom are a continuous inspiration to me and to countless other educators.

The dedicated scholarship of vocabulary researchers has certainly provided a solid base for insights shared in this book, and I appreciate and respect their contributions to the field.

Thank you to Holly Holland, dream editor at Stenhouse, who is a thoughtful and visionary colleague and makes writing a book a labor of love. I am so grateful for the expertise of people like Louisa, Jay, Chris, Chuck, Rebecca, and Chandra, who make the details flow into a finished product and enthusiastically support the work.

Of course, I owe much, much gratitude to the middle grades teachers and administrators who took a chance and loaned their time, attention, and expertise to this project. It is not always easy to change schedules and adjust priorities in order to try something new together and share ideas. My utmost appreciation goes to educators at Thea Bowman Leadership Academy, Eastside Middle School, and Bullitt Lick Middle School who worked to adapt *Word Nerds* to middle grades classrooms and thought so creatively about ways to make strategic vocabulary instruction a part of school lives for hundreds of students. They are

Christine Bolton
Gabrielle Brenston
Susan Carlisle
Julie Cox
Maurice Culver
Stephen Currie
Tabi Echols
Jennifer Geddes
Don Hollandsworth
Robert Kuprenas
Karen Muench
Brandi Odom
Trish Priddy
Michael Roccaforte
Kimberly Thompson

Tonie Weddle
Charles Williams

A million thanks for letting me learn from you and your students.

    As always, lots of love and gratitude go to my family, especially Jim and Obie, who gave me time and kept me going so I could write. I appreciate you more than you know.

INTRODUCTION

A bright June sun beckoned as the academic year slowed to an end at Eastside Middle School in Mt. Washington, Kentucky. Anticipation permeated the room—a mixture of excitement that the semester was almost over and early nostalgia for the kids and teachers who would soon disperse. I recognized the feeling, as the building began to transform from a place where students live and learn every day to an almost haunted space during the empty summer months.

Kerrigan and I were tucked into a corner of the library. She sat on a sofa across from me, cheerfully chatting about her vocabulary experiences during that spring of her eighth-grade year. After she explained why she thought it was important to learn new words, our talk turned to challenges.

"So, was there any particular word that gave you a hard time this year?" I asked.

Kerrigan tossed her long braid and thought a minute. "I don't know . . . Yeah, it was a word like coll . . . ? Cloak? Colloak?"

I took a guess. "Colloquial?"

She brightened. "Yes! *Colloquial*—I still can't pronounce that word! Like, I had never heard it or seen it before. So I was like, I don't even know what this is! And then when I found out, I thought it was ironic that it was such a big word and it just means something casual."

I hid my smile at the example of irony in her statement. Only a middle schooler could be so naive and so wise at the same time! And even though Kerrigan still had a hard time pronouncing this particular challenging word, she certainly knows what it means. She can recognize it in text and interpret the meaning in context, and she can use the word in her own writing. She also now knows the meaning of many other terms that will help her in high school and beyond. Kerrigan has learned to be fascinated by words and the turn of a phrase.

The Birth of a Vocabulary Plan

When Leslie Montgomery, Margot Holmes Smith, and I wrote *Word Nerds: Teaching All Students to Learn and Love Vocabulary* (2013), we set out to describe the strategic, intentional vocabulary plan we had implemented in their elementary school classrooms. I worked with Margot and Leslie for more than two years, observing lessons and working as a team to refine vocabulary instruction and assessment.

These two teachers are, quite frankly, remarkable at what they do. On our journey, we observed culturally diverse elementary grades students developing an enthusiastic desire to tackle the meanings of unfamiliar words in reading and to use the new words in their speech and writing. Most of Margot's and Leslie's students are growing up in poverty, and many had experienced little academic language outside of school. Before we began our vocabulary study, the students had rarely been challenged to learn the often sophisticated terms used in texts from various content areas. Because Leslie and Margot care deeply that their students are prepared for higher learning, they recognized that weak vocabulary knowledge was a major barrier to their success. Their kids did not have "word confidence" and were afraid to take risks with language.

Although there are many excellent resources available on both vocabulary research and vocabulary strategies, *Word Nerds* showed teachers how to implement comprehensive vocabulary instruction in ways that engage students. Leslie, Margot, and I described an easily adapted, research-based, five-part plan for teaching vocabulary and word-learning strategies. No special materials were needed—just good planning and teaching that meets the needs of all students.

The two-week word study cycle for elementary students described in *Word Nerds* includes the following:

1. Introducing, in context, five to seven carefully selected words and relating these words to the students' lives as they begin keeping vocabulary journals.
2. Adding two appropriate synonyms/examples and two appropriate antonyms/non-examples of each word and completing vocabulary journal entries.
3. Practicing vocabulary using active and engaging strategies involving art, music, drama, technology, literature, writing, movement, games, and test-taking skills.
4. Celebrating word learning with a vocabulary party, which secretly serves as a review.
5. Assessing students' knowledge of words from the two-week vocabulary cycle, as well as some words from previous cycles.

Leslie's and Margot's students thrived within this framework. They began learning and loving vocabulary, recognizing and relating words to concepts from subjects other than language arts, and using new vocabulary in their conversations and writing. And here's more good news: Teachers throughout the country, in varied schools and grade levels, shared how they used and adapted *Word Nerds* in their own classrooms to achieve similar results. Other high-poverty schools, including schools with large numbers of English language learners, as well as schools serving more affluent students have contacted us. Teachers of hearing-impaired students, speech language pathologists, and special education teachers have also shared their successes. We have found that all elementary children can learn and love new vocabulary when teachers learn and love teaching word study in ways that make sense to students.

Turning to the Middle Level

Word Nerds focuses on grades kindergarten through five and is ideal for teachers who have access to their students most of the school day. Since *Word Nerds* was published, however, many teachers, principals, curriculum directors, and staff developers have reached out to us and asked, "Are you planning to write a middle school version? We need to know how to adapt this for our older kids!"

Of course, we know that middle grades students greatly need vocabulary development. But the typical schedule of forty-five- to sixty-minute classes with a range of teachers looks very different from an elementary school schedule. This presents distinct challenges to the unified and comprehensive vocabulary model shown in *Word Nerds*. Students at the middle level are also different from elementary students in significant ways as they grow physically, emotionally, psychologically, and socially. This means a unique set of instructional needs must be met if students in the middle grades are going to be successful. While teachers of students in grades five through nine may understand that vocabulary is important, they often need to know more about how to teach students to become word learners beyond assigning vocabulary lists to memorize each week. And then there is the question of who should actually be responsible for vocabulary teaching in the middle grades as students travel from teacher to teacher.

How do I know? I spent twenty years in the classroom, teaching grades one through eight in city, suburban, and rural schools. I taught fifth and sixth grades in a self-contained elementary classroom and grades six through eight in a departmentalized middle school, and I was the leader of an interdisciplinary middle school team that was known for innovation. My classes have contained gifted students, students with disabilities, and students whose first language was not English. I also have some experience teaching middle grade mathematics, science, and social studies, but for the most part, I concentrated in English language arts. I am all too familiar with the juggling act of trying to balance reading instruction, writing instruction, and language development—while meeting the varied needs of students in one class period a day. When I decided to earn a doctoral degree, my dissertation focused on middle grades reading instruction across the curriculum.

What I learned about middle grades students and vocabulary development is that many young adolescents still have gaps in their word knowledge and lack a solid academic base to support their learning. They may have a basic understanding of a concept but lack the vocabulary to fully express their knowledge. Sometimes the vocabulary gaps keep them from learning a concept, and other times, they don't know that a new word is just a synonym for one they already know. When they look up words in the dictionary, they often choose the simplest definition, no matter that it does not fit the context of the sentence. Even students who have been labeled "gifted" often use words incorrectly or stick to words they already know when writing. Although my students needed good vocabulary instruction, as most middle school kids do, I was not always the best teacher when it came to word study. Quite frankly, there was little information about how to teach it well.

When I left the classroom, I became a middle school project coordinator at the Ohio Valley Educational Cooperative. I coached teachers and led staff development, with a special focus on literacy practices. It quickly became apparent that many teachers shared my frustration about how to engage students with rich vocabulary development, and they knew the learning gasps were hindering students' success. Here's an example I shared in *Word Nerds*:

Several years ago Brenda was leading a workshop with middle school teachers from nine different school districts. In Kentucky students are required to write short answers to extended response questions as part of the assessment in grades three through twelve, and these teachers said their students had performed poorly on the tests. The teachers were surprised and frustrated by the results because previous class work and practice tests had suggested that students knew the content covered on the exams.

"I know my kids! I know they know this stuff!" exclaimed Joe, a seventh-grade social studies teacher.

Heads nodded around the room, as other teachers agreed with his statement.

"Then why aren't they showing it on the test?" Brenda asked.

As a group, the teachers brainstormed possible reasons. Brenda encouraged them to think about student behaviors they had observed during the last test session.

"It's like some of them just quit trying in the middle of a question," said Margaret, a sixth-grade language arts teacher.

"Not just some of them. A lot of them," added Susan, a teacher of eighth-grade science.

After a moment, Joe quietly said, "Maybe they are shutting down because they don't know the vocabulary."

Immediately the other teachers caught fire with the same recognition. As they discussed the issue, many teachers acknowledged that they hadn't taught vocabulary explicitly or they had used less sophisticated words in class when the test required students to recognize and know appropriate subject matter terms. No wonder students were shutting down on the exams! As a result of that workshop, Brenda and the other teachers collaborated on a vocabulary list for each subject area and teachers learned new ways to teach vocabulary within content area classes. (Overturf, Montgomery, and Smith 2013, 29)

When I later became the coordinator for reading curriculum and assessment in a large urban school district and then a literacy instructor at the University of Louisville, I still did not see much intentional attention to vocabulary development that really helps kids learn. Then Margot and Leslie became my graduate students, and all that changed.

Developing Vocabularians

Skip forward to the fall of 2013. *Word Nerds* had been in the hands of teachers for a few months, and it seemed to resonate with elementary educators. But I was still thinking about the potential for the middle grades.

During my presentation at a national teaching conference, I included research about the need for vocabulary development in the middle grades and challenged teachers to think about ways they could add or enhance word study in their own classrooms and teams. Charles Williams, an assistant principal from Thea Bowman Leadership Academy in Gary, Indiana, approached me at the end of the session and shared that teachers at his school were struggling to integrate vocabulary instruction in their interdisciplinary teams. We agreed to collaborate on some action research that planted the first seeds of *Vocabularians*. Williams had been an English language arts teacher on a middle school team, and he was eager to adapt the ideas in *Word Nerds* at Bowman.

When I returned home to Louisville, I reached out to colleagues at Eastside Middle School in nearby Bullitt County, Kentucky. At Eastside, teachers have formed highly effective professional learning communities (PLCs) where they plan instruction and monitor student achievement together. Tabi Echols, the district resource teacher who leads all the content PLCs at the school, volunteered to help me figure out how to adapt *Word Nerds* to a schoolwide initiative.

A few weeks later, when I shared my presentation about *Word Nerds* to a K–12 audience at a state conference, my third collaboration was born. Tonie Weddle, an English language arts teacher at Bullitt Lick Middle School, a Title I school in Shepherdsville, Kentucky, reported having had some success with a beginning vocabulary plan. She volunteered to adapt *Word Nerds* in her classroom. I was thrilled! A group of excellent educators with a keen awareness of the importance of vocabulary development were eager to try the ideas in *Word Nerds*, and each had a plan to proceed.

Then reality hit—hard. The winter of 2013–2014 was the worst in decades. Local weather forecasters nicknamed the season "Snowmageddon." All three schools in my vocabulary partnership had multiple closings, late starts, and early dismissals due to dangerous weather conditions. The snow and subzero temperatures would not let up, and faculties struggled to maintain a routine with anything, much less unfamiliar vocabulary instruction. Many of my planned school visits had to be rescheduled, and I realized that we might not be able to finish this project on time. As Sinclair Lewis said, "Winter is not a season, it's an occupation."

In the face of extreme challenges, dedicated teachers at these schools still found ways to thoughtfully incorporate vocabulary instruction and assessment. It was not easy, but they were determined because they knew that vocabulary learning must be a priority for their students. As Weddle explained, "If my kids know things like problem and solution, cause and effect, or how to write short answers but can't support their thinking because they don't understand the words or the meaning of a phrase, then they are missing the whole thing. They need to know vocabulary and ways to understand words before they can think more deeply."

As teachers and I worked together to adapt *Word Nerds* to middle grades settings, we thought about ways to include vocabulary instruction into already tight schedules, ideas for transferring strategies across the curriculum, and how to assess for vocabulary learning. Teachers planned instruction to meet standards and tried creative and motivating activities with their students in varied subject areas. Most of all, educators engaged in collaborative dialogue about vocabulary teaching and learning in the middle grades as they explored how to make it a natural part of their classes.

Students Respond

Although the teachers' enthusiasm for integrated vocabulary instruction encouraged me to continue refining the model, the best inspiration came from the students. Through our shared practices, middle-level students learned that vocabulary knowledge can be transformative. They are becoming *vocabularians*—learners who use appropriate words with ease when reading, writing, and speaking across the curriculum.

Remember Kerrigan? She has learned that vocabulary is powerful life knowledge, and interesting words are not only found in the classroom. Kerrigan says, "It's nice having a big vocabulary because it makes you sound more intelligent in whatever you're writing or when you are taking a test, just anywhere really. Vocabulary also really helps in reading. And then once you learn a new word, it pops up everywhere! It's like once you get glasses you notice a lot of people have glasses. So once you get something, you're more attuned to noticing it."

Kerrigan's insightful comment actually has a basis in cognitive science. Known as *frequency illusion*, or the Baader-Meinhof phenomenon, it's the process of suddenly noticing a new word or idea almost everywhere. It may seem as if the word or idea has become explosively common, but in fact, the brain has merely developed selective attention and confirmation bias.

"And that's how it is with vocabulary," Kerrigan says. "A lot of times I'll learn a new word and that week I'll just be reading my book and all of a sudden I'll be like, 'Whoa! This word is actually used pretty commonly!' So it helps your vocabulary grow because you just didn't think about it like that before. You don't have to force that word into your vocabulary because it's not that weird to hear it."

Kerrigan is a vocabularian.

Then there's Carter, a young wordsmith who appreciates language and how it is used. Just a seventh grader at Eastside, he has already learned the power of word knowledge and the command that vocabulary can wield. At twelve, he understands that vocabulary is a key to learning.

"Vocabulary helps you because the more you know words, the more fluent you can be in reading, the better you can read and write, and the better your writing sounds," he says. "You can also read more challenging books. There's always going to be a time when you have to sound professional, whether you're applying for a job or anything else. You're just going to have to know how to use a good vocabulary."

Carter is a vocabularian, too.

As teachers, we want all students to be as confident as Carter, to have the knowledge and skills to determine the meanings of unfamiliar words and phrases when they read texts or listen to speakers. We want them to be able to show what they can do on standardized assessments in all subject areas because they are not disoriented or disrupted by the words on the test.

And like it or not, we are often judged by our command of vocabulary. As Steven Stahl (2005, 95) said, "The words we use define who we are."

Eighth-grader Ally at Eastside mirrored Stahl's observation when she earnestly explained, "I feel vocabulary is a big part of my life because I refuse to lower my standards. I'm trying to reach higher and I think expanding my vocabulary makes me expand who I am. It gives me more details to express myself and help me learn."

Vocabularians reach higher when it comes to word study, which, in turn, helps them prepare for college and careers. Ally is certainly a vocabularian as well.

Are you ready to help your students become wordsmiths like Ally, Carter, and Kerrigan? Join us as we work together to extend the reach and strength of middle-level vocabulary. Maybe, like Ally, we will also expand who we are in the process.

Chapter 1

WHY FOCUS ON VOCABULARY DEVELOPMENT?

The limits of my language are the limits of my mind. All I know is what I have words for.
—Ludwig Wittgenstein

It is an indisputable fact: Knowing more words usually leads to better success in school. At least one hundred years of research has demonstrated the importance of vocabulary development to academic progress. In one of the most prominent vocabulary studies, Keith Stanovich found that students who have a solid word base get ahead faster and achieve more in school, while students with a less-developed vocabulary tend to progress more slowly (Stanovich 1986). He named this theory the Matthew effect, after the Bible verse that is often paraphrased as, "The rich get richer and the poor get poorer."

Students with strong vocabulary knowledge make more extensive connections to words they already know, so they learn more new words at a faster pace. Students who do not possess such a vocabulary base also learn words but not as quickly or as extensively. This achievement gap often grows as students advance through school. Gaps in reading performance are typically associated with gaps in vocabulary knowledge (Anderson and Nagy 1991; Stahl and Fairbanks 1986).

The National Assessment of Educational Progress (NAEP), considered the nation's report card, began assessing vocabulary as part of reading passage comprehension in 2009 and conducted a further study to understand the results (National Center for Education Statistics [NCES] 2012). The NAEP study showed that students who scored higher on vocabulary questions also scored higher in reading comprehension and that students' ability to determine the meanings of words was directly related to reading achievement. Instead of testing words in isolation, NAEP asks students to read passages and determine how words are used in particular contexts. As the report states, "a reader may understand the meaning of 'acute' in the context of mathematics to describe the angles of a triangle, but may not have encountered the word used to describe human emotions, as in 'acute embarrassment.' Having a sense of words that is sufficiently flexible helps readers extend their understanding of the word and understand its use in a new context" (NCES 2012, 1). But not all students own this flexible sense of words.

Vocabulary deficits are often tied to poverty. Betty Hart and Todd Risley's (1995) far-reaching research on word knowledge and socioeconomic levels demonstrated the difference between the vocabulary of students who come from poverty versus those who come from more affluent backgrounds. Preschool children who grew up in homes with higher incomes (often correlated with the level of parent education) knew almost three times as many words before they began school than children who came from low-income homes. The difference was so stark that Hart and Risley called it the "thirty million word gap."

Vocabulary knowledge in the early primary grades has been found to be a significant predictor of reading comprehension in the middle and secondary grades (Cunningham and Stanovich 1997). When students reach the middle grades, concepts become more complicated and the words used to express them become more challenging. Researchers estimate that the average kindergarten student starts school with an oral vocabulary of about ten thousand words but naturally has a very small reading vocabulary. Students typically learn approximately three thousand to four thousand words a year, amassing a reading vocabulary of about fifty thousand words by the end of high school (Graves 2006; Nagy and Herman 1987). However, students who begin school with a linguistic disadvantage must play catch up throughout their education.

Although most educators understand that vocabulary is important, attention to developing language is not occurring for many middle-level students (e.g., Scott, Jamieson-Noel, and Asselin 2003; Watts 1995). The need is most acute in schools that serve students living in poverty. As Michael Kieffer and Nonie Lesaux (2010, 48) note, "In under-resourced schools in urban settings, a large number of students reach sixth grade without gaining the sophisticated vocabulary they need to read for understanding." Researchers agree that in the middle grades there should also be an emphasis on academic language, or the "word knowledge that makes it possible for students to engage with, produce, and talk about texts that are valued in school" (Flynt and Brozo 2008, 500). William Nagy and Dianna Townsend see academic words as "tools for communicating and thinking about disciplinary content" (2012, 105).

If vocabulary development is so essential, why does it not receive more consistent attention in the middle grades?

The Middle Grades Vocabulary Challenge

One of the reasons is confusion. Researchers do not always agree about the best ways to teach vocabulary. According to the Report of the National Reading Panel, *Teaching Children to Read* (National Institute of Child Health and Human Development 2000, 4–27), "a great deal is known about the ways in which vocabulary increases under highly controlled conditions, but much less is known about the ways in which such growth can be fostered in instructional contexts."

For example, some researchers believe that vocabulary instruction should focus on a small number of words (Graves et al. 2013; Kelley et al. 2010), while others advocate for a frequent avalanche of new words (Blachowicz and Fisher 2010; Brabham et al. 2012; Pressley 2008). Researchers also disagree about whether words included in vocabulary study should mostly be those that students will see in multiple contexts (Beck, McKeown, and Kucan 2002) or in specific content areas (Marzano and Simms 2013). Some researchers have found that many words can be learned through context (Nagy et al. 1987; Sternberg 1987; Swanborn and de Glopper 1999), while others share evidence that context is not so helpful in determining the meanings of unfamiliar words (Adams 2011; Beck, McKeown, and Kucan 2002). And some believe that teaching certain types of context clues is important (Baumann et al. 2012), whereas others think teaching context clue types is probably not a very worthwhile activity (Graves 2006).

In *Word Nerds*, we chose a balanced approach to vocabulary development. Our elementary grades students thrived with the intensive and consistent attention to word study. Let's take a look at how this work extends to the middle grades.

A Framework for Vocabulary Instruction

When Margot, Leslie, and I wrote *Word Nerds*, we based our plan on Michael Graves's (2006, 2007, 2009) four-part framework for vocabulary instruction. This is a framework respected by many vocabulary scholars that can increase vocabulary achievement (Baumann, Ware, and Edwards 2007). This framework, as depicted in Figure 1.1, can also become the backbone of a middle school vocabulary plan.

Graves's framework places vocabulary instruction within rich and varied language experiences in all content areas and throughout the school day. In our own experience, this means that

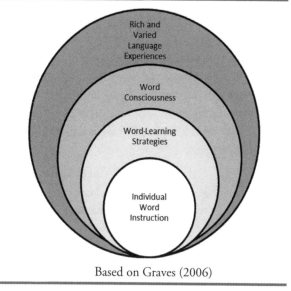

Based on Graves (2006)

Figure 1.1 *A model of strategic vocabulary instruction*

students read different types of texts in different types of groups (whole group, small group, pairs, reading for research, and independent reading). They write varied texts for authentic reasons. They engage in discussions, listen to teachers and peers read aloud with expression and purpose, listen to and critique speakers, and prepare and present multi-media experiences.

Within a classroom environment of rich and varied language experiences, we help students develop "word consciousness" by flooding the classroom with interesting and related vocabulary. We model new and unfamiliar words for students in classroom talk and encourage students to try them on for size in discussions. The classroom has a sense of fun with words and word learning.

We also help students learn how to determine the meanings of unfamiliar words and phrases by nurturing their growing capacity with word-learning strategies. When students learn to use context, become morphologically aware, and can use reference materials with ease, they are better equipped to figure out the meanings of new words they encounter.

At the same time, we recognize students must understand individual words and phrases that are germane to understanding content. These words are found in texts across content areas or represent disciplinary concepts important for comprehension of ideas. Engaging students in active experiences with words helps them internalize meanings and connections.

Nurturing Middle-Level Vocabularians

Students need opportunities to explore and learn vocabulary so they can deeply learn concepts. It is not enough to ask kids to look up words and write isolated definitions or to insert a brief, unconnected activity here and there. At the same time, middle-level teachers don't have unlimited teaching and planning time and must make the most of every second allotted to their subject areas. To develop vocabularians, we must plan strategically together, teach in ways that are motivating to middle-level students, assess for student learning, and base our instruction and assessment on the best vocabulary research available.

With that in mind, here is a guideline for a strategic, intentional vocabulary plan in the middle grades:

1. Carefully select a small number of words important to understanding upcoming lessons in different classes and that students will see in text. These are the words that will be designated for deep study for a two-week vocabulary cycle.
2. Introduce each selected vocabulary word in context. Encourage students to infer the meaning of the word and engage them in discussion that allows them to explore the context in which the word is introduced. Reinforce these words across the team or grade level.

3. Invite students to create a "vocabulary exploration" of each word selected for deep study. Add the vocabulary exploration to a journal or section of a binder to be used as a reference.
4. Flood each classroom with other words important to content or that students discover in reading.
5. Teach morphological awareness as multisyllabic words are introduced for deep study or as they are encountered in text.
6. Provide opportunities for active, engaging vocabulary practice that include movement, discussion, art, drama, music, writing, technology or media, and test-taking skills.
7. Assess vocabulary in ways in which students will be tested. Include words that students have studied previously so there is a cumulative effect. Provide ways for students to self-assess and monitor their own progress in vocabulary development.

Let's take a look at the major research findings that support our approach and see how they relate to the middle grades.

Some words are more important to teach than others.

In their wonderful book *Bringing Words to Life* (Beck, McKeown, and Kucan 2002), Isabel Beck and her colleagues talk about levels of words that they call Tier 1, Tier 2, and Tier 3. Tier 1 words are words that kids already know when they come to school—words such as *clock*, *baby*, *happy*, and so on. Tier 2 words are high-frequency words students will likely encounter in their reading across several contexts, yet probably don't know well. Examples of Tier 2 words are *coincidence*, *absurd*, *industrious*, and *fortunate*. Tier 3 words are domain-specific words that are used in content areas, such as *isotope*, *lathe*, *peninsula*, and *refinery*.

Most vocabulary researchers agree with this premise, and many use Tier 1, Tier 2, and Tier 3 as a guideline for vocabulary word selection. Beck and her colleagues suggest that Tier 1 words don't need to be taught because students already know them. They recommend that teachers plan most vocabulary instruction around Tier 2 words and explore Tier 3 words as part of content-area instruction in the disciplines. However, Marzano and Simms (2013) see content-area terms, or Tier 3 words, as just as important as Tier 2. (See Chapter 2 for more discussion about word selection.)

Students must learn words at more than one level.

Not all word knowledge is equal. According to Beck and her colleagues (Beck, McKeown, and Kucan 2002, 10), a continuum of word knowledge would look like this (emphasis added):

- No knowledge. *(I've never heard or seen the word.)*
- General sense of the word. *(I've seen or heard the word before.)*
- Narrow, context-bound knowledge. *(Even though a word may have several meanings, I only know one meaning in one situation.)*
- Having knowledge of a word, but not being able to apply it readily enough to use in appropriate situations. *(I may know the word has several meanings, but because I'm not sure which one to use, I sometimes use the word the wrong way.)*
- Rich, decontextualized knowledge of a word's meaning, its relationship to other words, and its extension to metaphorical uses. *(I know multiple meanings of the word, and I can use the word appropriately in different situations.)*

Students need to learn words deeply to get to the most sophisticated level of word knowledge. That means exploring vocabulary to understand related words, how words connect across ideas and subject areas, and the multiple meanings of words.

Students learn words when they experience them multiple times.

To really learn vocabulary, students need multiple exposures to new words over time (Stahl 2003). Jenkins, Stein, and Wysocki (1984) found that students need at least six exposures to learn a word, whereas McKeown et al. (1985) determined that it took twelve exposures. Through a systemic vocabulary plan, students can encounter words in context and engage in experiences that help them internalize meanings.

The structure of most elementary classrooms enables teachers to provide multiple exposures to targeted words throughout the day. However, this process is not so easy at the middle level. With compartmentalized classes and specialized disciplines, teachers must have an intentional plan to provide appropriate vocabulary instruction.

Asking students to look up words in the dictionary and write the definition does not help them learn many words.

Dictionary definitions may actually cloud a word's meaning rather than help a student learn it (Beck, McKeown, and Kucan 2002). In a study asking students to create sentences using dictionary definitions of words, Miller and Gildea (1985) found that 63 percent of the students' responses were judged to be "odd." Nagy and Scott (1989) found that students frequently interpreted one or two words from a dictionary definition as the entire meaning, and McKeown (1993) found that 60 percent of students' responses using dictionary definitions were unacceptable.

An episode of an old sitcom provides an example. Late one night I was flipping through TV channels (which I do often when I am writing) and came across a rerun of *The King of Queens*. In this episode, Carrie and Doug were discussing insurance with a salesman in their living room. The salesman asked if they wanted to add the "building code upgrade coverage" to their policy. When Carrie asked if they really needed it, the salesman answered that the "argument for it is fairly specious."

Carrie and Doug tried not to let the man see their confusion.

"So, yay or nay?" asked the salesman.

Carrie, searching for any type of context clue, ventured, "Well . . . that depends on how *specious* the argument really is."

"Well, I'd say in your case it is extremely specious," the salesman replied.

No help there. Carrie gave Doug a look that clearly said, "Rats!" Still perplexed, Doug distracted the salesman while Carrie slipped over to the side of the room to grab a dictionary. She quickly returned.

"Well, since the argument for it 'has the ring of truth but is actually false,'" Carrie quoted, "I say we take a pass."

This is a classic example of dictionary use, albeit for comic effect. I don't know about you, but I was still a little vague on the meaning of the word *specious* in that context. The definition might need to be restated in friendly language for it to be truly understood. And so it is with kids. Research shows that dictionary definitions are not always helpful to understand a new word, but putting definitions in student-friendly language helps kids learn words (Beck, McKeown, and Kucan 2002).

When students learn words, they need to think about patterns and networks of meaning.

In the late 1980s, William Nagy and Judith Scott (1989, 1990) coined the term *word schema* when discussing the many aspects of word knowledge. Schema means a framework or system of organizing and perceiving new information. (The plural is *schemata*, but we follow Nagy and Scott's lead and use "schemas.") Literacy instructors often talk about activating schema, or prior knowledge, in comprehension instruction. According to Nagy and Scott (1989, 9), "just as knowledge about the nature and typical organization of stories aids the comprehension of new stories, knowledge about the nature of words and the organization of the lexicon aids the understanding of new words."

Students with well-developed schemas about words can figure out the meaning of many words through use of context. They make connections to their background knowledge when deciding what a new word means and connect the new word to words they already know. Sometimes they use knowledge of syntax (sentence structure) or prefixes, suffixes, and root words. Sometimes they know a synonym or an antonym. Sometimes they have personal experience with the word that enhances their background knowledge. In *Word Nerds*, Leslie, Margot, and I appropriated the term *word schema* to mean making connections to meaning across webs of words.

Peter Fisher and Camille Blachowicz (2007, 6) also discussed the need for middle-level students to develop metacognitive understanding about the definition of a word. "It seems to us that in literacy education, we have done a good job of teaching students to be metacognitive about print skills (how to use all the cueing systems), about comprehension (making connections, visualizing, etc.), and even about fluency (monitoring appropriate rate, accuracy, and expression). What we haven't addressed thoroughly enough is teaching students how to think about what they know about words and how to learn them."

Fisher and Blachowicz suggest creating word maps to help students develop stronger word sense. A "concept of definition map" (Schwartz and Raphael 1985) is useful when learning nouns. Maps requiring students to think of synonyms and antonyms help students better learn the definitions of adjectives and adverbs.

Derek, a seventh grader, provided insight when he announced in an aside during one of my visits to his class at Bullitt Lick Middle, "You know you can't give a definition for the word *define*. The definition for *define* is to define the definition."

Students can learn some words through direct instruction.

There are obviously too many words in the English language to teach all of them individually, but Stahl and Fairbanks (1986) found that direct vocabulary teaching of some words can enhance achievement. Robert Marzano (2009) has found positive experimental research results on teaching and student learning of individual vocabulary words using this six-step instructional plan:

1. Provide a description, explanation, or example of the new term.
2. Ask students to restate the description, explanation, or example in their own words.
3. Ask students to construct a picture, a pictograph, or a symbolic representation of the term.
4. Engage students periodically in activities that help them add to their knowledge of the terms in their vocabulary notebooks.

5. Periodically ask students to discuss the terms with one another.
6. Involve students periodically in games that enable them to play with terms.

Some students need more intensive instruction with individual words, either because they are learning English as an additional language or because they come from home and community environments where academic language is seldom used. Marzano's steps to vocabulary learning can be used as a model for teaching individual words.

Students can learn some words through the use of wide reading.

At one time, wide reading was one of the major recommendations for developing vocabulary. We now know that, although words are learned through independent reading, we should not rely on independent reading as the only strategy to help students become skillful word learners. As Marzano (2004, 69) said, "The case for direct vocabulary instruction is strong. From a number of perspectives, the research indicates that wide reading probably is not sufficient in itself to ensure that students will develop the necessary vocabulary and consequently the necessary academic background knowledge to do well in school. In contrast, direct vocabulary instruction has an impressive track record of improving students' background knowledge and the comprehension of academic content."

Although it can't be the only strategy for vocabulary development, wide reading of different types of texts can certainly help build word schema and enable students to learn word meanings from context (Anderson 1990; Nagy and Herman 1987). Students see lots of new words as they read independently, and some of these will be words they learn for life.

Students can learn some words through rich conversations with adults and peers.

All students should participate in academic discussions on a regular basis. However, student-generated classroom conversation is vital for those who come from homes with limited language enrichment. Researchers at the Center for Research on Education, Diversity, and Excellence (CREDE) have consistently found that culturally and linguistically diverse learners achieve more success in school when they are regularly engaged in conversations with adults and peers in ways that can help them make connections, learn concepts, and learn the words for those concepts (CREDE 2014).

Instructional conversation is a research-based strategy for encouraging academic discussion with diverse students (Goldenberg 1991; Tharp and Gallimore 1988, 1991). In an instructional conversation, we decide what we want students to know by the end of the discussion, but we structure the discussion so that students can do most of the talking. During the instructional conversation, we weave in background knowledge the students need and teach skills or concepts directly when necessary. We ask open-ended questions, restate a student comment, pause strategically, or ask students to elaborate on an answer, such as, "What makes you think that?" (Goldenberg 1991). By engaging in instructional conversation about vocabulary across content areas, students can explore concepts as well. Instructional conversations can be a powerful tool, whether planned for whole-group lessons or small-group work.

Developing word consciousness helps students broaden their vocabulary.

Students become "word conscious" when they notice unfamiliar words and wonder about their meanings. Word consciousness can start as early as kindergarten, when young children learn to use sophisticated vocabulary ("The weather today is rather brisk!") in the classroom (Lane and Allen 2010). We want to help our students develop the habit of being curious about words, which can motivate them to take risks with new vocabulary.

Students also need opportunities to play with new words. We can promote vocabulary through games, art, music, and drama (Blachowicz and Fisher 2010; Graves and Watts Taffe 2002). When we use interesting vocabulary in class and include unfamiliar words and phrases in everyday conversations, students become more interested and curious about words.

Most middle-level students need to develop word-learning strategies to become independent learners.

One of the most important ways to help students succeed in school is by teaching them to use word-learning strategies (Blachowicz et al. 2013; Graves 2006, 2009). Three major word-learning strategies to help students become independent word learners include:

- Use of context: Students need instruction about how and when to use context clues to determine the meaning of new vocabulary.
- Use of word parts (morphology): Understanding word parts helps students piece together the puzzle of the English language. Students also need appropriate instruction

in morphology to determine the meaning of multisyllabic words. (Chapter 5 of this book delves into morphological awareness with middle-level students.)

- Appropriate use of reference materials to figure out the meaning of unfamiliar words: Students need to understand authentic uses of print and digital dictionaries, thesauruses, and glossaries, such as when context clues or word parts are not enough to determine meaning. Reference materials can also help students confirm definitions after an initial inference. (Chapter 4 includes authentic uses of reference materials as part of a strategic vocabulary plan.)

Middle-level students must be able to connect vocabulary concepts to their own lives.

Young adolescents are rarely motivated by traditional vocabulary activities. They are more willing to learn new words and learn new concepts when learning makes sense to them and is also fun. This means "making academic vocabulary personal" (Fisher and Frey 2008, 16), relevant, and engaging. Middle-level students are ready to engage in authentic conversations that help them explore deep aspects of word meaning. Drama and art can help young adolescents experience and connect concepts to their own lives and learn at higher levels. Such experiential activity across content areas leads to increased motivation and deeper understanding (Wilhelm 1997).

Robert Marzano (2004) reminds us that, for students of all ages to learn words, they have to experience and represent those words in both linguistic and nonlinguistic ways. Instruction where students are moving and interacting is often called *multisensory teaching*. Multisensory teaching involves a combination of visual, auditory, kinesthetic, and tactile (VAKT) activities to address the learning styles of all students. This kind of teaching has been found to be effective with diverse learners in literacy instruction (International Dyslexia Association 2009; Reinhart and Martinez 1996; Wadlington 2000).

Vocabulary instruction that includes multisensory activity can help students internalize new words and continue to develop word schema. In addition, multisensory vocabulary instruction creates novelty and excitement about words—a sure-fire motivator.

I was in Tonie Weddle's classroom at Bullitt Lick Middle one morning when Karen Muench, the social studies teacher on the team, peeped around the door frame. "Come and see what my kids are doing in vocabulary!" she entreated. I stepped across the hall and into a lesson about ancient Rome. The lesson contained a good deal of unfamiliar vocabulary, with the larger objective for students to be able to explain the two classes of society in ancient Rome and to discuss the basis of a democratic government in the Roman Republic. To help students learn important concepts and the vocabulary for those concepts, Karen had divided students into groups of four. She distributed a bag of marshmallows and a box of toothpicks to each group. One student was chosen to be a *patrician*, and the other three became *plebeians*. The patrician gave specific directions about how to build a structure, while the plebeians, using the toothpicks and marshmallows, were required to follow explicit orders. The lesson would quickly move to the secession of the plebeians and the formation of the Plebeian Council as a prelude to a study of the origin of the constitution. However, first students had to deeply understand the difference between the two classes of society and the reasons for the Conflict of the Orders in ancient Rome. There was no better way for students to learn the words for these important concepts than by having them experience it for themselves (see Figure 1.2).

Figure 1.2 *Students learn the words* plebeian *and* patrician *through a social studies activity.*

Some vocabulary instruction is better than no instruction.

"Thick" vocabulary instruction, in which young adolescents study various aspects of words and learn word-learning strategies through developmentally appropriate activities, is much more effective than "thin" instruction, in which students merely look up words in the dictionary and write the definitions. However, any attention to vocabulary can help students learn some words (Graves 2006).

Academic Vocabulary Development IS Concept Development

Most teachers are adept at "code switching." That is, we have the ability to use appropriate language for various situations, whether it is cheering at a basketball game, talking with eighth graders in class, or participating in a graduate seminar. We have words to use in everyday life, words for school, and specialized vocabulary for professional endeavors. Our vocabularies change with the venue and context.

Our students are not so adept at code switching. One of the difficulties in vocabulary teaching and learning is that the actual concept of vocabulary can vary. Michael Graves (2006) explains that our receptive vocabulary includes the words we understand when we hear them in spoken language, whereas our productive vocabulary encompasses the words we use when speaking. To break this down further, we actually use four types of vocabulary: (1) the words we can understand when we hear them (receptive-oral), (2) the words we understand when we read them (receptive-written), (3) the words we use when we speak (productive-oral), and (4) the words we use when we write (productive-written). These vocabularies vary in size. For example, young children have larger oral vocabularies than reading vocabularies, and college-educated adults often have larger reading vocabularies than the words they use when they speak (Graves 2006).

Academic vocabulary is the "language of schooling" (Snow and Uccelli 2009) and becomes particularly important for success in the middle grades. As seventh grader Carter related at Eastside, "I think vocabulary's pretty important because it kind of connects into everything and all the other subjects. Like you cannot do math without knowing good vocabulary. It's kind of like the base of all the subjects you have to know." Carter has hit on the very foundation of academic literacy—that vocabulary knowledge is vital for understanding in the content areas.

Although narrative text is still highly important in the middle grades, emphasis is placed on reading academic texts across the curriculum. There are a number of ways to describe the specific language used in content areas (Baumann and Graves 2010). Language Standard 6 of the Common Core standards calls it "general academic" (words that are important across content areas) and "domain-specific" (words that are important in particular content areas) vocabulary; *academic vocabulary* is generally used in the research literature.

Academic vocabulary is especially challenging for many students. Authors of academic texts usually write in a formal manner and use precise and technical vocabulary to explain concepts. Although the content of informational text can be interesting, the way the text is written is often not very motivating or clear to middle-level students. Students who have difficulties in comprehension usually find learning and interpreting academic vocabulary a daunting task (Blachowicz et al. 2013; Fisher and Frey 2008; Kelley et al. 2010).

Certain words and phrases are germane to specific content-area instruction. Most newer publications have a vocabulary section that precedes the text so that teachers can frontload terms students will need to know. But vocabulary development involves more than just learning words. With vocabulary instruction, we sometimes teach a new word for a term that students already understand. Other times, we may be teaching new information and the new words that correspond to that information. A concept is an idea or notion—a way to categorize information. Some concepts are familiar, but the word for the concept is unknown. Some concepts are unfamiliar, and the student is faced with learning both the concept and the corresponding words at the same time. The bulk of vocabulary learning in the middle grades may consist of unknown words that stand for unknown concepts in the content areas. Marco Bravo and Gina Cervetti (2008, 131) explained that "gaining control over disciplinary vocabulary is critical for conceptual understanding; knowing disciplinary terms is fundamental to the comprehension of content area concepts."

Students don't just have to learn words and concepts—they also have to learn the grammar of the subject discipline, which can affect how word meaning is perceived. In other words, the way that text is written in different subject areas makes a difference in comprehension and word knowledge. Math, science, and social studies texts all have different styles, such as the measurement terms commonly used in math and the clause connectors in science and social studies. Poetry is written in a different way than prose. Music, art, dance, and drama have their own ways of explaining concepts. Disciplines have unique text structures and ways of unveiling content that can be confusing to inexperienced learners.

The reader's interest and experience in the discipline can also affect comprehension and word meaning. Tim Shanahan and Cindy Shanahan (2008) found that a unique mind-set is required for comprehending reading materials in different content areas. They observed that each discipline possesses its own language, purposes, and ways of using text. For example, mathematicians emphasize rereading complex explanations and formulas and place great importance on small function words such as *of, into,* and *and* in mathematics texts. Scientists use charts, graphs, pictures, texts, and diagrams to convey concepts. Historians are most interested in the credibility of sources and the interpretations of different authors, which include the connotation of the words they choose to discuss concepts. A reader's background knowledge and experience in the discipline and the way the text is written will affect how words are interpreted and learned.

Let's take a look at how middle grades teachers focus on disciplinary vocabulary in mathematics, history/social studies, science, and English language arts.

Vocabulary Development in Mathematics

Michael Roccaforte, an eighth-grade math teacher at Bowman Academy, taught at the high school level before moving to middle school. He shook his head ruefully when thinking back to how he had to adapt to teaching middle-level students. "I was used to teaching older kids, so when I first started teaching math vocabulary, I kind of felt like I was teaching kindergarten. I mean, shouldn't these kids already know these words? I'll be honest—at first, I didn't do much with it because I thought they should already know what everything means. But they don't. Middle school kids need math vocabulary instruction." He paused. "And, surprisingly, I found out that teaching vocabulary really helps them learn the math concepts better." Word problems and explanations in mathematics use particular words, phrases, and sentence constructions that are different from other content areas. Blachowicz and her colleagues (Blachowicz et al. 2013, 100) observed that "mathematics texts may contain long noun phrases with complex grammatical patterning that result in complex meaning relationships." A noun phrase such as "three-sided figure with equivalent angles" can be confusing for middle-level students who don't understand that the phrase represents a thing (Helman 2013).

As more demanding concepts are introduced, middle-level students confront new and more challenging mathematics vocabulary. Elizabeth Moje and her colleagues (Moje et al. 2011, 469) explained that "Mathematics is a language, and algebra in adolescent classrooms, where symbolic notation may be confronted seriously for the first time, is as much about the language as the ideas expressed by it." Doug Buehl (2011, 62) observed that "mathematics vocabulary can be especially deceptive because many key mathematics terms are also used in more common ways in general conversation, such as *model, property, form, line, function, divide,* and *value.*" He goes on to say that readers in mathematics must be "particularly adept at discourse code-switching from informal everyday usage to precise mathematical meanings" (62). Lori Helman (2013) discussed the concept of word consciousness in math, saying that instruction should focus on specific words, use of context in math text, and generative morphology—that is, the recognition of word parts that hold meaning in mathematics, such as *tri-* (three), *medi-* (half), and *circum-* (around).

Vocabulary learning in mathematics is, in many ways, like learning to comprehend. According to Mary Lee Barton, Clare Heidma, and Deborah Jordan (2002, 26), "Students need to construct meaning—to grapple with how a concept such as prime numbers is similar to and yet different from other classifications of numbers that they have learned." When students understand the meanings of math terms and phrases and nuances of function words, they better understand mathematics.

Vocabulary Development in Science

Science vocabulary represents ideas about the way the world works. However, science texts can be difficult to read and interpret because of the surplus of unfamiliar terms (Groves 1995; Harmon and Hedrick 2005). And "science courses are all too often taught as a litany of facts leading many students to focus on rote memorization of terminologies instead of developing deep conceptual understanding" (Brown and Concannon 2014, 197).

In science, students must deal with dense language, visual information in the form of charts, graphs, and diagrams, and webs of related ideas. In addition, a great number of science words comprise Greek and Latin roots that, when combined, represent concepts. When students learn the meanings of common Greek and Latin roots, they can unlock the meanings of numerous science terms.

Vocabulary comprehension is crucial for students to be able to engage in discussions and science activities. When students engage in hands-on science and authentic discussion, they can often relate their own experiences to be able to learn science concepts at a deeper level.

Maurice Culver, an eighth-grade science teacher at Bowman, has observed the power of vocabulary study. In a recent team meeting, he discussed his students' progress. "Now they can make a correlation from an old word to a new one. For example, we had the word *convection* a couple of weeks ago. When we talked about the water cycle this week, instead of saying, 'The water is being heated,' the kids said 'convection.' I see students actually use correct terms instead of just reciting a definition."

Vocabulary Development in History/Social Studies

"I think a lot of my kids have anxiety issues around vocabulary," says Stephen Currie, a seventh-grade social studies teacher at Bowman. "And then when they do take a risk, they don't trust themselves. They will say, 'I'm probably saying this wrong . . .' If for no other reason, I've had to work on vocabulary to help my students feel more confident when they talk about ideas in my class."

Ally, an eighth grader at Eastside, shared her own difficulty with social studies vocabulary. "Probably the most challenging words for me this year were the ones in government and politics and social studies," she says. "I don't really understand politics, so the vocabulary was really hard for me and I had a hard time remembering the words. Those words just bugged me so much! Social studies is not my strong point. I just couldn't make any connections at first." Shaking her head, she says, "I guess I'm just not a politics girl."

Vocabulary in social studies is most often part of a web of complex ideas, and as such, definitions are rarely simple. The very nature of history and social studies is focused on relationships and concepts across time, ideas, people, places, events, visual sources, and titles. Blachowicz and her colleagues (Blachowicz et al. 2013, 81) summed up the difficulties in learning vocabulary in social studies by stating, "Very seldom will the one word with a single definition be very useful in social studies." Doug Buehl (2011, 58) noted that social studies words, including proper nouns such as Harriet Tubman, the Industrial Revolution, and the Magna Carta, "must be regarded as concepts and treated in many respects like meaningful vocabulary."

According to Blachowicz and her colleagues (2013, 81), social studies teachers should "build associations among terms and create a framework where new concepts can be related to other knowledge." Isabel Beck and Margaret McKeown (2001) discussed the importance of asking questions about social studies texts and teaching students to question the author. This process would include examining the vocabulary in a text to ask good questions about the author's word choices and intent. Kevin Flanigan (2013) observed that history and social studies contain many concept words that end with the suffix *-ism, -ist,* or *-tion*. He suggested a focus on generative morphology so that students could more deeply understand these social studies concepts.

Vocabulary Development in English Language Arts

In English language arts, word study is just as complex as vocabulary instruction in the other disciplines—perhaps more so. English language arts teachers usually carry the most responsibility for vocabulary instruction and are often working with at least four different types of vocabulary development, including teaching students how to

- determine the meanings of unfamiliar words when they encounter them in text,
- choose more expressive or accurate words in writing or speaking,
- analyze the word choices authors make, and
- understand and use English language arts concept words correctly.

In literacy, academic vocabulary enables students to engage in close reading or to discuss a text or their own writing (Blachowicz et al. 2013). They also need to be able to use this type of academic vocabulary when reading, writing, speaking and listening, learning new vocabulary, and thinking across the curriculum. In addition, many literacy terms are often found on standardized assessments. Some of these terms, outlined by Blachowicz et al. (2013), include

- comprehension process words, such as *schema, summarize, infer;*
- vocabulary process words, such as *definition, context clue, prefix;*
- writing process words, such as *draft, revise, edit;*
- craft words, such as *tone, argument, evidence;*
- text structure words for narratives, such as *plot, conflict, third person;*
- text structure words for informational text, such as *topic sentence, compare/contrast, cause/effect;*
- character trait words, such as *reliable, courageous, persistent;*
- genre words, such as *realistic fiction, fantasy, myth;* and
- figurative language, such as words and phrases that constitute idioms, similes, proverbs, and so on.

Gabrielle Brenston, an eighth-grade English language arts teacher at Bowman, shared her dilemma in teaching all types of vocabulary in her subject area. "I need to be teaching Tier 2 words to help kids learn to be expressive writers, but I also need to prepare them to be successful on ELA assessments," she says.

One way Brenston addressed this was to incorporate English language arts concept vocabulary when teaching students how to analyze poetry using a template posted on *Read-WriteThink*. This is a popular template called TP-CASTT, which stands for: title, paraphrase, connotation, attitude/tone, shifts, title revisited, and theme, and its related terms of *figurative language, imagery, sound, humor, sarcasm,* and *interpretive* (see http://www.readwritethink. org/files/resources/30738_analysis.pdf). Being familiar with these ELA terms provided a way for students to learn to think about critical analysis in literature as they interpreted figurative language and contemplated the author's word choices.

Vocabulary and the Common Core Standards

Attention to vocabulary development and instruction has been part of a pendulum swing in literacy education over the years. There was a flurry of interest from cognitive scientists and reading researchers in the 1980s, and then near silence during the whole-language movement of the 1990s. Vocabulary instruction again stood in the literacy spotlight when it was named one of the five pillars of reading education (along with phonemic awareness, phonics, fluency, and comprehension) as part of the No Child Left Behind Act of 2000. Today, there is a renewed emphasis on vocabulary development for all grade levels and content areas with the introduction of the Common Core State Standards (NGA/CCSSO 2010). Regular practice with complex text and its academic language has been considered one of the major instructional shifts in the English Language Arts Standards.

References to understanding word meanings are found throughout the ELA and Literacy Standards. The bulk of the standards related to vocabulary can be found in the Language Strand. Language Standards 4, 5, and 6 are focused on the skills needed to be able to infer and confirm meanings of words, to understand their relationships to other words, and to learn individual words important for comprehension. Although the value of vocabulary knowledge is not explicit in the Speaking and Listening Standards, academic conversation is certainly a crucial way to learn new words. The CREDE has consistently found that focusing on language development and instructional conversation across content areas helps culturally and linguistically diverse students to succeed in school.

Language Standard 4: The "Word-Learning Strategies" Standard and Indicators

According to Michael Graves, there are three major word-learning strategies: (1) the use of context to infer meanings of unknown words and phrases, (2) the use of word parts to figure out the meanings of multisyllabic words, and (3) the use of reference materials to find and confirm definitions (Graves 2006, 2009). When we explore the Language Strand of the Common Core State Standards, we see that Standard 4 focuses on these exact three word-learning strategies. In fact, College and Career Readiness Language Standard 4 states: "Determine or clarify the meaning of unknown and multiple-meaning words and phrases by using context clues, analyzing meaningful word parts, and consulting general and specialized reference materials, as appropriate" (CCR.L.4). These three word-learning strategies constitute an important part of vocabulary instruction for middle-level students.

Word-Learning Strategy: Use of Context

By the time students reach grade six, the first indicator for Language Standard 4 in the ELA Standards is the same until the end of high school:

> *Use context (e.g., the overall meaning of a sentence or paragraph; a word's position or function in a sentence) as a clue to the meaning of a word or phrase.*

Teaching students to analyze the context of a sentence or passage for clues to help them infer the meaning of unfamiliar words and phrases helps kids become better readers. This skill is called *contextual analysis*. Chapter 3 will focus on the use of context as a word-learning strategy as we introduce words for intentional vocabulary study.

Word-Learning Strategy: Use of Word Parts

Language Standard 4.b for grades four through eight states:

> *Use common, grade-appropriate Greek or Latin affixes and roots as clues to the meaning of a word.*

Competent readers are able to determine the meanings of many words they have never seen before by considering the meanings of prefixes, suffixes, and roots. This is called *morphological awareness*. Using word parts to determine the meanings of words can be called *morphemic analysis* and is also known as *structural analysis*. Chapter 4 will focus on helping students develop the ability to use morphemic analysis as a word-learning strategy.

Word-Learning Strategy: Use of Reference Materials

The ability to use grade-appropriate reference materials begins at grade two in the Common Core State Standards for Language. Language Standard 4c has this to say about the use of reference materials in grades six to eight:

Consult reference materials (e.g., dictionaries, glossaries, thesauruses), both print and digital, to find the pronunciation of a word or determine or clarify its precise meaning or its part of speech.

Language Standard 4d in grades six to eight says:

Verify the preliminary determination of the meaning of a word or phrase (e.g., by checking the inferred meaning in context or in a dictionary).

Obviously, students should use reference materials frequently so it becomes second nature to check for accuracy when writing or preparing a presentation. The use of reference materials should be naturally embedded across the curriculum and interwoven throughout a plan for vocabulary instruction.

Language Standard 5: The "Word Schema" Standard and Indicators

Language Standard 5 for grades four to twelve states:

Demonstrate understanding of figurative language, word relationships, and nuances in word meanings.

Just as students activate prior knowledge to comprehend text, they have to build and activate networks of words to have a place for new words. When students explore figurative language and are able to make semantic connections between and among words, they are better able to comprehend an author's meaning and have better word choices at their fingertips when writing. Working on the aspects of Language Standard 5 helps students develop word schema. We will explore these concepts in Chapter 5.

Language Standard 6: The "Words to Teach" Standard

Language Standard 6 for grades six to eight states:

Acquire and use accurately grade-appropriate general academic and domain-specific words and phrases; gather vocabulary knowledge when considering a word or phrase important to comprehension or expression.

This standard actually helps us decide which words to teach. General academic words and phrases found across contexts are the same as Tier 2—words such as *analyze, culture,* and *generic.* Domain-specific words and phrases that a student is most likely to encounter in content-area texts are the same as Tier 3—words such as *desalination, triptych,* and *integer* (a deeper discussion about how to select words to teach is part of Chapter 2).

Vocabulary Development Is Key

Although research is sometimes vague about the particular instructional methods that are best to use, there is no doubt that vocabulary development is one of the keys to student achievement. Our students need us to make vocabulary development a priority in every class, helping them expand their knowledge and learn strategies for determining unknown words in challenging texts and assessments.

Teachers like Tonie Weddle understand this. As I visited her classroom at Bullitt Lick Middle School one afternoon, she invited her seventh graders to work together in small groups to decide which vocabulary words fit certain clues. A murmur began around the room as students started to figure out words that matched the information on the sheet she had given them. At a table near the back of the classroom, Cindy, Alex, and Tomas began reading the clues, preparing to take on the challenge. Danny, the fourth member of their small group, looked perplexed. Suddenly, he exclaimed, "Oh, my, gosh! It's going to be so hard. Out of millions of words, we have to pick one. Watch it be something we were already supposed to know!"

Cindy gave him the look that only a seventh-grade girl can bestow and then repeated their teacher's directions. The students were supposed to use any vocabulary word they had studied during the school year as a choice. "Oh, yeah," said Danny sheepishly. Then he, too, got to work figuring out the clues.

A kid like Danny, who makes excellent grades, can still be easily overwhelmed when he thinks about the voluminous number of words there are to learn. However, we can focus the task and make it easier to accomplish by using research-based ideas and strategies to help students develop "word confidence."

The rest of this book is devoted to making vocabulary learning something to anticipate, rather than to fear. I will describe how teachers and administrators have explored vocabulary teaching and learning with students in the middle grades, and along the way, we will connect vocabulary plans with the research outlined in this chapter.

Let's start this journey together by thinking about different ways to organize vocabulary instruction for students at the middle level.

Chapter 2

ORGANIZING FOR MIDDLE GRADES VOCABULARY DEVELOPMENT

The secret of all victory lies in the organization of the non-obvious.

—Marcus Aurelius

Middle-level students can be like the wind—a gentle breeze one minute, a tornado the next. They can be thoughtful, funny, embarrassed, exasperating, curious, wise, and innocent all in the same five minutes. They strive for independence while they simultaneously cling to the known. As my old principal used to say, "You either love middle school kids or you hate 'em. If you hate 'em, you have no business teaching in middle school." To me, they are at a fascinating age.

The Association for Middle Level Education (AMLE) considers students between the ages of ten and fifteen to be early or young adolescents (www.amle.org). Young adolescents are in the middle of the second most rapid physical development period of their lives, the first being from birth to age three. Kids can grow up to four inches and gain eight to ten pounds per year in the middle grades. This rapid development has a definite effect on appropriate vocabulary instruction for students in the middle grades.

Effective teachers of middle-level students understand that this age group has specific physical, social, emotional, and intellectual needs that must be met to help kids learn. It is the rare middle-level learner who doesn't need attention to one or more of these needs at any given moment. According to AMLE (2010), an education for young adolescents must be developmentally responsive, challenging, empowering, and equitable. As middle-level educators, we must make instructional decisions based on the unique natures and needs of middle-level kids. We need to hold every student to high expectation and ensure that all students have the knowledge and skills they need to succeed. Making sure that all middle-level students receive an equitable education means advocating for their right to learn. It is also up to us to provide challenging and relevant learning opportunities for them. When we help middle-level kids develop their vocabulary knowledge, we need to do so in a way that meets their needs and motivates them to learn (Lesaux, Harris, and Sloane 2012).

AMLE (2010) has outlined five characteristics for appropriate curriculum, instruction, and assessment for middle-level students. Each of these five characteristics comes into play when planning deep vocabulary instruction appropriate for young adolescents.

1. *Educators value young adolescents and are prepared to teach them.* Teachers of young adolescents understand their development and are prepared to help them learn vocabulary in ways that are developmentally appropriate. Fluctuating hormones sometimes makes it difficult for kids to keep emotions in check, so students need ways to express their emotions. Students need an opportunity to learn words in thoughtful ways that allow them to express their creativity and use new words in academic conversations. Bones and muscles are growing rapidly, often making it physically uncomfortable for students to sit still for long (one reason that a seemingly quiet boy will suddenly need to sharpen an already sharp pencil—or maybe throw a paper wad). This rapid and uncomfortable growth means that students need physical activity as a planned part of their instruction. And a burgeoning desire for independence will make a student challenge authority in a way she would not have done just weeks before. This means that middle-level kids need choice within a student-centered classroom. Effective teachers of young adolescents understand and value their kids and take their needs into consideration when planning vocabulary instruction. This also means that effective middle-level teachers purposefully gain the knowledge they need to be able to teach their students, including knowledge about vocabulary development.

2. *Students and teachers are engaged in active, purposeful learning.* Active learning requires young adolescents to engage rather than merely sit and listen. Inviting them to participate in strategies where they move, manipulate objects, discuss, and make connections helps them learn at higher levels. Also, a developing sense of fairness and autonomy means many young adolescents need to see the purpose in a lesson before they can fully engage. Authentic vocabulary activities where students are thinking and learning together make more sense than worksheets or other activities that do not take much thought, such as merely looking up words in a dictionary and writing a definition.

3. *Curriculum is challenging, exploratory, integrative, and relevant.* Planning curriculum that includes a focus on exploring and developing challenging vocabulary helps make learning new words relevant. When I was the leader of a middle school team, we worked hard to plan integrative curriculum to ensure that students could make connections across English language arts, science, social studies, and math. It wasn't always easy, and as teachers we had to plan carefully together, but we felt it was best

for our students. Vocabulary is the same way. Students need to be able to make vocabulary links across subject areas and their daily lives. This means that vocabulary development needs to be integrated across the entire curriculum, and students need opportunities to deeply explore relevant new words.

4. *Educators use multiple learning and teaching approaches.* Young adolescents need routine to know what to expect, but they also need variety to be motivated to learn. Each student also has different learning styles, needs, and abilities. We want to plan vocabulary instruction using an array of approaches within a routine that makes sense so that all students can learn. Vocabulary activities that incorporate art, music, popular culture, technology, movement, drama, creative writing, discussion, and interesting text will motivate students to learn vocabulary in a variety of ways.

5. *Varied and ongoing assessments advance learning as well as measure it.* Formative assessments should be learning experiences for students and provide valuable information about student learning for teachers. Planning for student self-assessment and peer assessment is also an important step in students learning to evaluate their own work. When we engage students in analyzing their own vocabulary assessments, we teach them ways to succeed on future assessments. (See Chapter 7 for a deeper look at vocabulary assessment.)

Many, if not most, middle school teachers include vocabulary lessons here and there, but implementing an intentional, strategic vocabulary plan is a different animal altogether. When Leslie, Margot, and I worked on *Word Nerds*, our vocabulary plan was designed for an elementary structure in which a single teacher can easily teach, reinforce, and integrate vocabulary instruction throughout the day. However, middle school students usually travel from teacher to teacher as they change subjects. This is obviously a different kind of challenge and one that is not always simple when trying to meet the instructional needs of middle-level kids.

Sometimes, with the best of intentions, we make the process harder. Teachers who understand that vocabulary is important for knowledge of their subject area may decide to reinforce terms associated with their classes. A middle-level student (let's call him Matt) goes to his English language arts class on Monday, where his teacher gives him twenty words to learn for Friday's vocabulary test. Matt then goes to social studies, where he is assigned another twenty words. Add the ten words in science, numerous terms in mathematics and special areas such as library/media, art, music, and physical education, well, do the math. Matt could easily be expected to learn eighty to one hundred new vocabulary words at the same time. Even if each teacher assigns just five words, it can still be overwhelming for young adolescents, most of whom still do not have a strong command of vocabulary concepts and connections (never mind that if they pass each test, they still often don't remember or use the words).

Published research on content-area vocabulary development often overlooks the fact that students are in multiple classes a day. If each middle-level teacher implemented methods suggested by researchers in their content classes, students would be expected to concentrate on a sizeable number of new words all at the same time across the school day. As we try to do the right thing, we sometimes don't realize the cumulative expectations that kids may carry with them from class to class.

Choosing Vocabulary Words for Deep Study

I have chosen to discuss word selection in this chapter, because it is such an issue for many middle-level educators and, in many ways, dictates how vocabulary development can be accomplished. There are so many words for students to learn! William Nagy and Richard Anderson (1984) estimated that there are at least 88,500 word families in printed school English. How do we know which words to choose? How do we know we are making the right choices? How do we organize for teaching vocabulary? Most published vocabulary programs come with a set of words to teach at each grade level, all neatly tied in a bow, but that doesn't guarantee that these are the right words for our particular kids or that the words will be retained.

There is a converging sense that deep vocabulary study should be restricted to a small number of words that kids can build on (Graves et al. 2013; Kelley et al. 2010; McKeown and Beck 2004). According to Steven Stahl and William Nagy (2006), "Complex concepts require multidimensional teaching techniques" (77). Stahl and Nagy go on to say that to teach a concept, "one must (a) identify the critical attributes of the word, (b) give the category to which it belongs, (c) discuss examples of the word, and (d) discuss non-examples of the word" (77). Because of the time it takes to teach in such a deep way, Stahl and Nagy suggested choosing a few key words for such emphasis.

Joan Kelley and her colleagues (Kelley et al. 2010) agree, saying it is best to "choose a small set of high-utility academic words students need and then use those as a platform for teaching word learning, increasing academic talk, and promoting more strategic reading" (9). I wholeheartedly agree with this premise. We need to carefully choose a small number of words for what Karen Bromley calls "direct deep teaching" (2012, 48) and others call "direct and rich vocabulary instruction" (McKeown and Beck 2004, 13) to get the most out of our vocabulary time. Along with individual words, we need to intentionally teach students word-learning strategies (Graves 2006) so they can "learn to learn" vocabulary, concepts, and connections and help them develop word consciousness (Blachowicz and Fisher 2010; Graves 2006) in ways that will open the world of words to our kids. This means that those who teach middle-level students need to make decisions together for a vocabulary development plan that best meets the needs of their particular students.

Given the time middle school teachers can realistically allot for vocabulary instruction within their tightly packed schedules and the academic load students may already carry, I suggest that teachers come to consensus on five to seven words for this type of deep study for a two-week vocabulary cycle. This doesn't mean that other words aren't important for kids to know; it does mean that we focus on just five to seven words for deep study during each two-week vocabulary cycle so that kids learn how to become vocabulary problem solvers as well as how to own these words for life.

So if we select just a few words for deep study, how in the world do we choose? First, it is important to remember that all words are not equal.

Tier 1 Words

Tier 1 words are usually described as basic vocabulary words that do not have multiple meanings. For our purposes, Tier 1 words are words that kids already know. It may seem obvious, but if students already know the meaning of a word, that word should not be chosen for vocabulary study. But seemingly easy words can also be deceptive. For example, a word like *run* seems to easily fit the bill as a Tier 1 word. It means to "move at a speed faster than walking," right? It would seem so, but my dictionary actually lists twelve definitions of the word *run* as a verb, and thirteen definitions when it is used as a noun. Some of these meanings are a bit obscure, such as a "run of bad luck" or to "run a series of tests." Sometimes a simple word has multiple meanings that make it more complex.

It is fairly straightforward to assess the basic vocabulary knowledge of kindergarten children. After all, words such as *baby* and *look* are words that students probably know when they first come to school, whereas words like *subtract* and *horizon* may not be. It is much harder to gauge which words are Tier 1 words for older students. Middle school students have had a range of school and life experiences by the time they get to us. The number and types of books they have read, depth of technology use, and the media have also influenced their vocabulary knowledge. In some home environments, students engage in conversations with adults that build their vocabulary. In other environments, kids rarely participate in that type of discussion. And even if young adolescents do regularly engage in discussion with adults, English may not be their fluent language, or a regional dialect may affect the words they know and use in conversation.

It is probably good to remember that a Tier 1 word for one group of students may not be a Tier 1 word for another. The time we have for teaching vocabulary is precious, so we need to be especially careful with words that have already been selected by a publisher or are included on a standardized word list. Some of these words may be Tier 1 words for our students and should not be included in vocabulary study. How do we know? One way, suggested by Janet Allen (1999, 19), is to ask students to rate their level of knowledge of words using these categories:

- "Don't know at all"
- "Have seen or heard, but don't know the meaning"
- "I think I know a meaning"
- "I know a meaning"

If we ask students to work in partners or small groups to analyze the results, we immediately get a gauge on whether these words are appropriate for the group we are teaching. Another way is to carefully observe students and their comfort level with words. We can listen intently to ways students use vocabulary in conversation and in writing. We don't want to waste instructional time on words kids already know and can use well. If students already know words, these words fit into the Tier 1 category and are not worth the class time.

Tier 2 Words

Language Standard 6 in the English Language Arts Standards for grades six, seven, and eight states:

Acquire and use accurately grade-appropriate general academic and domain-specific words and phrases; gather vocabulary knowledge when considering a word or phrase important to comprehension or expression.

In the Common Core standards, Tier 2 words are the same as "general academic words." Tier 2 words are words that students will encounter across texts in all content areas or that help them discuss concepts in more detail—words such as *analyze, diminish,* and *obscure.* Isobel Beck and her colleagues (Beck, McKeown, and Kucan 2002) recommend that most vocabulary study should focus on Tier 2 words, as these are the types of challenging words students will meet most often in text.

Tier 3 Words

Tier 3 words are called *domain-specific words* in the Common Core standards. Tier 3 words are words that students will encounter in content-area study, such as *isotope, Renaissance,* and *coefficient.* Tier 3 vocabulary sometimes stands for important concepts in the disciplines of mathematics, science, social studies, arts and humanities, and others—concepts that students must deeply know to understand content in a discipline. Robert Marzano and Julia Simms (2013) suggest that Tier 3 terms are just as important for learning as Tier 2 words. We should choose Tier 3 words that are most vital to understanding a particular unit of study and its accompanying disciplinary texts.

Selecting "Just Right" Words

Selecting words for deep study at the middle level is often a conundrum. We sometimes want to throw up our hands and scream, "Just give me a list!" The problem is that school communities are different and students have varying levels of background knowledge. In the past, vocabulary instruction has frequently been based on lists handed to educators by a publisher or from a website, but that doesn't mean the words are right for our kids.

So how do we identify "just right" words? From working with middle grades students and teachers, this seems to make sense:

1. Examine the unit or lessons you will teach. What texts will students read? What Tier 2 or Tier 3 words will they see, hear, or need to know to understand the concept you are teaching?
2. Make a list of words students need to understand for a concept in a text or lesson. This list would include words they really need to know, not words that may just be unfamiliar.
3. If students will see these words in text, which words might they be able to predict by using context? Teach them how to use context, and empower students with a word-learning strategy as they use contextual analysis to figure out the meanings.
4. Which words should students be able to predict by using the meanings of word parts? Teach them how to use the meanings of prefixes, suffixes, and roots to understand the meaning of a multisyllabic word.
5. Which words can just be mentioned as "cool" and interesting words but not words they really need to know? These are probably not words for deep study.
6. Words that are key to understanding and that students will see outside the walls of your classroom are the ones that probably should be considered. Add your words to the team or grade-level list of possibilities.
7. As a team or grade level, choose five to seven of the words on the list for students to study deeply during a two-week cycle.

Incorporating Word Consciousness

Obviously, students won't learn many new words if they only focus on five to seven new words every two weeks. Most teachers have a whole list of words they believe students should know, and students vary in their understanding of vocabulary to describe the world around them. There are thousands of words to learn, and middle-level students have plenty of vocabulary gaps they need to fill. Besides teaching students the vocabulary we choose for deep study, we can also emphasize "word consciousness" to make students attentive to an array of additional words. Developing word consciousness means an awareness and appreciation of the myriad words in the English language. When we take delight in words and play with language, we create a sense of significance as well as fun around words and word learning (Bromley 2007).

For students to become more word conscious, we can create vocabulary floods where classrooms are inundated with interesting words and phrases (Blachowicz and Fisher 2010; Brabham et al. 2012; Pressley 2008). In literacy-rich classrooms flooded with vocabulary, students are surrounded by a wealth of words even in content areas.

Adding Synonyms and Antonyms

One way to generate a vocabulary flood and begin to expand our students' web of words is to add synonyms or examples and antonyms or nonexamples to the words we choose for deep study. If students learn six vocabulary words and then two synonyms/examples and two antonyms/nonexamples for each word, they are actually learning six vocabulary networks containing thirty total words during a two-week cycle. Adding synonyms and antonyms also reinforces word relationships and connections, which is key to learning new vocabulary (Mountain 2007). From those thirty words, students' word networks expand even further. This is an essential part of the vocabulary plan we described in *Word Nerds* and is described in more detail in Chapter 5 of this book.

Concept Word Walls

A concept word wall is an alphabetical list of terms and phrases representing important concepts in the disciplines to be used as a reference. The words are often written on cards or sentence strips and then placed prominently on the classroom wall or on a bulletin board where students can refer to them in writing and discussion. When we create concept word walls and introduce the words to kids, we help them become more aware of words that are related to the topic under study. For instance, at Bowman content-area teachers posted word walls of important content words for the units that corresponded to their discipline. Teachers drew attention to the words throughout the unit of study, teachers and students used the words in discussion, and students were expected to use the words in written assignments.

Word walls have been found to be effective in providing a "conversational scaffold" about words and their meanings (Brown and Concannon 2014) and can be an important tool to help students to develop disciplinary vocabulary. An interesting idea that middle grade schools can replicate is to place a large word wall containing color-coded content-area words (science green, English language arts yellow, and so on) in the hallway. Content-area teachers then post the same color-coded words in their respective classrooms. By engaging students in discussions about the words and how they relate, teachers can help students encounter new terms and reinforce content-area words in all classes (Yates, Cuthrell, and Rose 2011).

Fast Mapping Related Words

Some words seem to be learned merely by brief exposure to them, a process called *fast mapping* (Carey and Bartlett 1978). Fast mapping is learning a new word through a single experience to get a sense of a word's meaning. Kids don't deeply learn words by fast mapping. To be retained for the long term, new words have to be connected to an existing knowledge base (Braisby, Dockrell, and Best 2001). Although fast mapping begins the process of learning a word, it is not enough to help students develop full meaning and use. *Extended mapping*, where students get to the richer, deeper level of word use, takes more meaningful instruction. There are instances where fast mapping can be useful, however. Kevin Flanigan and Scott Greenwood (2007) make the case that middle school teachers, especially in the content areas, need to carefully analyze the text they will be using and categorize words according to importance. Some words do warrant deep study, but some words only need to be mentioned or introduced briefly for content-area learning to progress. For example, Robert Kuprenas, a seventh-grade math teacher at Bowman, might focus on the word *volume* as a term that represents a concept for deep vocabulary study, but he also embeds the related words of *surface area*, *area*, and *perimeter* as students study *volume*. These related words can be quickly learned as students build deeper knowledge about the concept of volume.

Academic Conversation

Vocabulary study helps students become better able to express their thoughts accurately when participating in a discussion. The flip side is also true. Classroom discussion, where students are doing more talking than the teacher, can also promote vocabulary learning. As Jeff Zwiers and Marie Crawford (2011, 102) stated, "Word meanings tend to stick in the brain longer when used multiple times in real communication, which involves the need and desire to listen, learn, express, and get something done with language."

Ensuring that we make space in the curriculum for frequent academic conversations will help students not only learn words but also become word conscious. Brandi Odom, a seventh-grade English language arts teacher at Bowman, explains that "one of the most beneficial things I've done is to give students the opportunity to discuss the concept first instead of asking them to just look it up the dictionary. Putting them in small groups and asking them to come up with their own interpretation of a word really helps. It is important for my kids that they talk about the words."

For students growing up in poverty and students learning English, taking part in collaborative conversations is not only important, it is vital for school success. Nancy Frey and Doug Fisher (2010) have noted that academic conversations don't just happen. We have to plan carefully for these types of rich classroom conversations to include vocabulary necessary for understanding. By establishing content, language, and social goals for academic conversations, we can ensure that every student has an opportunity to learn (Fisher, Frey, and Rothenberg 2008).

Read-Alouds of Brief Texts

Another way to develop word consciousness is by reading aloud intriguing literary and informational passages that can spark discussion of words and their meanings. Middle-level students love to listen to teachers read aloud with enthusiasm and often rate it as a preferred literacy activity (Ivey and Broaddus 2001). Including brief read-alouds of high-quality texts from newspapers, magazines, or related fiction in content-area classes can ignite new ideas and spark engagement with content (Albright and Ariail 2005).

By taking a minute to discuss a few of the challenging words and phrases in the read-aloud, students will not only learn more about the topic of the text, but they will also become more cognizant of word choices that authors use to make their points. Asking questions such as "How does this word fit into your life?" or "What do you know about this word?" will often encourage kids to try to use the word in their own context. Asking "Why did the author choose this word instead of another one?" leads students along a path of critical thinking.

An out-of-the-ordinary way to flood the classroom with interesting words is to occasionally read aloud a picture book that is appropriate for older students. Picture books are not just for little kids anymore. Indeed, many picture books include rich, sophisticated vocabulary or use snippets of the original text of classic literature with contextualized images (Cairney 2014). Hayes and Ahrens (1988) have estimated that children's literature, with the exception of texts that have been simplified for beginning or inexperienced readers, contains two times as many rare words (those not found in the top ten thousand most frequently used words in the language) as in a conversation between two college-educated adults and more than all adult conversation except in courtroom testimony. The number of rare words found in adult television speech is not much more than adult conversation.

Consider this page from the picture book *Weslandia* by Paul Fleischman (2002), a story about a misfit middle-level kid who creates his own civilization as a summer project:

His schoolmates were scornful, then curious. Grudgingly, Wesley allowed them ten minutes a piece at his mortar, crushing the plant's seeds to collect the oil. This oil had a tangy scent and served him both as a suntan lotion and mosquito repellent. He rubbed it on his face each morning and sold small amounts to his former tormentors at the price of ten dollars per bottle.

A great picture book for middle-level classrooms makes a specific point and contains interesting vocabulary but is written in a way that resonates with early adolescents (Albright 2002; Lightsey, Oliff, and Cain 2006). For example, *Pink and Say* by Patricia Polacco (1994) is a captivating and emotional story about the unlikely friendship between two fifteen-year-old Union soldiers, one black and one white, trapped in the South together during the Civil War. This intense and moving picture book is based on a true story from the author's family and would be an excellent way to demonstrate the personal impact of the war during a social studies unit as well as to introduce new terms.

Math Curse (1995) and *Science Verse* (2004), both by Jon Scieszka and Lane Smith, are humorous looks at math and science that amuse middle school kids but also contain relevant content-area terms. *Sir Cumference and the First Round Table* (1997) and the other Sir Cumference books by Cindy Neuschwander are tongue-in-cheek ways to introduce math vocabulary. *Leonardo: Beautiful Dreamer* (Byrd 2003) and *Starry Messenger: Galileo Galilei* (Sis 1996) are beautifully written biographies of early scientists that include not only a story and challenging vocabulary but also accompanying biographical information with primary source journal excerpts. *William Shakespeare's Macbeth* (Coville 1997) and *The Extraordinary Mark Twain (According to Susy)* by Barbara Kerley (2010) are picture books that embed lively vocabulary and can be used to jump-start classic literature lessons in a motivating way for middle-level students. Picture books can feel safe, especially for struggling readers and students learning English. The art fits the words and the theme or information the author has chosen and provides solid context clues so even an inexperienced reader can feel confident enough to participate in the vocabulary discussion. When teachers read aloud children's literature with attention-grabbing vocabulary and engage students in interactive discussions about some of the rare words heard in the text, they can help students extend their vocabulary schemas (Beck and McKeown 2001).

Wide Reading

Another stream that adds to a vocabulary flood is pleasure reading. Rudolf Flesch and Abraham Lass said, "You can't build a vocabulary without reading. You can't meet friends if you . . . stay at home by yourself all the time. In the same way, you can't build up a vocabulary if you never meet any new words. And to meet them you must read" (quoted in Graves 2006). We have known for years that readers learn new words from encountering them in text

(Anderson 1990; Nagy, Anderson, and Herman 1987; Nagy and Herman 1987). We will explore more about that notion in Chapter 3.

Nancie Atwell (1987), the brave pioneer of the reading workshop in middle school, shared that student choice, time to read, and opportunities for response are what motivate young adolescents to read independently. Stephen Krashen, one of the most respected experts in language acquisition theory and strategies for English language learners, would support that. He has strongly advocated for what he calls free, voluntary reading as a powerful way for all students, including English language learners, to develop reading ability, writing style, spelling, grammatical competence, and vocabulary. Free, voluntary reading means reading for enjoyment with no book reports and no questions at the end of the book. It also means that students can choose their own reading materials (Krashen 2004a, 2004b).

To help build vocabulary as well as comprehension, middle-level students need time and encouragement to read all types of materials they find fascinating. One study on the leisure reading habits of urban adolescents found that students enjoyed reading magazines the most, followed closely by comic books, stories and information on the Internet, books for pleasure, and newspapers (Hughes-Hassell and Rodge 2007). Magazines about sports, video games, and music were especially motivating to boys, as well as a variety of comic books and graphic novels.

Comic books and graphic novels are actually a great way to develop higher-level vocabulary. If you haven't read a comic book recently, look again. Remember the study about the complexity of language in picture books? According to those same researchers, the level of complex language in comic books is even higher, with 53.5 rare words per thousand (Hayes and Ahrens 1988). Stephen Krashen shared that a typical comic book has about two thousand words and that a student who reads one comic book per day will read about five hundred thousand words per year (Krashen 2004b). The positive literacy value of teaching with comic books, graphic novels, and *manga*, which are Japanese-style comic books, has been well documented (Bitz 2010; Cary 2004; Frey and Fisher 2008; Thompson 2008). Comic books and graphic novels based on historical events can provide an introduction and overview of social studies concepts and relationships. Comic books have even been suggested as a major vehicle for vocabulary study for struggling students and students learning English (Carter and Evensen 2013; Cary 2004).

Encouraging students to read widely helps them become better readers and enriches vocabulary. Making sure that students have access to a variety of motivating texts in the classroom will encourage them to read more.

Vocabulary Mini-Lessons

Sometimes, we can sneak in a vocabulary mini-lesson while the kids aren't even looking. Robert Kuprenas, a middle-level math teacher, often embeds brief, quick vocabulary tutorials to help kids deepen their understanding of mathematical terms. For example, during a recent lesson on statistics, he included a mini-lesson on the word "outlier." After teaching about different types of graphs, he asked all the students to line up on the left side of the room. He then asked DeShawn to stand by himself on the right side of the room. As the students chuckled at DeShawn standing all alone, Kuprenas asked them what mathematical term DeShawn represented (see Figure 2.1).

The students thought for a minute. "Is he an outlier?" Tina finally ventured.

"Great! Okay, let's check why. What parts does the word 'outlier' have?" asked Kuprenas.

"Out" and "-lier" were the answers.

"'Lier' in this instance means 'something lying somewhere.' The point on the graph is lying somewhere. What other words have the word 'out' in them?" asked Kuprenas. Students responded. "Outside!"

"Outsider!" (The seventh graders had recently finished a novel study on *The Outsiders* in English language arts and this word was fresh in their minds—a case of an unintentional connection.)

"Outlaw!"

"That's right. What does the word 'out' mean?"

"Something separate," stated Isis.

"Something apart?" Ronald pondered.

"That's right. When a word has 'out' as one of its parts, the 'out' means 'apart.' So *outlier* means…"

"The point that lies apart."

"Excellent thinking!" replied Kuprenas. Kids took their seats, and the lesson continued. Kuprenas did not plan more instruction on the word "outlier," but did continue to use it as a natural part of academic conversation as students practiced statistics problems. Within the rest of the lesson on graphs, he reinforced that the Latin root *medi-* means "middle" and is the origin of the word *median*.

By getting kids up and moving, connecting words to their lives, and focusing on visual ways of learning, we give kids a solid experience to link to words. It won't be forgotten, because they have made connections to other learning. Embedded vocabulary mini-lessons take very little time but can make a big impact on kids who learn in active ways.

Figure 2.1 *Math vocabulary lesson on* outlier

Word of the Day

Many middle-level teachers help motivate students to become word conscious by introducing a "Word of the Day." Tonie Weddle shares a new word each day from *100 Words Every Middle Schooler Should Know* from the American Heritage Dictionary series. Most of the words on the list can fit into the category of "general academic words." A list of the selected one hundred words can be found on the *American Heritage Dictionary* website (http://ahdictionary.com/word/hundredmiddle.html).

Weddle writes the Word of the Day, the part of speech, origin, pronunciation, brief definition, and a sentence containing the word on a small whiteboard at the front of the class (see Figure 2.2). As each class comes in, she introduces the word and then tries to use the word during class as many times as possible. She also encourages students to use the Word of the Day in discussion and in writing.

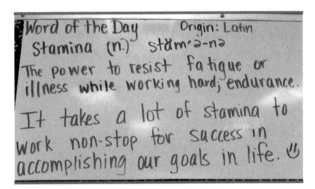

Figure 2.2 *Word of the Day board*

Another way to go about this is to encourage students to collect interesting words to be added to Word of the Day. When we ask students to self-collect noteworthy words from texts or reference materials, we not only get a sense of the kinds of words that students find fascinating or confusing but also get a chance to nurture independence in vocabulary learning (Ruddell and Shearer 2002). Invite students to write a word they find thought-provoking on one side of a card. On the other side, ask students to write the part of speech, origin, pronunciation, brief definition, and a sentence containing the word. Collect the words in a jar or box each month, and draw out a word per day. This will help make the Word of the Day a community activity where kids are learning together and play to the middle-level learners' developing sense of autonomy.

Intentional Word Play

When I was a classroom teacher, occasionally I would intentionally introduce words into the classroom conversation that I knew would be unfamiliar, maybe a little goofy. For example, I might announce to my students, "I observe a plethora of writing implements on the foundation of this dwelling." After an initial sea of puzzled faces, the kids would try to figure out what I had said ("I see a lot of pencils and pens on the floor of this room."). I repeated variations of sentences using the words several times throughout the week. After a few days, I invariably had students saying they would love to have "a plethora of pieces of candy" or that "this dwelling is too hot today."

For this type of word play to occur, we have to create a safe and risk-free environment where vocabulary development can thrive. We all feel more comfortable when we are welcomed and appreciated. We know we can take appropriate risks and that those risks will be celebrated. Our students are no different. Middle-level students are highly egocentric with a nagging sensation that everyone is looking at them. They are often worried about being embarrassed or humiliated in front of their peers if they volunteer an answer. With the rise of bullying, especially over social media, they may not be far off. We have to make our classrooms a place where it is acceptable and encouraged to take academic risks and become word conscious together.

Organizing for Middle-Level Vocabulary Development

I sat at a table in the back of a classroom the last period of the day, trying to be unobtrusive while observing and enjoying the vocabulary lesson. Heterogeneous small groups of students worked together in teams, fully concentrating on the task at hand. Suddenly, the crackling of the intercom invaded the room and a voice boomed, "Will seventh-grade boys who think they might want to play football next year please come to the gym at this time?" In a flash, every boy in the room was headed out the door, even the ones who didn't look as though they could lift an average sack of flour. Taken aback, the teacher and I made eye contact and then just starting laughing and shaking our heads helplessly at the inevitability. The vocabulary lesson, for all intents and purposes, was officially over. Experienced middle-level teachers will recognize this fact of daily school life, as this was hardly an isolated incident.

Time for vocabulary development seems to be a luxury at the middle level, but it is an expense we must make. Young adolescents need strategic, rich vocabulary instruction, and to implement such a plan the adults in schools have to work together. Let's take a look at a few organizational approaches to middle-level vocabulary development that cover the spectrum.

Vocabulary Development Across an Interdisciplinary Team

Thea Bowman Leadership Academy is located in Gary, Indiana, a small industrial town of about eighty thousand residents on the outskirts of Chicago. Like many steel cities at the beginning of the twentieth century, Gary once provided good jobs and security to its workers but now is only a shade of its former glory. According to the most recent census data, the median income for a family in Gary is $32,205. The National Center for Children in Poverty reports that the average income for a family of four should be at least $44,700 to meet basic needs in the United States (Addy, Engelhardt, and Skinner 2013).

Bowman is a nonreligious charter school named after Sister Thea Bowman, an African American nun, teacher, and scholar. Bowman includes 227 students in grades seven and eight as part of a secondary school of grades seven through twelve. Ninety-seven percent of the students are African American, and 74 percent of the students receive free or reduced-price lunches. Test scores for grades seven and eight are currently a bit below the Indiana state average, but students at Bowman achieve as well as or better than most of the schools in the community that include middle-level students.

Charles Williams, a former middle-level English language arts teacher, was (at the time I met him) the assistant principal in charge of the middle school section. Williams is a dynamic young administrator and had already encouraged the middle school teachers to infuse vocabulary across their teams. However, after hearing about *Word Nerds*, Williams thought that the school could become even more vocabulary focused and invited me to his school to get to know the students and the faculty.

Organizing for Vocabulary Study at Bowman

At Bowman, teachers work together in interdisciplinary teams—one seventh-grade team and one eighth-grade team. Each team includes the four major content teachers representing mathematics, science, social studies, and English language arts. A Spanish teacher is also part of each team. After much thoughtful discussion, the middle school teachers at Bowman decided to adopt a team-based vocabulary approach for their school. Core teachers would work together to develop vocabulary in a unified effort across each team. The Spanish teacher would continue with the language curriculum but would incorporate some of the vocabulary strategies into classes.

A discussion by the faculty about how to best organize their time for schoolwide vocabulary instruction produced several ideas. One thought was to create a dedicated time in the schedule each day for vocabulary study. This was quickly discarded after the teachers realized that vocabulary, because of the myriad of ways in which it can be used, should be taught within the context of the discipline. For example, if the science teacher selected the term *solution*, the term would have a very different meaning than if taught by the math teacher. Because of these disparities, the teachers at Bowman decided it was essential to teach the word as it was being used within the lesson. Their belief was that vocabulary study must be embedded within each content-area class.

Terms were introduced at the beginning of the cycle (Monday), and students explored vocabulary words using graphic organizers. Teachers were then free to choose whatever activities they thought best for their students to engage more deeply with vocabulary and any related words. Bowman teachers gave a common team assessment on the last day of the two-week cycle during the students' eighth-hour class.

Selecting Words to Teach at Bowman

After much debate, the teachers at Bowman Academy ultimately decided to have each teacher on the team select a Tier 3 term (domain-specific word) related to their unit of study. The word selected was one that students would see in text or were expected to use in discussions and know on assessments. Williams also selected one Tier 2 (general academic) word to be taught schoolwide. This made a total of five words for deep study during each two-week vocabulary cycle.

Each Bowman teacher focused on selected terms, tried to tie in the terms of their colleagues, and incorporated vocabulary strategies during their lessons. Teachers continued to include related words in content-area lessons, but the five selected words and their word networks received sustained attention. Bowman students enjoyed activities that included drama, art, and music, so that impromptu acting, artwork, and singing easily became part of vocabulary instruction in some classes. This helped all students develop rich representations of word meanings (Kucan et al. 2007) and provided a natural outlet for creative kids. It also made vocabulary learning enjoyable and motivating.

Vocabulary Development Within an English Language Arts Department

Eastside Middle School is a public school located within the city limits of Mt. Washington, Kentucky. Although once a booming independent economy in the 1800s, Mt. Washington is now considered a bedroom community for the city of Louisville. The population is approximately nine thousand and consists of a couple of main streets and spreading subdivisions. Like many rural towns, fast-food restaurants and chain stores are rapidly filling the sides of the road leading into town that once bordered farmland. The median income for a Mt. Washington family is $46,507, placing it slightly above the basic-needs income level.

Eastside houses 593 students in grades six, seven, and eight. Ninety-seven percent of the students are white, and 24 percent of the students receive free or reduced-price lunches. Kentucky has the distinction of being the first state to adopt the Common Core State Standards in 2010, and students in Kentucky were also the first to participate in an assessment based on the CCSS. Eastside's staff members have worked exceptionally hard to plan and implement instructional strategies that will help their students succeed on these assessments. The teachers participate in content-area professional learning communities (PLCs), where they work to align curriculum, plan instruction, discuss assessment results, and make decisions together.

Tabi Echols, an innovative district resource teacher assigned to the school, plans and leads the PLC meetings in all content areas. Echols brings in new ideas, facilitates teacher sharing, and helps plan common assessments. Teachers keep careful records of student progress and needs. Prior to adapting this vocabulary plan, Eastside had already celebrated a rise in student achievement, and in a recent year had been ranked as a top-achieving middle school in the state.

Organizing for Vocabulary Study at Eastside

At Eastside, the English language arts PLC consisted of all ELA teachers, along with collaborating special education teachers and the school library media specialist. Teachers participating in this PLC took on the responsibility for selecting a small number of core words for deep study while content-area teachers reinforced these words and other content-area vocabulary words across grade-level teams. English language arts teachers introduced the vocabulary words selected for deep study, engaged students in active learning of words, and administered vocabulary assessments. Echols created the vocabulary assessments for each grade level and helped teachers keep track of students' vocabulary progress.

Selecting Words to Teach at Eastside

Eastside students participate in an English language arts assessment three times a year to gauge their progress toward meeting standards. The teachers in the ELA professional learning community decided the best place to start would be to simply ask students to remember some words they found difficult on the progress monitoring assessment. When the ELA teachers analyzed student responses at a PLC meeting, they were astonished at some of the words that students had noted. Tier 2 words such as *elaborate*, *depict*, and *convey* were words that teachers (and test makers) assumed that kids knew, but the pattern was clear—students needed vocabulary work to even understand the assessments they were expected to take.

Together, the English language arts teachers discussed options for vocabulary words. By using information they gathered from students and by pinpointing vocabulary words that would be important for upcoming English language arts lessons, they chose five or six words for deep study for each grade level. Because Echols facilitated all the content-area meetings, she was able to reinforce vocabulary with teachers across the curriculum.

Vocabulary Development Using an ELA Published Program

Bullitt Lick Middle School is a public school located on the banks of the Salt River about twenty miles from Louisville and has a rich pioneer history. In 1773, Captain Thomas Bullitt surveyed the area's natural salt licks where wild animals came to get nutrients, and Bullitt's Lick was named after him. The town of Shepherdsville is the county seat and has a population of approximately 11,500. Shepherdsville is located right off I-65, and a number of fast-food restaurants and gas stations make it a busy intersection for interstate travelers. Several small industries also make their home in the Shepherdsville area. The median income for a family of four is $40,878, hovering near the low-income bracket.

Bullitt Lick houses 441 students in grades six, seven, and eight. Ninety-five percent of the students are white, and 68 percent of students receive free or reduced-price lunches. This school has had some tough times in the past but certainly seems to be in the midst of a turn-around, having demonstrated gains in all academic areas on the state assessment in the past few years. Tonie Weddle, a seventh-grade English language arts teacher, has earned National Board Certification and represented the school district as a member of the Kentucky Department of Education ELA Leadership Network to study the standards.

Organizing for Vocabulary Study in Weddle's Classroom

Because Bullitt Lick is a Title I school, it receives extra funds to address the needs of students who need more time and attention to achieve. The faculty made a decision to use some of the funding to purchase a published literacy program specifically designed to help kids meet the expectations of the Common Core State Standards. Although the program has excellent authors and the vocabulary strategies are better than most, Weddle still saw a need to focus even more instructional time on helping kids learn how to determine the meanings of unfamiliar words and phrases.

Weddle followed the literacy program as a guide, but she made a number of significant changes in vocabulary instruction. First, she introduced words in sentence context instead of in isolation on a chart. Then she helped students add to their word networks, included more active practice activities, and evaluated in ways that matched how students would be formally assessed.

Selecting Words to Teach in Weddle's Classroom

The published literacy program at Bullitt Lick Middle has about twelve words selected by the authors for each unit of study. These words are included in the texts that students will read and will be on the assessments that students take that are part of the program. Weddle regularly asked students to rate their knowledge of the words but usually had so many students who needed instruction that she ended up using all twelve words from the program for deeper study.

Figure 2.3 *Smack Down words*

She called the vocabulary words Smack Down words and kept a list of the words on charts in the room (see Figure 2.3). Whenever students saw a Smack Down word in text, they smacked the word with their hand and then engaged in a discussion about how it was used. This helped students become more aware of the vocabulary words in text.

Weddle arranged her classroom so that heterogeneous groups of students could sit together and planned for a lot of small-group work. This arrangement helped support those who needed more help during vocabulary study and throughout the rest of the class period.

Vocabulary Study as an Integral Part of Instruction

Students need vocabulary instruction to succeed across the curriculum, and planning for connected, integrated vocabulary study that meets the needs of students in the middle grades is a piece of the academic learning puzzle.

Middle grades students are in the middle of rapid physical, emotional, social, and academic change. As their teachers, we must be cognizant of those needs and plan for vocabulary instruction to increase student learning. But we certainly have a challenging job when it comes to incorporating vocabulary study across a school day. There are so many words and so little time! What we do with that time, how we organize our classes, and how we think about kids and their word learning matters.

As Steven Stahl (2005, 99) said, "Vocabulary instruction should be part of the fabric of the classroom—an integral part of all instruction." He also reminded us that word learning should be part of a knowledge curriculum in which words are embedded, "rather than taught as isolated factoids" (99). The typical middle grades schedule makes it difficult to keep this sentiment in mind. However, we know that young adolescents need more, not fewer, connected experiences across their school day. For vocabulary instruction to be deep, rich, and abiding, there has to be a strategic plan to emphasize a small number of words for each instructional cycle.

In addition, when we enrich our classrooms, hallways, and common areas with remarkable and intriguing words, we show we love words no matter where we are. And when adults and peers love words, students learn to love them, too. Together, we become a word-learning community.

Chapter 3

WORDS AND CONTEXT

The beginning of wisdom is the definition of terms.

—Socrates

In one of my graduate literacy classes, Dr. Ellen McIntyre introduced a paragraph from a famous experiment on comprehension and recall by John Bransford and Marcia Johnson (1972, 722). If you are not familiar with it, see if you can infer what the paragraph is about:

> The procedure is actually quite simple. First you arrange things into different groups. Of course, one pile may be sufficient depending on how much there is to do. If you have to go somewhere else due to lack of facilities that is the next step, otherwise you are pretty well set. It is important not to overdo things. That is, it is better to do too few things at once than too many. In the short run this may not seem important but complications can easily arise. A mistake can be expensive as well. At first the whole procedure will seem complicated. Soon, however, it will become just another facet of life. It is difficult to foresee any end to the necessity for this task in the immediate future, but then one never can tell. After the procedure is completed one arranges the materials into different groups again. Then they can be put into their appropriate places. Eventually they will be used once more and the whole cycle will then have to be repeated. However, that is part of life.

Do you know the topic? Many people don't until they hear the title, which is "Washing Clothes." If you read the paragraph again, the clues are plain to see. Dr. McIntyre introduced this passage so we would understand the power of context in comprehending text. Although all the clues are available on the page, we often have to infer the meaning based on the context.

Using context is also a useful strategy for understanding unfamiliar words and phrases (Graves 2006), if the text provides sufficient clues to support an inference. However, from my own experience and from visits to middle grades classrooms, I know that many students struggle with using context to figure out the meanings of words.

What Is Context?

When I was in sixth grade, my teacher would peer at us over the top of the glasses perched at the end of her nose and exclaim, "Read between the lines!" The other kids and I would glance at one another and shrug. I was a good reader, yet I didn't know what she was talking about. I'm sure that the students who needed help in reading didn't understand the reference either. Of course, now I realize that Mrs. Rogers meant for us to use the context of the passage to understand the meaning of the word. As a teacher, I also understand that most middle grades students need guidance in how to use context.

Sometimes a reader can use the information within the word, such as deciphering the meaning of prefixes, roots, and suffixes. Sometimes the reader can find hints in the sentence to figure out what the word means. In other instances, the reader has to search for clues in sentences coming before or after, look at the larger passage, or decide whether the inferred definition makes sense within the type of text (Blachowicz et al. 2013). Students also make connections to their own background knowledge when deciding what a new word means (Nagy and Scott 1990). They connect the word to words they already know. Sometimes they know a synonym or an antonym. These patterns of word learning are called *word schemas*.

When Molly encounters an unknown word in a text, for example, she doesn't have to guess every word in the English language to figure it out. Instead, she activates her word schema about the type of word that would make sense. Her brain begins to race: Is it a noun or verb? Does the word have a prefix or a suffix? What do the prefix and suffix mean? What does the root mean? Have I seen the word used somewhere before? How does the word connect with other words I know? What are words that would make sense in this sentence? Molly's brain can quickly narrow down her choices for what the right word might be. She can then hypothesize (infer) about the meaning of a particular word.

Context and the Common Core State Standards

The word *context*, as it refers to word recognition or determining the meaning of words, appears approximately thirty-eight times in the K–12 Common Core English Language Arts Standards. The expectation that students should be able to use context to determine the meanings of words and phrases actually begins in first grade. By the time students reach grade six, the first indicator for Language Standard 4 in the ELA Standards is the same until the end of high school:

Use context (e.g., the overall meaning of a sentence or paragraph; a word's position or function in a sentence) as a clue to the meaning of a word or phrase.

According to the ELA Language Standards, students should be able to use sentence- and passage-level context, with increasing sophistication, to determine the meanings of unfamiliar words and phrases in the increasingly complex texts they read. Reading Standard 4 in Literature, Informational Text, History/Social Studies, and Science and Technical Subjects also focuses on the ability to determine the meaning of unfamiliar words and phrases when reading stories, poetry, drama, and nonfiction, including historical documents as well as scientific and technical materials. Using context is one way to do that.

Standardized Assessment and Use of Context

The ability to identify context clues also becomes highly important in the way new standardized assessments have been designed. We can all probably remember taking standardized tests that relied heavily on reading passages containing a few unfamiliar words and phrases. Whether we realized it or not, we had to use context to comprehend the passage and to determine the correct meaning of these words. The National Assessment of Educational Progress (NAEP) vocabulary test, which I described in Chapter 1, assesses vocabulary in context in a more overt way to "capture students' ability to use their understanding or sense of words to acquire meaning from the passages they read" (National Center for Education Statistics [NCES] 2012, 1). Vocabulary on the NAEP is assessed in context. In some new assessments, students are also asked to identify the context clues (or "evidence") that helped them understand the meaning of the word or phrase.

The ability to use context to determine the word that might complete a sentence is an important test-taking skill as students participate in state assessments, tests of intelligence, and scholastic aptitude throughout their school years. See Chapter 7 for more discussion about context in standardized assessment.

Is Context Really That Important?

Some researchers have theorized that most vocabulary is learned from context (Sternberg 1987). Michael Graves (2006) considers use of context to be the most important word-learning strategy.

However, other researchers have found that context is much more helpful to older students and better readers (Swanborn and de Glopper 1999) than younger and less-experienced readers. In *Bringing Words to Life*, Isobel Beck, Margaret McKeown, and Linda Kucan (2002) disputed the conventional wisdom that students learn vocabulary from context for three reasons: (1) it's difficult to learn words from context because many natural contexts are not very informative; (2) students must read widely and deeply enough to encounter unfamiliar words; (3) many students do not have the necessary skills to be able to infer the meanings of words they do not know.

Does this mean that we should not teach students to try to determine the meanings of unfamiliar words in context? Of course not! Middle-level students need to understand that looking for context clues can often help them determine the meaning of unfamiliar words if the context contains enough information to make an inference. When we introduce words in context for deep vocabulary study, teachers can make sure that context clues are apparent. We also can show students that some sentences or passages do not have many clues. This prepares them to adopt multiple strategies for word leaning.

It is also true that students must read widely and deeply enough to encounter unfamiliar words. Many studies on learning words from context were conducted at a time when students read more traditional text than they typically do now. Recent studies have found that text complexity in school materials and the amount of independent reading have actually been declining since 1962 (e.g., summarized in Appendix A of the English Language Arts Standards found at www.corestandards.org). A feature of complex text is more challenging vocabulary, and many students are likely to encounter more difficult words in close reading lessons than they may come upon naturally in their independent reading. Students need to learn to approach unfamiliar vocabulary with confidence when reading challenging texts.

If students do not have the skills to infer meanings of words, we must teach them! As Jennifer Geddes, a teacher at Eastside Middle, mused, "Back before the idea of schema in reading comprehension was really big, we would ask students about their background knowledge and they didn't know what we were talking about. Now I ask about schema, and they immediately begin telling me the connections they can make. It's almost like the phrase *context clues* is something they have just never heard before. We have to teach them how to look for clues so they can figure out word meanings."

When we introduce words in context, students gain practice in inferring word meanings. This is a skill they will need to draw on again and again.

Vocabulary Circles of Knowledge

Consider the way Bowman teacher Brandi Odom reinforces this point for her students. When Bowman students struggled with long, unfamiliar words in text, Odom realized that part of the problem was her students' lack of word confidence. "Some of my students get very nervous, and I have to assure them it's not the end of the world when they see a word they don't know," Odom explained. Most students could decode words but then didn't always know what they meant.

She decided to adapt a concept they already understood to help ease their fears. In a professional development session, she had learned about Circles of Knowledge, a graphic organizer that can assist students when they are brainstorming writing topics (www.smekens-education.com). Like a target, this diagram contains expanding circles for sources of things to write about. In the bull's-eye is personal knowledge or experience. The circle surrounding the bull's-eye is someone or something you know or have heard. Books or media are contained in the third circle, and the circle surrounding all the others contains the phrase: "make it up." All students had a copy of this chart and had been using it successfully in their writing workshop to generate topics.

Odom decided to relate Circles of Knowledge to vocabulary and used it to conduct a think-aloud (Davey 1983), showing kids how she figures out an unknown word. She shared how they could use the same type of thinking when figuring out the meaning of a word they have never seen. Instead of shutting down and skipping the word (what Odom calls "running and hiding"), students would have strategies they could use.

Odom began, "Say, there is a word I don't know."

The kids were astonished. "What? You don't know a word?" "I can't believe it!" You're the language arts teacher!"

Odom chuckled. "Well, I don't know everything, but I can try to figure it out. I'm your teacher, but I do not know everything. I have to use strategies, too. And I can show you how to find out."

The kids looked at her expectantly. "The dot in the middle represents me, or my personal experience with the word," she explained. "So I ask myself, have I ever used this word myself? If the answer is no, I go to the next circle, which is someone else. So maybe I don't use that word, but I've heard someone else use it." She continued, using the word *insubordinate* as an example. "Like, maybe the principal saw a group of students running down the hallway screaming and yelling, and he called them *insubordinate*. Then I have to think about what he meant."

As Odom looked around the room, she could see that most of the kids were still puzzled. They had heard this word several times but had always been a bit baffled by its meaning. She decided to try another example, "Say you are in a store and a small child is throwing a tantrum. The child is screaming and crying, 'I want a toy now!'"

"We used to do that all the time, Ms. Odom," called a voice from the back of the room. Odom smiled and continued. "If the mother is telling the child to stop being insubordinate or we will leave this store, what does that mean?"

The kids discussed for a few moments. "Does it mean not following rules? Is that what it means?"

"Yes, *insubordinate* means not following the rules," said Odom.

One of the girls called out, "Ooh! Big, fancy word!"

As the class laughed, Odom said, "Yes, we are learning big, fancy words that can help you understand reading better.

"So that's the second level. The next level is something you may have seen or heard in the media or on a TV show or the news. Maybe it's a word you have seen in another book. The last level in our Circles of Knowledge for writing was to make it up. For vocabulary, we are going to say 'predict the meaning.' We want to look at the sentence or passage and think about what the word might mean based on what the other words are around it."

With that, Odom left her students with a strategy to try rather than running and hiding from words they can pronounce but don't understand.

Types of Context Clues

When we teach students to use context clues to determine meanings of words, we are teaching them to engage in *contextual analysis*. Savvy readers almost subconsciously scan and analyze the surrounding text when they spot an unfamiliar word or phrase. However, identifying context clues is often a difficult task for middle-level students. Sometimes the problem lies with the text—for example, if there are not enough clues available to hypothesize a meaning. In other instances, the clues may seem clear to an experienced reader but not always to a middle grades student. Trish Priddy, a seventh-grade ELA teacher at Eastside Middle School, was surprised when she began asking students to circle the context clues in sentences containing vocabulary words. "I was shocked!" she exclaimed. "This is the hardest thing in the world for them to do. The clue is blatantly there, and they don't see it. No wonder they are struggling with everything else, because they just do not have that skill."

Studies are mixed about whether there are consistent benefits to teaching students to identify specific types of context clues to define unknown words (Graves and Silverman 2011). Michael Graves (2006, 27) concluded, based on the findings of several researchers, that instruction in how to determine context clues by type can be beneficial, but "only well-planned, powerful, and relatively lengthy instruction is likely to prove effective." As Charles Williams, the assistant principal at Bowman, said, "When I taught in high school in a neighboring town, one of the strategies we were supposed to teach was to identify the type of context clue. As a teacher, I didn't really care if they could tell me (whether) it's a definition clue or a synonym clue. I just wanted them to be able to look at the sentence and see if there are clues available to help them."

Because of the renewed emphasis on identifying context in standardized assessments and the positive studies that support contextualized learning, it seems worth the time to introduce types of context clues as part of an intentional, strategic plan for deep vocabulary study. Let's take a look at seven types of context clues appropriate to teach middle school students.

1. Definition

In some sentences, the definition of a word is directly stated and is often found right after the word. The following sentence contains an example of a definition clue for the word *marsupial*:

> A <u>marsupial</u> is an animal that bears its young in a pouch outside the mother's body.

Signal words for definition context clue are words such as *is, is called, which is, means,* and *refers to*.

2. Example/Illustration

Sentences can sometimes include examples of a certain word. In this sentence, the word *persecuted* is illustrated:

> Galileo was <u>persecuted</u> for his idea that the earth revolved around the sun; for example, his book was banned, he had to leave the church, and he was sentenced to prison.

Examples of signal words include *for example, for instance, like, such as, to illustrate,* or *including*.

3. Synonym/Restatement

Sometimes writers include another word or phrase that means the same as the focus word. The synonym can either be found in the sentence with the word or sentences before or after that sentence. An example of a synonym clue follows:

> Thomas worked <u>laboriously</u> on the project. After spending many hours of backbreaking effort, it was finally finished.

In this example, the reader would need to read the next sentence to see a phrase that is a synonym for the word *laboriously*. Sometimes the synonym clue is in the form of a restatement enclosed within commas or dashes:

A <u>malodorous</u> smell, a really foul odor, filled the basement of the old house.

4. Antonym/Contrast

When using the antonym context clue, the reader can figure out the meaning of an unknown word from an opposite word or phrase. An example of a sentence with an antonym clue for the word *congruent* is the following:

Lines A and B are <u>congruent</u>, but Lines C and D are not the same length.

Signal words are *but, though, unlike, in contrast to, instead of, yet, on the other hand, however,* and *whereas.*

5. Inference

Inference clues are based on logic and reasoning. The reader has to think about what the author is trying to say and make a prediction about the meaning of a word based on what would make sense. An example of a sentence with an inference clue is the following:

Anita loved to play soccer so much that on game day she often felt <u>exuberant</u>.

The reader can infer that since Anita loves soccer she would be excited and happy on a game day.

6. Grammar and Punctuation

Another context clue is grammar. Sometimes figuring out a word's part of speech can help narrow down the meaning. Also, the English language has a distinct syntax, which means parts of speech usually follow an order. For example, adjectives usually come before nouns in English (whereas in Spanish adjectives follow nouns).

Using Lewis Carroll's "Jabberwocky," I can use what I know about the grammar of the English language to understand more about the nonsense words in the poem:

'Twas brillig, and the slithy toves
Did gyre and gimble in the wabe;
All mimsy were the borogoves,
And the mome raths outgrabe.

Punctuation helps me figure out *'Twas*—a contraction for "it was." In the English language, the way *brillig* is placed after "it was" leads me to think it is a noun or an adjective. The word "the" comes before *toves, wabe, borogoves,* and *raths,* which means they are probably nouns. *Slithy* seems to describe *toves* and is most likely an adjective, as are *mimsy* (describes *borogoves*) and *mome* (*raths*). The word *did* is a helping verb for *gyre* and *gimble,* so they are verbs. *Outgrabe* could be a verb (what the *mome raths* did). This doesn't help me determine all the meanings of the nonsense words, but it does help me narrow them down.

7. Use of Word Parts

A "within word" use of context is the ability to analyze the parts of a word to better understand its meaning. Interpreting the meaning of the prefix, root, and suffix of a multisyllabic word and then checking it against the larger context of the sentence can be a useful strategy in determining the meaning of the word. Chapter 4 of this book is dedicated to this strategy.

Practicing Word Context with *Baloney*

A fun way to practice the use of context that I have used with middle-level students is to select text containing nonsense words (or what seem to be nonsense words). We have already taken a look at the poem "Jabberwocky," which is a classic poem full of nonsense words. A more modern (and possibly more motivating) example is Jon Scieszka and Lane Smith's (2001) wonderful picture book *Baloney (Henry P.).* In this book, a space alien boy is late for school. Miss Bugscuffle is set on giving him Permanent Lifelong Detention unless he can come up with a good excuse. Using strange "space" words, Henry P. Baloney relates a tall tale about why he is late. "Well I would have been exactly on time . . . , "said Henry. "But . . . I misplaced my trusty *zimulis*." Henry then relates that he found the *zimulis* in his *deski,* and someone had put his *deski* in a *torraku*. The story continues, getting wilder and wilder, and students have to use picture and context clues to decipher the unfamiliar words in the text.

By giving students access to the text alone (and not the pictures), we can create richer and higher-level experiences with context. Ask students to work with a partner or in a small group to figure out the meaning of the strange words. There are lots of clues hidden here and there among the sentences, passages, and even within the words themselves. Students can identify the clues, making a list of the words and the clues they used to determine the meanings of the words and continually checking to make sure they still make sense as the story progresses. To conclude the lesson, share the "decoder" from the end of the story, which reveals that the apparent nonsense words are actually words from a variety of languages.

To extend the lesson into nonfiction, invite students to read and discuss Ben Macintyre's tongue-in-cheek review of *Baloney* from the *New York Times* (http://www.nytimes.com/books/01/05/20/reviews/010520.20macintt.html). The review is full of fantastic vocabulary, providing another training ground for learning how to use context to determine the meanings of words.

Introducing Words for Deep Vocabulary Study

In *Word Nerds*, we discussed how we introduce vocabulary words in context by using a procedure with cloze sentence strips in a pocket chart. A cloze sentence is one that has a blank where the vocabulary word should go. We make sure that the cloze sentences we write to introduce vocabulary words contain appropriate context clues. We start by asking students to brainstorm words that might fit into the blank, and then we introduce each word written on a card. Students repeat the word and clap the syllables. We discuss the meaning, relating it to students' lives, and then ask a student to place the correct card into the sentence.

Encouraging young students to think about how new words might fit into sentences prepares them to use context to determine the meanings of unfamiliar words they encounter in text. But we also should not overlook the importance of emphasizing to older students that words often have multiple meanings. Using context to determine the meaning of a word helps readers understand the way the word is used in a particular sentence or passage.

As I worked with middle-level schools, I suggested using this procedure to introduce the words selected for deep vocabulary study:

1. Show the students a sentence or passage with a blank where the vocabulary word would go. Make sure to include a good context clue when you write the sentence or passage so that students can have enough information to make an appropriate prediction. As lessons progress, teach students different types of context clues so they can identify clues during this introduction.
2. Make sure all students can see the sentence or passage. A pocket chart with sentence strips, a magnetic board with word cards, or computer projection is best so the whole class can work together.

3. Ask students to predict a word that might go in the blank based on context clues. Give them a moment to brainstorm. This brainstorming is helping them connect to their background knowledge about words.

4. Show each word. Discuss its part of speech. If the word has a meaningful prefix, suffix, or root, point that out to students (as study progresses, they should recognize these on their own). Let students brainstorm what the word means and why they think so. Ask engaging questions to guide them to think about and discuss the word meaning as it relates to your content area.

5. Do not initially tell students what the words mean unless absolutely necessary. We want them to use context clues to figure out the types of words that might go into the blank. At the conclusion of the discussion, affirm the definition you want them to use using a student-friendly explanation that relates to their lives.

Good teachers often adapt to meet the needs of their students, whether working as an interdisciplinary team, as an English language arts professional learning community, or as a teacher working alone with a published literacy curriculum. The teachers at Bowman, Eastside, and Bullitt Lick were no exception.

Introducing Words on an Interdisciplinary Team

One way to introduce words is to make vocabulary a shared experience across an interdisciplinary team. At Bowman, Charles Williams demonstrated a way for teachers to introduce words based on a popular game.

Students at Bowman had been enthusiastically playing a game on a mobile phone app called "What's the Word?" In this game, the player is presented with four pictures and blanks where the letters of a word should go. The bottom of the screen includes a group of letters to choose. The object is to think of a way that all four pictures are connected and then choose letters that create a word that links the four pictures. For example, recent pictures shown included: (1) a lakeside; (2) a ceramic pig; (3) a close-up of the numbers on a credit card; and (4) a beach with kayaks. There were four blanks for the word. Kids were working to think of a word that connected the pictures, when Kenneth called out, "I know! It's *bank*!" He pulled B-A-N-K into the blanks and the program rewarded him with a happy little ding. A fun way to think about multiple meanings as well as practice inference!

Williams decided to use the "What's the Word?" game to motivate students in vocabulary study. He created a PowerPoint presentation with pictures to represent each of the five words being introduced across the seventh-grade team. The seventh-grade words for this vocabulary cycle were *adversary* (general academic word); *plot* (ELA); *confederation* (social studies); *solution* (science); and *slope* (mathematics). Williams created four slides for each word. The word *adversary* was depicted by an animated GIF of a cartoon villain with the sentence "The hero had to defeat his _____ in order to save the day." On this slide, students predicted the word that would fit into the blank. The second slide showed the sentence with the word *adversary* inserted into the blank. The third slide showed the dictionary definition. The fourth slide was entitled "Our definition." On this slide, students were invited to work together to come up with a student-friendly definition.

To begin, each teacher showed this PowerPoint in one class to introduce all the words for the team. Kids were excited: "Hey! It's like our game! Cool!" In subsequent vocabulary cycles, each teacher was responsible for introducing the word for his or her content area.

Figure 3.1 *Introducing words in context in social studies*

The seventh-grade social studies teacher, Stephen Currie, took this idea to heart. During one lesson, he showed the class a five-slide PowerPoint he created to introduce *interdependence*, the new word for deep vocabulary study. Currie introduced the first slide (see Figure 3.1) with a drumroll sound effect followed by a "You can do it!" sound effect. The first slide showed three clip art pictures: a photo of Walmart, a picture of a Walmart logo with "Made in China" written underneath, and a picture of a cartoon globe with a tag that says "Made in China" attached. The sentence said, "There is no Wal-Mart without China is an example of _____."

Students brainstormed ideas about the word that might go into the blank. Currie then showed them the next slide. Animated GIFs of Mufasa and Young Simba from Disney's *The Lion King* were placed at the top. The dialogue between Mufasa and Young Simba was written out so students could read along as an audio clip played:

Mufasa:	Everything you see exists together in a delicate balance. As king you need to understand that balance and respect all the creatures, from the crawling ant to the leaping antelope.
Young Simba:	But, Dad, don't we eat the antelope?
Mufasa:	Yes, Simba, but let me explain. When we die, our bodies become the grass and the antelope eat the grass. And so we are all connected in the great Circle of Life.

After giving students a brief moment to discuss the second slide, Currie then flipped to the third slide, which was a picture of an automobile with all the parts labeled. The diagram clearly showed how various parts of a car were made in different parts of the world. Currie gave students a minute to discuss the facts found on the slide, such as "Tires come from a number of countries, including Mexico, South Korea, or Chile," and "Many cars feature windows manufactured in Venezuela or the United States." Students began to speculate. Kevin mused, "I know it has something to do with the world is connected . . ."

Currie then displayed the Walmart slide again. This time, the sentence was completed, "There is no Walmart without China is an example of <u>interdependence</u>." Currie asked students to repeat the word *interdependence*. Then he asked, "What might be other examples of 'interdependence'?"

"Maybe oil in the Middle East? If we don't have oil, people can't drive cars or heat houses," ventured Ambrose.

Kennedy nodded and said, "When countries need money or weapons they go to their allies. That's interdependence."

"Bananas," added Diamond. "The countries we get them from may have had a drought. Then we wouldn't be able to get any."

Ramon volunteered, "Well, in World War II mostly all countries joined together to help each other."

"Right," said Currie. "Those are all good examples of interdependence." He then flipped to the last slide. This slide was entitled "The Dictionary Says . . ." It included the syllabication, pronunciation, part of speech, dictionary definition, alternate form, and origin, as shown in Figure 3.2.

After quickly discussing the slide, Currie said, "Let's take a look at the origin of *interdependence*. What words have you seen with 'inter' and 'dependence'?" Students brainstormed words they knew and what they meant, such as *depend, independence, dependent, interfaith, interaction,* and *intercouncil.*

The Dictionary Says...

in·ter·de·pend·ence [in-ter-di-**pen**-duh ns]
noun
the quality or condition of being <u>interdependent</u>, or mutually reliant on each other: *Globalization of economies leads to an ever-increasing interdependence of countries.*

Sometimes, **in·ter·de·pend·en·cy.**

Origin:
<u>inter-</u> + <u>dependence</u>

Figure 3.2 *Thinking about a dictionary definition*

Currie continued, "What does 'inter' mean?" Students quickly came to the conclusion that "inter" means "between."

"What does 'dependence' mean?" After a discussion of the word "depend" (something you can count on), Currie said, "So what does the word 'interdependence' mean for this class?"

"I think it means social and economy depending on each other," concluded Brian. The class decided that was a pretty good student-friendly definition.

Brandi Odom introduced words differently in her language arts classes. She presented the word she had chosen for their English curriculum connections and assigned students to small groups to interpret the concept. She asked, "What words do you associate with this word? What comes to mind?" Then students came up with different concepts that extended their understanding of the word.

The next day, Odom introduced a topic that was related to the word. Discussion naturally flowed from the word to how it relates to the topic. For example, when students were reading about Anne Frank, Odom asked them to think of examples of *injustice* and immediately got responses.

"They treated her like that just because she was Jewish. That's not right!"

"She had to go into hiding!"

"They made her go to a concentration camp!"

"She had to stop going to school. She couldn't see her friends! That's an injustice!"

Students next thought of a number of examples related to Anne Frank, and Odom later reinforced the word with a vocabulary art activity.

A few days later, when the projector in Odom's classroom blew out, one student quickly sympathized and showed how well she had internalized the vocabulary lesson. "See, Ms. Odom? This is an injustice!" Tina said, shaking her head. "You put in a work order to get that projector fixed a week ago!"

Introducing Words in an English Language Arts PLC

At Eastside Middle School, each ELA teacher was responsible for introducing five selected vocabulary words for their grade level. The ELA teachers introduced the words as their schedules permitted, with some introducing the five chosen words all on one day, and others introducing them one word at a time throughout the first week of the vocabulary cycle.

Trish Priddy, a seventh-grade ELA teacher, introduced one word each day for the first week of the vocabulary cycle. Students then completed a graphic organizer adapted from *Word Nerds* that required them to deeply explore aspects of the word (see Chapter 5 for vocabulary journals, the next step in instruction). Priddy shared the word she had introduced that day with the other content-area teachers on her team. She posted the word in the hall and made sure other adults in the building also knew to use the word. The kids were totally immersed in the word all day long. They heard it every period, from all their content-area teachers. "They came running back to me, saying, 'The library/media specialist used that word you taught us!'" she said. "Even though they are seventh graders, they get excited to hear their other teachers slip the word we are learning into their conversations."

Susan Carlisle, an eighth-grade ELA teacher, created vocabulary "bell ringers" that were available as soon as her students walked into class. This was a quick activity to get the class settled and into the lesson. The bell ringer consisted of a passage displayed on the electronic whiteboard, and students had to find evidence for the definition of the highlighted word in the passage. Carlisle said, "They touch base with the definitions, and then I introduce the bell ringer. We talk about how writers write passages and also how test makers write questions—how there might be a repeated word or some other type of clue."

One day her bell ringer consisted of three sentences for the words *indigenous* (science), *arrogant* (general academic word), and *bias* (English language arts). The student task was as follows: "For each item circle the words/phrases that are the context clues which help you determine the definition of the vocabulary word."

1. In Bernheim Forest there are a variety of plants *indigenous* to Kentucky. Several ornamental grasses thrive in the hot summers and relatively mild winters. The root systems of the pine and maple trees grow and develop easily in the clay soils and take full advantage of the underground springs in the area.
2. A condescending attitude, unjustified confidence and general rudeness toward others have collectively led to the label of *arrogant* for Kanye West.
3. When I drive by a store or restaurant marquee and see misspelled words or improper grammar, my *bias* becomes obvious. I literally will groan aloud or snort in disgust. I want to either get out my purple pen and circle the errors or make a phone call to the manager to urge them to correct the problems!

Carlisle had written these sentences with vocabulary words placed within rich contexts so that students could determine the meaning of the word through contextual analysis. Even so, determining the meanings of words from the context is not an easy task for many students. While the context may seem obvious to educated adults, it takes a lot of practice and reading experience for middle-level kids.

Jennifer Geddes, a sixth-grade ELA teacher, also connected vocabulary with what she was already doing with the Common Core Reading Standards. "Before, vocabulary was always something separate—like a thing that you did on the side. Now I find it easier to tie it into what I am actually teaching," she said. "For example, we were working on poetry, so I asked students to write a haiku about their vocabulary words. It kind of killed two birds with one stone. And it helped reinforce words like *convey, elaborate, connotation, depict,* and *analogy* for sixth graders."

Introducing Words Within an Existing Literacy Curriculum

Tonie Weddle teaches in a middle school that has adopted a published standards-based literacy series for English language arts. Although the published program was written by respected literacy educators, she often supplements the materials to meet her students' needs. This includes beefing up vocabulary instruction so students are more actively involved. As she said, "My kids are smart, but a lot of them are behind. Part of this is due to a lack of vocabulary knowledge. They just need more instruction."

The first year of the vocabulary enrichment plan, Weddle concentrated on the words that had been suggested by the publisher since she knew they would appear on assessments that accompany the literacy series. She introduced new vocabulary words by creating a context-rich cloze sentence for each word. She typed the cloze sentences on a half sheet of paper and included a word bank of the new vocabulary words. The kids then predicted which word from the word bank might complete each sentence. This strategy helped them connect to their background knowledge and knowledge of sentence structure.

After the students completed their predictions, Weddle asked them to flip their papers over. She then stapled a new set of cloze sentence strips to a bulletin board. This time, the sentence was extracted from texts that the students were preparing to read. Weddle pinned index cards with the vocabulary words written on them above the sentences (see Figure 3.3).

The first time she introduced words in this way, she guided her students as they examined the first two sentences. "In the first example, I gave them the regular form of the word, but in the sentences from the text, the words might have prefixes, suffixes, or inflectional endings. For example, the vocabulary word was *fathom*. The word was *fathoms* in the text.

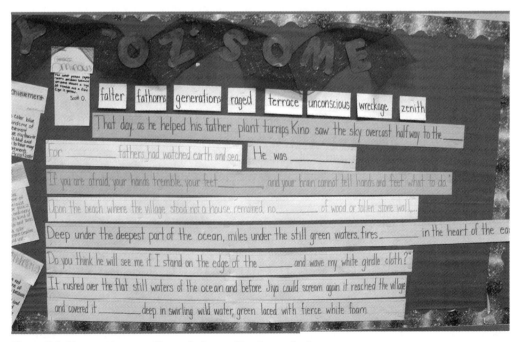

Figure 3.3 *Cloze sentences with words from a literature selection*

The kids noticed the differences." In classes where students needed more support, she first encouraged them to work together as a large group to figure out the words that go in the sentences. In classes where students were more independent, she facilitated work in small groups to determine the word that might fit into each sentence and the context clues that helped them know.

After students had discussed the possible word choices, Weddle handed out a graphic organizer. Students wrote the definition of each word and then worked in groups to find synonyms and antonyms to go with the word using electronic devices or a hard-copy dictionary or thesaurus. They also sketched a quick picture but didn't write a sentence until after they had completely explored the word. "Their sentences were a lot better," Weddle reflected. "I feel like they have a much richer understanding of that word. When they wrote their sentences there wasn't as much structural weirdness, and their sentences were constructed more solidly. They also used the word as a particular part of speech more accurately."

It's All in the Context

As the great British economist Alfred Marshall said, "In common use almost every word has many shades of meaning, and therefore needs to be interpreted by the context." Although he wasn't a reading researcher, Marshall's observation is dead on. Context helps us understand nuances of meaning. It tells us how to pronounce words such as *lead*, whether with a long *e* sound as in, "The head of the line will lead" or with a short *e* sound, as in "Get the lead out!" The context of a sentence or passage also helps us understand the meanings of unfamiliar words.

Being able to infer the meaning of words in rich context is an important word-learning strategy for students to know. As Kim Thompson, a middle-level library media specialist at Eastside, said, "It warms my heart when I have kids come up to me and say, 'I didn't know this word, but I used my context clues to figure it out.'" Understanding the word-learning strategy of using context helps foster independent learning.

Chapter 4

Developing Morphological Awareness

Hyperpolysyllabicomania is a fondness for big words.

—Unknown

Leslie Montgomery stands in front of her fifth-grade class and holds up a card with the word *abolitionist*. She does not say anything. The students buzz as they briefly contemplate the new word and its meaning.

After conferring with his group, Jacob states confidently, "Well, *-ist* means someone who does something."

"Yeah, like a scientist does science!" exclaims Portia.

"And *-tion* means the act or process of doing something," Tianna adds.

Then Maria joins the conversation: "The first part looks like the word *abolish*. Wasn't that word a synonym for *repeal*? And *repeal* means to take something away. So *abolish* must be to take something away or stop something."

"So it means a person who is in the act or process of taking something away. It means a person who stops something from happening. I'm sure that's it," Richie finishes the discussion.

Leslie glances at the clock on the wall. In a single minute, her students have boldly and skillfully dissected unfamiliar vocabulary, using their knowledge of word parts. The conversation was generated entirely by the students, not the teacher. Leslie's students, most of whom did not begin school with a solid academic vocabulary base, have discovered the power of determining the meanings of words they have never seen before by analyzing the prefixes, roots, and suffixes. They have become unabashed word nerds because of the rich and comprehensive vocabulary instruction that Leslie provides.

Now contrast that scenario with the following comments expressed by middle grades teachers before their schools began exploring integrated word study.

"One of our challenges is that kids don't know very elementary prefixes and suffixes. Like 'un-' in front of a word. They don't know that 'un-' means 'not.'"

"They have an initial fear of a big word. If I put a word longer than about five or six letters on the board, you can see the reaction. They have already decided they can't figure it out."

"I don't think my students have any idea that word parts mean something."

Sound familiar? Vocabulary researchers say making educated guesses about the definition of an unfamiliar word by analyzing its parts is an effective literacy strategy (Carlisle 2010) and some say one of the most important word-learning strategies we can use (Graves 2006, 2009). Yet Graves points out that "many upper elementary students do not know even the most common prefixes" (2006, 30). And students in middle school also struggle to understand derivations (Kieffer and Lesaux 2010). How can we make sure our students develop these skills?

First, we have to recognize the importance of including morphology, or the study of the form and structure of words, in our systemic vocabulary plan.

Morphological Awareness—A Key to Word Knowledge

When students learn the meanings of common prefixes, suffixes, and roots and know how to manipulate the parts, it is like giving them a golden key. With the key, they can unlock many of the multisyllabic words in texts they encounter in every content area. When it becomes second nature to analyze words and connect them to related words for deeper understanding, students can be considered to be morphologically aware. Lee Mountain (2005, 744) concluded that "morphemic analysis may be one of the ways to narrow the gap between the vocabulary 'haves' and the 'have nots.'"

Ally is a middle school student who was fortunate to have a teacher who taught her how to break down words to understand them. "In sixth grade, we had to infer the definitions based on the parts of the words. That's the main thing I remember from sixth-grade language arts, and it's really helped me in all my classes. It helps me find meanings of words if I don't know them," Ally explains. "Like on tests, it'll say, 'What's your best inference on the definition of this word?' And I'll have to look at the word parts. When I look at a big word I always divide it up and see if I can find parts that I recognize."

From their research into middle-level vocabulary instruction, Michael Kieffer and Nonie Lesaux (2007) offered the following four principles for teaching students to use word parts as a word-learning strategy:

1. *Teach morphology in the context of rich, explicit vocabulary instruction.* This means that the study of word parts should only be one component of vocabulary study. Students should also learn to explore individual word meanings, as well as develop use of context, use of reference materials, and word consciousness. Morphology can be embedded into classes across the curriculum as teachers introduce multisyllabic words as part of vocabulary study, or as students encounter them in text.

2. *Teach morphology as a cognitive strategy.* Middle-level students must learn to be strategic when they come to a multisyllabic word they don't know, employing effective thinking strategies instead of panicking. We can model this type of cognitive strategy by doing "think-alouds" (Davey 1983) where we demonstrate how we ourselves break down a word we don't recognize. We can also provide opportunities for students to practice breaking down and inferring the meanings of unfamiliar words.

3. *Introduce important word parts systematically and with opportunities for reteaching and practice.* When selecting words for strategic vocabulary study, include at least one important multisyllabic word that contains a prefix, a suffix, and a Greek or Latin root. When students participate in explorations and practice activities that include multisyllabic words, they learn more about how to figure out complex words on their own.

4. *Situate explicit vocabulary instruction in meaningful contexts.* Vocabulary should be an integral part of instruction. Providing lists of isolated multisyllabic words or quick vocabulary activities out of context do not help students make deep connections.

Second, we must learn or refresh our knowledge of morphology.

Understanding Our Language Heritage

English has a rich and varied history, much of it borrowed from other languages. Booker T. Washington's famous expression reminds us: "We don't just borrow words; on occasion, English has pursued other languages down alleyways to beat them unconscious and rifle their pockets for new vocabulary." We also constantly create new words—the *Oxford English Dictionary* is actually revised four times a year to accommodate evolving vocabulary (Block and Siegel 2014).

If you have ten minutes, search for *The History of English (Combined)* on YouTube. This Open University production reminds me of the segments of "Mr. Peabody's Improbable History" on the old *Rocky and Bullwinkle* show (the modern version is the 2014 movie *Mr. Peabody & Sherman*). It is a tongue-in-cheek summary of how modern English came to be. Just be careful about using it with students without previewing first because a few parts may be a bit risqué for middle school kids!

Vocabulary found in most content areas relies heavily on Greek and Latin roots. Scholars estimate that more than 60 percent of all words in an English dictionary stem from Greek or Latin; in science and technology, it is closer to 90 percent (Moats 2000). As Amanda Goodwin, Jennifer Gilbert, and Sun-Joo Cho (2013, 39) explain, "By middle school, many of the content-specific vocabulary words that carry important meanings for academic contexts (e. g., *thermosphere, circumscribe, dormant, migratory*) are low-frequency words made of multiple affixes and Latin or Greek roots that cannot stand alone." William Nagy and Judith Scott (2000, 275) agree: "It is hard to overstate the importance of morphology in vocabulary growth."

The ability to determine the meanings of unfamiliar words by analyzing the parts is also a component of the Common Core State Standards (CCSS) for middle school students. Language Standard 4.b for every grade from grades four through eight states:

Use common, grade-appropriate Greek or Latin affixes and roots as clues to the meaning of a word.

- In grade five, *photo-* is the Greek root given as an example. *Photo-* means "light" and the examples are *photograph* and *photosynthesis*.
- In grade six, the examples are *audience, auditory,* and *audible*. If we know that the Latin root *audi-* means "to hear or listen," it is easy to see how these words are related.
- In grade seven, the examples are *belligerent, bellicose,* and *rebel,* which all come from *belli-,* the Latin root meaning "of war."
- The eighth-grade examples come from the Latin root *ced-,* which means "move or go." Examples are *precede, recede,* and *secede*.

The CCSS Language standards expect early primary students to know the meanings of common prefixes and suffixes, and the study of Greek and Latin roots is expected beginning at fourth grade. However, as we saw in the middle school examples at the beginning of the chapter, many middle-level kids do not yet know the meanings of even the simplest affixes and roots. When students are able to break down a new word and figure out its meaning from the meanings of its parts, they have learned a strategy that can significantly enhance word knowledge and increase comprehension. Students who are morphologically aware can read more challenging text independently. Knowledge of the meanings of word parts can be considered a type of "in word" context clue.

Clearly, the time has come for including morphology in our students' knowledge base. Tim Rasinski and his colleagues (Rasinski et al. 2011, 135) suggest that "the next quantum leap in vocabulary growth . . . will come when the systematic study of Latin-Greek derivations is embedded into vocabulary programs for the elementary, middle, and secondary grades."

Developing Morphological Awareness

Morphemes are the smallest units of meaning in a language and are made up of prefixes, suffixes, and roots. Morphemes can be "free," which means they can stand alone as an independent word, or "bound," which means they have to be attached to another morpheme to make sense. An example of a free morpheme is *sweet*. An example of a bound morpheme is the suffix *-ly* (which means "characteristic of"). Put these parts together and they make the word *sweetly*. Take them apart and *sweet* can stand as a word by itself, whereas *-ly* cannot. Compound words combine two free morphemes to create a new word, such as *skateboard*, *earthquake*, or *keypad*. Using the meanings of these word parts to understand the unfamiliar word is called *morphology*.

When we use morphemes to determine the meaning of a longer word, we are using morphemic analysis (also called *structural analysis*). Consider the quote at the beginning of this chapter. *Hyper-* is a Greek prefix that means "excess or exaggeration." *Poly-* also originates from Greek and is another prefix that means "many." *Syllabic* is a Latin root, by way of a Greek root, which can be defined as "consisting of syllables." *Mania-* is also Latin and means "excessive enthusiasm." Sometimes this knowledge can be overgeneralized (as when President George W. Bush famously said, "Don't misunderestimate me").

Competent readers use morphemic analysis to figure out the meanings of many unfamiliar multisyllabic words when they encounter these words in more complex texts. If they see a new word, they immediately make connections to words they already know containing the same root (Goodwin, Gilbert, and Cho 2013; Moats 2000). When students become aware of word parts, they can see connections between words and use those connections to understand text in a new and deeper way. Connected words are remembered words, and remembered words are applied words. Morphological awareness is an aspect of powerful lifelong learning, and morphemic analysis is a strategy most middle-level kids need to learn (Kieffer and Lesaux 2010).

The Power of Prefixes

Prefixes appear at the beginning of most multisyllabic words, and their function is to change the meaning, such as adding the prefix *re-*, which means "again," to *live*, to create a word that means "something that lives again." Adding a prefix can also change the connotation of a word. For example, by adding the prefix *dis-*, to *approve* (a positive word), we create *disapprove* (the opposite, negative word).

My husband reminds me that what we think we know about prefixes is not always reliable. When he worked at a gas station in college, some gas cans were labeled "flammable" and some were labeled "inflammable." It would seem that inflammable would be the opposite of flammable, but that is not so. The prefix *in-* in this instance is derived from the Latin preposition *en-*, which means "cause to" (like *cause to burst into flames*) instead of the meaning "not" as it is used in many other words.

There are many prefixes in English, and some have multiple meanings, depending on the ways they are used. Sometimes a word has two or more prefixes attached. Recognizing all the permutations might seem an overwhelming task, until we realize there are some good shortcuts. At Bullitt Lick Middle, Tonie Weddle solved that problem by teaching her students that 97 percent of the words with prefixes in English begin with one of these:

dis- = not, opposite of

im-, in-, il-, ir- = not

re- = again

un- = not

This was powerful knowledge for Weddle's students and made the study of word parts far more streamlined. Her students were able to figure out the meanings of hundreds of words with just this small bit of knowledge.

The website *ReadWriteThink* (readwritethink.org) features many vocabulary activities appropriate for middle-level students. Mary Callahan's activity You Can't Spell the Word *Prefix* Without a Prefix helps students explore the role and function of prefixes. After being introduced to prefixes, students brainstorm as many examples as they can. Then, working in small groups, they brainstorm all the words they can think of that begin with an assigned prefix and write the words on chart paper with markers. Next, they analyze the function of a prefix and how it changes the original word. All the groups then review one another's charts. Finally, they play a matching game with prefixes and roots. (For complete directions, find the activity at http://www.readwritethink.org/classroom-resources/lesson-plans/spell-word-prefix-without-399.html.)

The Stamina of Suffixes

Suffixes are added to the end of a word and always change the meaning. The smallest suffix in the English language is the letter *s* to make a noun plural (such as book*s*). Suffixes can be either inflectional or derivational (Moats 2000).

Inflectional suffixes are bound morphemes that cannot stand alone. These types of suffixes do not change the original word's part of speech. According to Louisa Moats (2000), an inflection can do any of the following:

- Change the tense of a verb (*shouted*)
- Show possession (*hers*)
- Show comparison (*higher, highest*)
- Show gender (alumna)

Young children begin using inflections by age two and often overgeneralize, such as saying "goed" for *went* and "mans" for *men*. However, they begin to use more accurate forms as they hear others use the correct forms around them. Middle-level students usually understand simple inflectional suffixes, but they need to explore more sophisticated inflections for deeper word knowledge.

Suffixes can also be derivational. Derivational suffixes are "derived" from Latin or Greek words, and these types of suffixes often do change the original word's part of speech. For example, by adding *-ment* (which means "the act of" or "the state of") to the verb *adjust*, we can make the noun *adjustment*. Sometimes the spelling changes as the derivational suffix is added (*face* to *facial*), and sometimes the pronunciation of the root changes as well (*type* to *typify*). Derivations often impact the way texts are written from fourth grade on and become important for both word knowledge and reading comprehension (Blachowicz and Fisher 2010).

Although fewer than prefixes, suffixes can still challenge middle grades students. Tonie Weddle taught her students that 97 percent of the words with suffixes end with one of these (see Figure 4.1):

-ing = verb form; past participle
-ed = past tense verbs
-s, -es = more than one
-ly = characteristic of

Teaching the most common suffixes can provide a jump start, but deeper word knowledge comes when students learn the meanings of more challenging suffixes, such as *-cracy* (which means "rule") and *-ology* ("study or science of"). One way to increase students' awareness of suffixes is

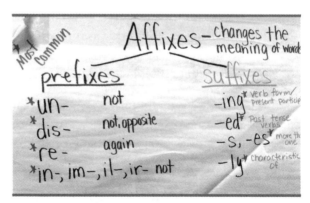

Figure 4.1 *Most common affixes*

to do a "suffix search." Invite students to work in small groups and search newspapers, magazine articles, textbooks, or websites to find words with suffixes. Ask them to make a list of the words written in one color and the suffix written in another color on chart paper—only one word per suffix. Then students can work together to research the meaning of each suffix they find and decide how the suffix changes the word. After searching for suffixes, each group can create a Suffix Web (adapted from Bromley 2012). Each group should choose a derivational suffix and write the suffix in the center of a chart. Group members then draw spokes from the suffix as they brainstorm all the words they can think of that include that suffix.

Word Roots Can Boost Language Learning

Research has shown that a middle school reader's ability to analyze a root word is a good predictor of his or her ability to read a larger derived word. Middle-level students are less able to apply root word knowledge when the pronunciation of the root word changes in the larger derived word (Goodwin, Gilbert, and Cho 2013). For example, students more easily recognize that the word *dependence* is derived from *depend* than that *ferocity* comes from *ferocious*.

Teaching students to be aware of Greek and Latin roots helps them reveal the deep meanings of multisyllabic words and how they are related to other words. Most vocabulary researchers have found that students should learn the meanings of common Greek and Latin roots such as *graph* (to write), *therm* (heat), and *port* (to carry) so they can determine the meanings of unfamiliar words they encounter in text.

Figure 4.2 is a chart of common prefixes, roots, and suffixes. This is not a comprehensive chart but does show the meanings of many word parts that students can use to think about the meanings of unfamiliar words. I have also included the grade level where particular word parts are mentioned in the Common Core State Standards.

If students' first language is Spanish, teaching them morphology can speed English learning. Because Spanish is a Latin-based language, the two languages share many affixes and roots. For example, the prefix *re-* comes from Latin and when attached to a verb means "again." Spanish verbs that contain this prefix include *reactivación* (reactivation), *redescubrir* (rediscover), and *reutilizar* (reuse or recycle). One reason for the large number of cognates—words that seem almost the same in both languages—is the Latin similarities between English and Spanish. Studying word parts can help Spanish speakers better grasp academic vocabulary (Fisher, Rothenberg, and Frey 2007).

Making Connections Across the Curriculum

Middle grades students often enjoy exploring the history of word origination. The technical term for these stories is *etymology* (the word *etymology* comes from Greek and means "the true sense of a word"). When I first read *Vocabulary Their Way: Word Study with Middle and Secondary Students* (Templeton et al. 2010), I was interested to note the etymology of these academic domains:

Common Prefixes

Most Common Prefixes—Account for 97% of words with prefixes			
Prefix	Meaning	Examples	Mentioned in Language Standards
dis–	not, opposite	disagree, disappear	
in–, im–, il–, ir–	not	incorrect, impossible, illegal, irregular	
re–	again	retell, rebuild	K, 2
un–	not	unhappy, uncomfortable	K, 2, 3
Other Common Prefixes			
anti–	against	antisocial, antibiotic	
bi–	two	bicycle, bilingual	
de–	opposite	decode, deactivate	
en–, em–	cause to	enable, empower	
fore–	before	foretell, forecast	
inter–	between	interact, international	
mid–	half	midway, midnight	
mis–	wrongly	mislead, misinterpret	
non–	not	nonfiction, nonsense	
tri–	three	tricycle, triangle	
semi–	half	semiannual, semicircle	
sub–	under	submarine, substandard	
tele–	far off	telescope, telegraph	4
trans–	across	transport, transform	
under–	below	underachieve, underpass	

Common Root Words

Common Roots			
Root	Meaning	Examples	Mentioned in Language Standards
aud	to hear	audience, audible	6
auto	self	autograph, autobiography	4
belli	of war	belligerent, rebel	7
bene	good	benefit, benevolent	
cede, ced	move, go, yield	precede, secede	8
cred	believe	credit, credible	
dict	say	prediction, dictionary	
duc	lead, make	produce, introduce	
graph	writing	photograph, biography	4
jur, jus	law	jury, justice	

Figure 4.2a *Common prefixes, roots, and suffixes for grades K–8*

Common Root Words (continued)

Common Roots			
log, logue	thought	logical, dialogue	
phon	sounds	telephone, phonics	
photo	light	photograph, photocopy	4, 5
port	carry	portable, airport	
scrib, script	write	describe, prescription	
spect	look	inspect, spectacle	
struct	build	destruction, reconstruction	
tract	drag, pull	tractor, distract	
trans	across	transatlantic, transport	
vid, vis	see	evidence, visible	

Common Suffixes

Most Common Suffixes—Account for most words with suffixes			
Suffix	Meaning	Examples	Mentioned in Language Standards
–ing	present verb form	singing, walking	
–ed	past tense	baked, smiled	K
–s, –es	more than one	dogs, wishes	K
–ly	characteristic of	softly, easily	
Other Common Suffixes			
–able/–ible	able to	comfortable, responsible	3
–al, –ial	having characteristics of	personal, spatial	
–en	made of	golden, wooden	
–er	comparative (more)	bigger, happier	
–est	comparative (most)	greatest, sweetest	
–ful	full of	hopeful, beautiful	K
–ic	having characteristics of	artistic, fantastic	
–ion, –tion, –ation, –ition	act or process of	addition, persuasion	
–ist	one who	scientist, artist	
–less	without	careless, homeless	K, 3
–ment	condition of	excitement, government	
–ness	quality or act	neatness, kindness	
–y	having the quality of	windy, noisy	

Figure 4.2b *Common prefixes, roots, and suffixes for grades K–8*

- Mathematics: The word *mathematics* comes from a Greek word meaning "to learn."
- Arithmetic: The word *arithmetic* comes from the same root as the words *arm* and *arthritis*, which means "to fit" or "join." Arithmetic means to fit and join numbers together.
- History: The word *history* comes from a root that means "to inquire."
- Science: The word *science* comes from a root that means "to know."
- Art: The word *art* is related to the same root as arithmetic. It means "fitting together" colors, shapes, and materials.
- Music: The word *music* comes from Greek mythology. The *Muses* were the goddesses who oversaw music, arts, and sciences.

Exploring etymologies can help students develop not only morphological awareness but also curiosity about words. For example, Shane Templeton and his colleagues described an activity they called Explore-a-Root (Templeton et al. 2010) that is appropriate for any subject area. In this activity, students search the origin of a root and then research to find words that are derived from that root. For example, the root *sal* comes from Latin and means *salt*. *Salinate* means to make salty, and *saline* means containing salt. Other words derived from the same root include *desalinate, salimeter, salami, salad, saltines, sauce,* and *salsa. Salary* also comes from the phrase "salt money" because ancient Roman soldiers were paid in salt. Middle-level students can work in pairs to create illustrated posters of an assigned root or contribute to a class media presentation of etymologies.

Numerous other charts depicting common prefixes, suffixes, and roots can be found online by conducting a simple search. An especially interesting list of common content-area roots and affixes was created by Valerie Ellery and Jennifer Rosenbloom and can be downloaded from *ReadWriteThink* at http://www.readwritethink.org/classroom-resources/printouts/common-content-area-roots-30842.html. Just think of the power of teaching students how the same Greek or Latin root, prefix, or suffix can be used across content areas!

Scaffolding Morphological Knowledge for Comprehension

Tonie Weddle helped students develop morphological awareness as she facilitated close reading and text analysis in her English language arts class. Students were rereading a passage from a myth about the Greek goddess Pandora, which had been used on a teacher-created practice assessment. After describing all the dreadful things that Pandora accidentally released from the box because of her curiosity (greed, jealousy, and so on), the next sentence in the text read, "And now they had all flown out into the world because of an undisciplined woman!"

As students were discussing the passage, Weddle called attention to the word *undisciplined*. "What do you see?" she asked the class.

Jonathon answered the question. "Oh! I see *discipline*!" Weddle wrote the word *discipline* on the whiteboard with a marker (see Figure 4.3 for Weddle's chart).

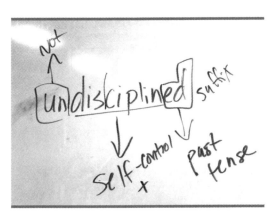

Figure 4.3 *Breaking down a multisyllabic word*

"What else do you see? Taylor?"

Taylor replied, "*Un-* and *-ed.*"

Weddle prompted, "What do we call *-ed*?"

"It's a suffix," the students responded.

"So, wow! If I look over here at our chart I see that that word has two of the most common prefixes and suffixes in the English language. So what does *un-* mean?"

Savannah, "*Un-* means not."

Weddle reinforced Savannah's answer and wrote the word *not* on the board with an arrow pointing to the prefix. "And what does *-ed* mean?"

"It's past tense," Chris replied.

The teacher wrote "past tense" on the board with an arrow pointing to the suffix. "Yes, the suffix *-ed* means past tense. So what does the word *discipline* mean?" Weddle queried.

There was a brief murmur, and then Sam said, "Well, it usually means correction."

Weddle, anticipating a misconception, said, "Now, Sam said something really interesting, and I think that people get confused by this. So often we want to go straight to the negative. When we were talking about connotation we were thinking about how we apply words and maybe levels of feeling or shades of meaning. Remember?"

Heads nodded in agreement.

"Let's think about the word *discipline*. Is there another meaning? Sam said it usually means correction. Could *discipline* be correction?"

The students agreed that correction could make sense. Then Brett added, "But discipline could also mean self-control."

With a doubtful look, Mindy said to Brett, "But that would make it *not self-control*. That doesn't make sense either."

Weddle continued to probe. "Well, let's think about that. Self-control could be a type of discipline. Some of you might think of discipline as punishment. And that would be a negative connotation. But if we think about it as self-control as meaning things like [quoting two points she often makes to help kids make good decisions] 'if it's doubtful don't do it' and 'just because we can, doesn't mean we should,' is that a positive thing?"

Students agreed that it was.

"So that would be a positive connotation. Okay, what does *undisciplined* mean?" Weddle asked. "Take a minute to work with your group to decide how the word *undisciplined* is used in this passage."

Kids conferred with their peers. From one group, a boy's voice questioned, "So could it be *not* self-control?" His partner was emphatic—that didn't make sense. After about a minute, Weddle pulled them back to a whole group.

"So we've got self-control here, or maybe *not* self-control. We can use our prefixes and our suffixes to help us figure out what words mean, but sometimes we have to also connect with context clues so we know which meanings to use. What did you come up with? What did your table group talk about? Meagan?"

Meagan answered. "The way it's used in the paragraph, we think it means a lack of self-control."

"Okay, what context clues, or evidence, helped you know that?" Weddle asked.

The students decided that a phrase in the story that described Pandora as "just a little too curious" was a clue to the meaning of the word.

Weddle exclaimed, "There we go! She was just a little too curious. That's a clue. Do we need to focus on the things that flew out of the box or do we need to focus on the person who made the things fly out of the box?" After another brief small-group discussion, the students decided that *undisciplined* was a word to describe Pandora because she was just a little too curious and lacked self-control. Then they moved on to the next part of the text. In Figure 4.3, observe how Weddle showed students how to break down the word *undisciplined*.

This was an embedded vocabulary mini-lesson focused on making sure that students knew to use prefixes, suffixes, and context to figure out the meaning of a word as they read a challenging text. To expand their vocabulary knowledge, students could explore the origin of the word *discipline*. They would find that it is based on the Latin word *disciplina*, which means "instruction or education." Related words are *discipline* (meaning subject area) and *disciplinary*. *Disciple*, meaning *pupil*, is a distant relative.

Stephen Currie, the seventh-grade social studies teacher at Bowman, also teaches students to use word parts in his subject area as a strategy for learning content. For instance, the social studies word for vocabulary study was *colonialism*. Currie encouraged his students to tackle a multisyllabic word they had never seen before by saying, "You guys can figure out the meaning of a long word! Remember, focus on the meaning of the prefix, the root word, and the suffix."

In previous lessons, Currie had already taught students that the suffix *-ism* is used to indicate social, political, or religious beliefs or ways of behaving, and students had explored *monotheism* and *polytheism*. This day, Currie helped his students build on that knowledge to understand the word *colonialism*.

He wrote the term on the board. Some students seemed hesitant about venturing a guess. "Remember, anytime you see the prefix *mono-*, what does that mean?" Currie asked.

"One!" replied a majority of students, many holding up one finger in the air.

"Of course, *mono-* means one. And when you see *poly-*?" Currie continued.

"That means a lot!"

"Okay, so stick with that theme," Currie said. "Look at *colonialism*. What do you see right away?"

"Oh!" several students exclaimed as the realization hit them. "Colony!"

"The suffix at the end . . . *-ism*! That means a belief!"

Mental lightbulbs flashed as students discussed. They decided that *colonialism* can mean a belief in forming colonies. Currie was delighted. "In the years before we started including vocabulary strategies, when we got to the word *colonialism* I would always get that blank stare. After I taught them to look at the root word and suffix, they could figure out the word on their own and they still know it." Currie was teaching his students to become morphologically aware as a tool for understanding important terms in social studies.

Teaching Morphemic Analysis

If students have not had much experience with morphemic analysis, they may struggle at first, but regular practice will build their confidence. Let's explore some instructional activities to help middle grades students increase their skills with morphemic analysis.

Crystal Ball Words

In *Word Nerds*, we described a graphic organizer that Leslie and I called Crystal Ball Words (a blank version can be found in Appendix A). We used it to introduce students to morphemic analysis in a way that would give them confidence when encountering longer words with prefixes, suffixes, and Greek or Latin roots. The graphic organizer was headed by a clip art picture of a crystal ball and had three columns—one for a prefix, one for a root, and one for a suffix. With her intermediate grades students, we began with the word *transportation*. We taught students that *trans-* means "across," *port* means "to carry" in Latin, and *-ation* means "act or process of." Then we asked students to look deep into the word to discover its meaning. As a whole class, students brainstormed all the words they could think of that had the prefix *trans-*, such as *transform*, *transcribe*, and *translator*. Words with the root *port* included *import*, *portable*, and *airport* (their favorite was *Porta-Potty*, of course!). Students thought of a number of words with the suffix *-ation*, including *acceleration*, *location*, and *population*. From the word *transportation*, the class was able to derive forty-one words. Leslie's students love Crystal Ball Wednesdays. Because her students are excited about words and have developed word consciousness, they think it is a game to see how many words they can brainstorm. It is also a nonthreatening way to introduce the idea of morphemic analysis.

Crystal Ball Words can easily be adapted for middle school students. After modeling how to break words into meaningful parts, we can introduce a multisyllabic word that is relevant to the curriculum. Invite students to work in small groups to complete graphic organizers by brainstorming words that include the prefix, the root word, and the suffix. Students can use reference materials to find other words and to clarify that the words they choose fit the list. Working in small groups to explore words that are related to the selected word can generate thoughtful discussion about the meanings of prefixes, roots, and suffixes as well as the meanings of words that fit into the columns. Accountability is assured when each student completes his or her own graphic organizer. Figure 4.4 shows our original Crystal Ball Words.

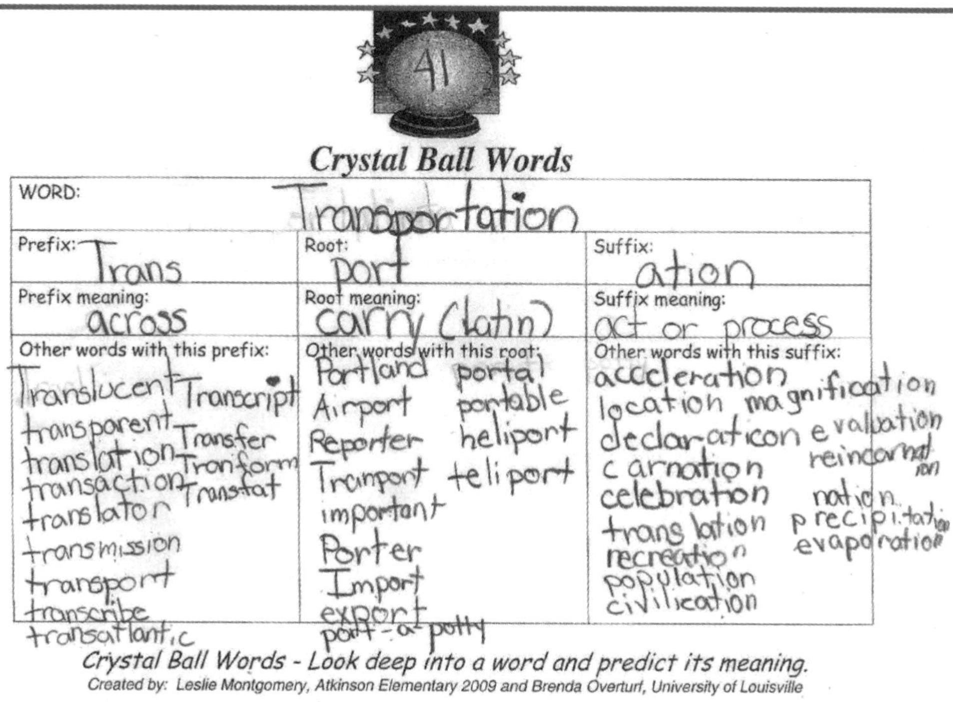

Figure 4.4 *Crystal Ball Words*

Morpheme Triangles

Rod Winters (2009, 686) developed an inverted triangle approach for students to create ownership of word parts through a "recurrent process of brainstorming, analysis, and confirmation." In Morpheme Triangles, the teacher selects a multisyllabic word containing a Greek and Latin root from the text students are preparing to read (many multisyllabic words do not have both prefixes and suffixes, but the idea can be adapted). The teacher then breaks the word into morphemes and places it in the center of an inverted triangle. For example, *subterranean* might be the selected vocabulary word. The word is written in the middle of the triangle as: *sub-terr-anean*. The teacher pronounces each morpheme, provides a short situational context for the word, and explains the meaning of the word. Students then discuss situations where the word might be used appropriately and inappropriately.

Beginning outside the top left corner of the triangle, students brainstorm five to six other words that appear to have the same prefix and make a list of them. For *sub-* (a Latin prefix meaning "under"), students may come up with words such as *subtraction, subdivision, submarine, subflooring, subtotal,* or *substitute* (and for music fans, *subwoofer,* of course). As they add words to the list, students explore and discuss the possible meaning of the prefix *sub-* and its relationship to the word *subterranean.* A plus sign goes in front of words that share a meaning as it is used in the word *subterranean.* A question mark goes in front of words where no connection can be found. Kids engage in lively discussions about the meanings of morphemes as they decide whether to place a plus or a question mark in front of each brainstormed word.

Students repeat the process with the root *terra* (a Latin root meaning "earth or land"), maybe coming up with words such as *terrain, terrace, terrorist, interrogate, extraterrestrial,* and *Mediterranean.* These words are written outside the top right corner of the triangle, and students again decide whether a plus sign or a question mark should go in front of each word. In this example, the word *terrorist* and *interrogate* are actually "impostors" and not related to the word *subterranean,* which can actually lead to an even richer discussion.

Finally, students brainstorm words that end with *-an* (Latin suffix meaning "belonging to"), such as *American, Russian, civilian, magician,* and *pedestrian.* They list and rate these words at the bottom of the inverted triangle. Together, the class comes to conclusions about the meanings of these roots and is on the road to developing morphological awareness as well.

Word Building

Two of the best resources I know for extensive morphology instruction are *Words Their Way: Word Study for Phonics, Vocabulary, and Spelling Instruction* (Bear et al. 2008) and *Vocabulary Their Way: Word Study with Middle and Secondary Students* (Templeton et al. 2010). Both of these resources use word building as a hands-on activity where students explore the meanings of roots and affixes and then build words from the parts. Sets of cards containing common prefixes, Greek and Latin roots, and suffixes can be written on index cards or printed out on perforated business card templates and stored for reuse. By manipulating cards to rearrange the parts, students can build and deeply explore lists of multisyllabic words.

A game-like variation of word building is an activity called Flip-a-Chip (Mountain 2002). Lee Mountain used white poker chips with word parts written on them (PRO and

RE on the front and back of one; DUCE and VOKE on the other). Students flipped the chips to make words that make sense, such as *reduce, provoke, revoke,* and *produce.* Her students then found new words and made their own sets of chips for other students. As an extension, Mountain required students to write a cloze passage (a paragraph with blanks where the words should go) for other students to complete, making it also an exercise in using context clues. An interactive, online version of Flip-a-Chip can be found on the *ReadWrite-Think* website at http://www.readwritethink.org/classroom-resources/student-interactives/flip-chip-30031.html.

A creative word-building activity based on the genius of William Shakespeare is called Be the Bard (Rasinski et al. 2011). Shakespeare is considered the greatest wordsmith of the English language, inventing approximately two thousand new words and phrases before his death in 1616. Many terms we use every day were actually created by the Bard, including *exposure, blood-stained, submerge,* and *circumstantial.* In Be the Bard, students are invited to use prefixes, suffixes, and roots they have already learned, create new words by combining roots and affixes in original ways, and explain their thinking. Students as young as primary grades have learned to create nonsense words from Greek and Latin roots such as *terramater,* which they explained as a device to measure land or *automand,* meaning an order that one gives to himself or herself (Rasinski et al. 2011). By manipulating word parts to invent new words and defending their "definition," students better understand and remember the meanings of roots and affixes.

Discussion Is the Key

As we have seen in this chapter, students need to be encouraged to think about and share new knowledge and discoveries about the origin of word meanings. But as Leslie reminds us, "Kids have to be able to talk about word parts. The big key to developing morphological awareness is fostering a discussion-based environment."

Discussing and exploring word parts can boost students' word confidence. Brandi Odom has seen the changes in her seventh graders at Bowman. Before she made morphemic analysis a regular part of her vocabulary instruction, students would sometimes "panic when they came to a longer word in the text. They would just stop," Odom explained. "I had to remind them just to take it slow, and that if we don't know a word we can break it down and figure it out."

She chuckled as she told me about one of her students. Terrance was reading an excerpt of a text aloud when all of a sudden he stopped at an unfamiliar multisyllabic word. Normally, Terrance would have just looked at Odom and silently appealed for help in pronouncing and understanding the term. This time, after sounding out the word, he said, "Wait! I know what that word means!" and continued to read. Later, during the classroom discussion, it was clear he was right when he used the word in conversation.

"I see them breaking down words to understand their meaning," Odom said. "I just see them becoming better, more independent readers."

Chapter 5

A Deeper Dive into Words and Phrases

News release: Two trucks loaded with thousands of copies of Roget's Thesaurus collided as they left a New York publishing house, according to the Associated Press. Witnesses were aghast, amazed, astonished, astounded, bemused, benumbed, bewildered, confounded, confused, dazed, dazzled, disconcerted, disoriented, dumbstruck, electrified, flabbergasted, horrified, immobilized, incredulous, nonplussed, overwhelmed, paralyzed, perplexed, scared, shocked, startled, stunned, stupefied, surprised, taken aback, traumatized, upset.

—Anonymous

"You are just a *hypocrite*!" exclaimed Sonia to Janie, eyes blazing, as the girls burst into Don Hollandsworth's eighth-grade social studies class. The girls were usually best friends, so this exchange was quite extraordinary.

Hollandsworth intervened. "Whoa, Sonia! Slow down! Why are you calling Janie a hypocrite?"

Sonia took a breath and replied, scowling, "I don't know. It's just a word I heard."

"Do you even know what it means?" asked Hollandsworth.

Sonia dashed over to the side of the room and grabbed a dictionary off the shelf. She flipped through the pages, found the word, and jabbed at it with her index finger. "This is what it means, Mr. H." She read aloud, emphatically, "A person displaying the opposite belief of what he or she states." Then she slammed the book shut with a bang and glared at him.

It was definitely a teachable vocabulary moment. Before this class, Hollandsworth's students were already used to hearing him ask, "What does this mean?" when reading a dictionary definition. Several times they had worked in small groups to create student-friendly definitions after interpreting dictionary definitions. Now Hollandsworth asked Sonia, "Well, what does that definition mean? Say it in your own words."

A brief discussion ensued about the definition of the word *hypocrite* and then whether Janie was or was not displaying those characteristics. Apparently, Janie had borrowed Sonia's notebook without asking, didn't sit with her at lunch, and had talked to a boy Sonia liked. Wrapping up the discussion, Hollandsworth said, "So should you really call Janie a hypocrite? I don't want you to call each other names, but if you're going to, be educated about it. Either use words you know or learn new words."

"Okay, Janie. I'm sorry I called you a hypocrite," Sonia murmured with a slight smile (leaving us to wonder what new words she might learn by the next time).

As Sydney J. Harris once said, "The right word is as important to the writer as the right note is to the composer or the right line to the painter" (1961, 266). Words have nuances and shades of meaning and are connected to other words in webs of relationships. Choosing exactly the right word means knowing a variety of ways to express thoughts. Understanding semantic connections to other words, nuances of meaning, and figurative language is important for deep comprehension of text.

After vocabulary words have been introduced in context, the next step is to invite students to engage in vocabulary explorations that will help them understand the relationships between and among words. Let's take a look at the types of vocabulary explorations that students need in the middle grades, including understanding how words are related, such as synonyms and antonyms, multiple meanings, word nuances, and connotation and denotation. We will also think about figurative language, verbal analogies, and word play, which are all considered part of vocabulary instruction.

Visual Representations of Words and Concepts

When students understand connections between and among words and phrases, they expand their word schemas. Words are rarely isolated, and understanding different strands of the web that connects a word to other words and ideas is a powerful learning tool. As Steven Stahl (2005, 95) said, "Vocabulary knowledge *is* knowledge; the knowledge of a word not only implies a definition, but also implies how that word fits into the world." To deeply understand a word is to have, as Beck, McKeown, and Kucan (2002, 10) put it, "rich, decontextualized knowledge of a word's meaning, its relationship to other words, and its extension to metaphorical uses such as understanding what someone is doing when they are *devouring* a book."

Semantic mapping has been identified by research as an effective way to enhance students' knowledge of words and their relationships to other words (Johnson and Pearson 1984; Johnson, Pittelman, and Heimlich 1986; Margosin, Pascarella, and Pflaum 1982). The word *semantic* means "meaning," and that is exactly the purpose of this strategy. When students create a simple semantic map, they write a focus word in the middle of a piece of paper. Related words are written at the end of spokes extending from the focus word. Around each of these related words, students write more related words. The semantic map (that when completed can look almost like a nest of spiders on the page) is a highly effective tool for students to think about word relationships that also activates their background knowledge about a topic and boosts comprehension of a text being read.

Semantic maps are useful for learning new vocabulary, but research has speculated that class discussion around the maps is what makes them most effective for students (Stahl and Vancil 1986). Collaborative academic conversation creates active processing with students thinking about how their own experiences relate to the words discussed. As a result, students own new words and phrases and better understand them in context.

Word Maps

Word maps are visual representations of definitions (Schwartz and Raphael 1985). These types of semantic maps provide a way to organize information so that students can see how a particular word connects to other words and ideas (see Figure 5.1). Some vocabulary words are just new names for ideas students already understand. However, other words represent names for more encompassing concepts that help them better understand the world.

Word maps can be informal yet powerful tools. When Michael Roccaforte, an eighth-grade teacher at Bowman, began emphasizing vocabulary in his math classes, he asked students to write the definitions of words from the beginning of each lesson in the book. Roccaforte soon realized that his students were not learning the meanings of the words by copying definitions, so he decided to model how to make a vocabulary map of connected terms. The concept was algebra, specifically relations and functions. Before Roccaforte could teach students how to do a vertical line test to determine whether a given graph represents a function, he needed his students to understand how words such as *domain*, *range*, *input*, and *output*, connect to *relation* and to one another. Roccaforte taught

Figure 5.1 *Student creating a word map in science*

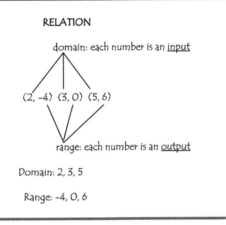

RELATION

domain: each number is an <u>input</u>

(2, -4) (3, 0) (5, 6)

range: each number is an <u>output</u>

Domain: 2, 3, 5

Range: -4, 0, 6

Figure 5.2 *Math vocabulary map about* relation

students to make a math vocabulary map, such as the one pictured in Figure 5.2.

This process helped students to get a visual map in their heads of how the words were related and what the connections look like. Students quickly caught on. "For the word *relation*, students were able to give me the words and the parts before I drew the diagram," Roccaforte said with a smile. "I started with two ordered pairs and the kids gave me the rest." Students then made their own vocabulary maps with other sets of ordered pairs.

From there, Roccaforte began expecting students to use correct vocabulary in word problems. "They look at the context and decide which part of the problem represents which term. They also tell why it makes sense." Roccaforte's students kept completed vocabulary maps in a three-hole-punch notebook and used them as a reference in math class. "For kids to understand algebra concepts," he says, "the best thing I've seen is making word maps."

Concept of Definition

In 1985, Robert Schwartz and Taffy Raphael (1985) maintained that many students do not really understand the concept of a definition and found that a better way to help understand meaning was asking them to consider three questions about a word: (1) What is it? (2) What is it like? (3) What are some examples? These questions correspond with the general class to which a concept belongs (*dog*, for example, is a type of animal), the primary properties of the concept and those that distinguish it from other members of the class (barks, tail that wags, domesticated, man's best friend), and examples of the concept (German shepherd, hound dog, poodle). According to Schwartz and Raphael, exploring this type of information about a word also helps students figure out new words on their own. Because students better understand how to use context clues and background information attached to a word, they can be more independent in word learning and comprehension of text. Various versions of their concept of definition map are available online.

Maureen McLaughlin and Mary Beth Allen (2009) adapted the concept of definition map to deepen students' conceptual thinking by asking them to use the map to also write a summary of the information. With this map, students consider the different aspects of words as they complete a template like the one shown in Figure 5.3.

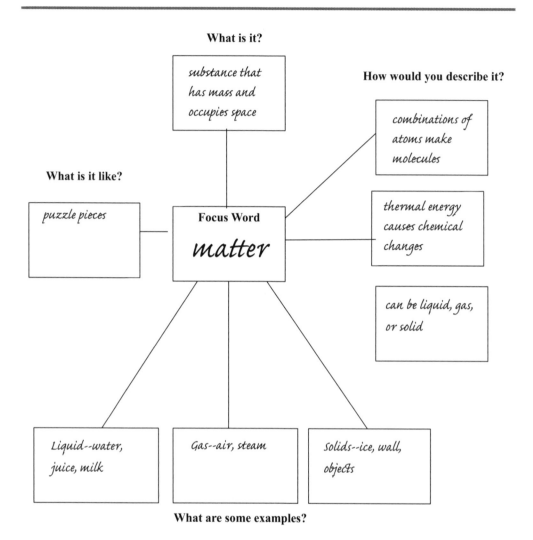

What is it?

substance that has mass and occupies space

How would you describe it?

combinations of atoms make molecules

thermal energy causes chemical changes

can be liquid, gas, or solid

What is it like?

puzzle pieces

Focus Word

matter

Liquid--water, juice, milk

Gas--air, steam

Solids--ice, wall, objects

What are some examples?

Summary

Everything is made of matter. Matter is substance that has mass and takes up space. It is made of combinations of atoms that make molecules. Thermal energy causes chemical changes. Matter can be in the form of a liquid, gas, or solid. Examples of liquid matter are water, juice, or milk, Gasses are like air or steam. Solids can be ice, a wall, or other objects. Matter is like puzzle pieces.

Figure 5.3 *Concept of definition about* matter

Students write the focus word in the center box. In the box at the top labeled "What is it?" they enter the appropriate category (solar system, algebra, geography, dogs, and so on). In the three boxes at the right marked "How would you describe it?" students jot down brief descriptions of the concept. In the boxes at the bottom, students record examples. In the box at the left ("What is it like?"), students note a synonym or comparison. When students make a comparison, they think about how the object being defined can be compared to another object, which helps them think about the concept at a higher level. At the very bottom of the organizer, students use the information in the map to write a summary describing the concept. This serves not only to help students better understand a concept but also to teach them to write a succinct summary of it—always a challenging task. See Appendix B for a blank concept of definition map.

Semantic Feature Analysis

A semantic feature analysis grid (Johnson and Pearson 1984) is a research-based strategy that is especially useful for helping students identify important characteristics or features of words. According to Patricia Anders and Candace Bos (1986), a semantic feature analysis not only enables students to learn the relationships between and among the conceptual vocabulary and the major ideas in a content-area text, but it also provides background knowledge for better comprehension. This strategy also helps students understand similarities and differences among words. Basically, it is an expanded compare-and-contrast chart (McLaughlin and Overturf 2013).

Semantic feature analysis is often used as a prereading strategy to introduce words before reading a content-area text. Words or phrases related to the concept are written in the left-hand column of the chart. Characteristics are listed across the top. Students think about what they already know about the words and make a prediction. They place a "+" if the characteristic relates to the word, a "–" if it does not, and a "?" if they are not sure. When everyone has completed the semantic feature analysis chart, students discuss and explain their predictions. Then they read the text and discuss whether their predictions were accurate. Students can change the chart as their knowledge of the words and concept increases.

Robert Kuprenas, the seventh-grade math teacher at Bowman, used a semantic feature analysis chart to help students understand similarities and differences among words that stand for concepts. For example, he placed the words *volume*, *surface area*, *area*, *perimeter*, and *circumference* in the left-hand column. He led students in a brainstorming session to think of features of these geometric concepts. Students came up features such as *2 dimensions*, *3 dimensions*, *plane*, *space*, and *distance*. Kuprenas then placed these features along the top row of the chart. Students worked in pairs to decide whether the terms in the left-hand column shared the feature at the top of the chart (see Figure 5.4).

Topic: Volume and Related Words

Words	Features				
	2 dimensional	3 dimensional	plane	space	distance
volume	-	+	-	+	-
surface area	-	+	+	-	-
area	+	-	+	-	-
perimeter	+	-	+	-	+
circumference	+	-	+	-	+
Response Key:	+ = Yes	- = No	? = Don't Know		

Figure 5.4 *Semantic feature analysis about* volume

The research on the semantic feature analysis strategy has consistently shown student growth in vocabulary knowledge, as well as comprehension of content-area texts. A blank semantic feature analysis chart can be found in Appendix C.

Adding Synonyms and Antonyms to Word Networks

Steven Stahl and William Nagy (2006, 64), well-known vocabulary scholars, stressed that "often, a synonym is all a person needs to understand a word in context." Although this is a sound observation about figuring out words from the context of the passage, research has shown that middle and high school vocabulary instruction is often relegated to only learning synonyms that may be important on standardized tests (Beck, McKeown, and Kucan 2002, 85), which is "a bankrupt way to teach word meaning."

Including synonyms and antonyms in vocabulary instruction benefits students in many ways. In his extensive work on vocabulary development, Steven Stahl (1999) explained that teaching synonyms and antonyms helps students grasp a word's meaning. Louisa Moats (1999) placed vocabulary study squarely in the field of semantics, writing that words are learned in relation to other word meanings and that students should be able to "identify antonyms, synonyms, analogies, associative linkages; classes, properties, and examples of concepts; and denotative and connotative meanings" (25) in order to truly know a word. Moats also recommends including "context clues, semantic mapping and comparison, analogies, synonyms, antonyms, visual imagery, and other associations to teach meaning" (37). Camille Blachowicz, Peter Fisher, and Susan Watts Taffe (2005) discussed the importance of teaching synonyms and antonyms to help students understand denotative (literal) and connotative (interpretive) meanings of words.

In *Word Nerds*, we taught elementary students to add synonyms (or examples) and antonyms (or nonexamples) to the words we introduced for deep vocabulary study as one way to help them build their word schemas. Our aim was to help kids construct strong networks of words so that they were able to talk and write about that word as well as related words. As fifth grader David announced, "Knowing more words makes me feel smarter in my brain. It gets the synapses coming."

When we introduce individual words in the middle grades, we want to ensure that we link them to related words. For example, if students learn *analysis*, they might also learn related synonyms (or examples) such as *investigation* and *scrutiny* and antonyms (or nonexamples) such as *unexamined* and *conjecture*. When we add two synonyms and two antonyms to each of five vocabulary words, we are surreptitiously teaching a connected web of each of twenty-five words in all. Or maybe we aren't as sneaky as we think. Elementary students usually accept adding synonyms and antonyms as a routine part of a systematic vocabulary plan, but middle-level students are a little quicker to catch on. When Trish Priddy introduced vocabulary words and required her seventh-grade students at Eastside Middle School to add synonyms and antonyms, they realized immediately that they weren't just concentrating on the five words selected for deep learning. Kim Thompson, the library/media specialist at Eastside, reported with a laugh, "Some of Trish's students said to me, 'Ms. Priddy says we only have five vocabulary words. But then we add synonyms and antonyms so we are really learning a lot more words than that. She's really tricky!'"

Using Reference Materials to Discover Multiple Meanings

To progress in school, middle grades students need to be able to use reference materials to clarify the meaning of a word in context, figure out the pronunciation of a word, or find more precise or thought-provoking words to use in writing. In fact, one of the three word-learning strategies for determining the meaning of an unfamiliar word or phrase is the use of reference materials (Graves 2006). Yet there may be a problem hiding in plain sight in the classroom. When I first introduced the idea of searching for synonyms and antonyms as part of a strategic vocabulary plan that builds word relationships, it became quickly apparent that many middle grades classrooms did not have adequate access to reference materials such as dictionaries and thesauruses. This was especially true for content-area classes. Once we realized the problem, some administrators immediately found ways to provide sets of print resource materials for students. Some educators also guided students to use classroom digital sources. Others decided to take advantage of a BYOD—bring your own device—policy, where kids have access to their own reference materials at their fingertips through smartphones, tablets, or e-readers they bring to school (see Figure 5.5).

At Eastside Middle, Susan Carlisle took a novel approach. When she first began vocabulary study, she distributed an old set of collegiate dictionaries for her eighth-grade English language arts students so they could search for synonyms and antonyms. Then it occurred to her that she could combine vocabulary learning with her students' weekly trip to the library/media center so they could have more authentic experiences. Students entered the library/media center once a week and not only found a book to read but also scattered to the computers and print reference materials where they began looking for synonyms and antonyms for the words they were

Figure 5.5 *Students use electronic devices to find synonyms and antonyms.*

studying. This opened up a lot of discussion, not only about appropriate synonyms and antonyms but also about multiple meanings of words.

"It has brought me, as the teacher, into their world. I was so stuck in that old school thinking of Must. Use. Hard. Copy. Dictionaries," Carlisle stated, shaking her head. "I'm now realizing some of the limitations. For example, some of the sources give a lot of synonyms and antonyms or provide examples and nonexamples and some don't. In an eighth grader's mind, if they see only one synonym listed they think, 'That's cool. There's only one synonym I have to worry about.'"

After Carlisle's students found their words, she facilitated a quick group activity to combine all of the synonyms and antonyms they discovered. This discussion reinforced the idea that it isn't always best to rely on one resource.

"They have also been quite engaged in discussions about multiple meanings of words," Carlisle said. "When we discuss as a whole group, kids realize that some of the synonyms or antonyms they have chosen don't make sense for the definition we have introduced in class."

Exploring Word Nuances with Semantic Gradients

A semantic gradient is an array of related words placed along a continuum (Blachowicz and Fisher 2010). These words are not always synonyms, but they do demonstrate varied shades of meaning. For instance, *savvy*, *wise*, and *erudite* are all adjectives that can describe a person who possesses knowledge, but the subtle differences in meaning also say something about the personality of the person. Another example is the poster, popular in many writing classrooms, entitled *100 Ways to Say "Said."* Although there are various versions of this poster (easily retrieved online), they mostly list the same information—different choices for the verb *said* to make writing more lively. Groups of words from the poster can easily be arranged in a semantic gradient from a hushed *whisper* at one end to an anxiety-ridden *scream* at the other (see Figure 5.6).

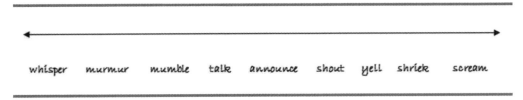

whisper   murmur   mumble   talk   announce   shout   yell   shriek   scream

Figure 5.6 *Semantic gradient chart*

Students can work with a partner to complete a semantic gradient chart where they begin with antonyms at each end and write selected words from least intense to most intense. A variation of this activity is to write synonyms on cards and invite students to physically arrange themselves into a semantic gradient line while holding up the cards (a thought-provoking activity that also includes movement). Students can also write related words on paint samples from the hardware store, going from light to dark to literally demonstrate shades of meaning (Fisher and Frey 2008).

The word of the day in Trish Priddy's seventh-grade English language arts class at Eastside was *nuance*. She introduced the word within a sentence, saying, "Let's try to predict the definition of *nuance* based on the clues in the sentence." After making some predictions, students used electronic devices to find an official definition and a list of synonyms for *nuance*.

Priddy continued, "Now I'm going to ask you to work with a partner to think of pairs of antonyms. You know, something like 'light' and 'dark' or 'good' and 'bad.'" When students had created a list of antonyms, she asked each pair to pick one set to work with. Olivia and Jason chose *happy/sad*. Olivia then used a thesaurus to find synonyms representing nuances of meaning for the word *happy*, while Jason did the same thing with *sad*.

Next, Priddy asked students to pick six words that showed how one antonym transitioned to the opposite and write the words on paint samples along with their definitions to show shades of meaning or nuance (see Figure 5.7). When students had completed this activity, each student wrote an individual story using the words on their paint sample. This helped them apply the concept of nuance to further cement the meaning.

Working on semantic gradients is a good way to help students understand more about the relationship between and among words and can help students develop word consciousness. When students think about and arrange similar words on a semantic gradient beginning with least intense meaning and progressing to most intense meaning, they better understand nuances of word meanings and the way authors use these words to convey a message. In this way, semantic gradients can become a bridge to teaching connotation and denotation.

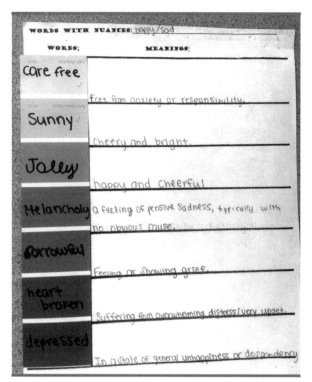

Figure 5.7 *Paint samples to show shades of meaning*

Connotation and Denotation

I'm not a huge sports fan, but I do thoroughly enjoy the rivalry of college basketball in my home state of Kentucky. After the 2014 NCAA tournament, I made sure to watch Stephen Colbert, at the time the star of Comedy Central's *Colbert Report*, interview John Calipari, the head coach of the University of Kentucky program (mostly because I am a University of Louisville fan, and I wanted to see what he would say).

"You have a reputation for 'one and done.' What does that even mean?" asked Colbert, referring to a controversial decision to recruit highly regarded players who would most likely turn pro after just one year in college.

Calipari looked nonplussed. "I don't like the connotation of 'one and done,'" he replied. "I like 'succeed and proceed.'" Of course. Said the first way, the phrase has a negative connotation, whereas said the other way, it has a positive connotation. But the denotation of the phrase is that guys go to school one year on a basketball scholarship, become successful basketball players, and then leave for the pros without completing their education. That's the difference.

When we teach connotation and denotation, we help students understand that there is a difference between a literal definition (denotation) and an implied or inferred definition (connotation). Authors use connotation when they make specific word choices to set a tone or a mood or to manipulate the reader's emotions and thoughts. Students can explore connotation and denotation by using an emotion-laden passage of text, whether it is literary or informational. Editorials, poetry, biased articles, and passages in literature can all be used as examples. Take, for instance, the enigmatic poem "Richard Cory," published in 1897 by Edwin Arlington Robinson and traditionally included in many literature anthologies. The poem begins:

> *Whenever Richard Cory went down town,*
> *We people on the pavement looked at him:*
> *He was a gentleman from sole to crown,*
> *Clean favored and imperially slim.*
>
> *And he was always quietly arrayed,*
> *And he was always human when he talked,*
> *But still he fluttered pulses when he said,*
> *"Good morning," and he glittered when he walked.*

Of course, if you remember the poem, it ends badly with the narrator wishing he could be Richard Cory and Cory abruptly taking his own life. Besides the intense discussion about interpretations of this poem and the parallels that students can draw to modern-day celebrity, this text is ripe for exploring connotation. Why did the poet choose words such as *crown, imperially, quietly, arrayed, human, fluttered,* and *glittered?* How did the poet set the mood and tone and relay his message through the use of these words? And, of course, many of us can't read this poem without thinking of the Simon and Garfunkel song by the same name. Playing the folk version of "Richard Cory" (easily found on iTunes or YouTube) will provide a song for students to compare with the original poem, and the discussion about word choice will grow with another interpretation.

One way to invite thinking about connotation and denotation is to ask students to work in small groups and list synonyms for a simple word like *house* (for example, *dwelling, home, shack, residence, mansion, crib,* and *abode*). Each group can have a different word or the whole class can work on the same word for a deeper discussion. This is a case where kids will beg to use reference materials. Allow them to find as many synonyms as possible in any way you feel is appropriate. After the groups have made a list of words, ask them to write them on colored sticky notes—words that show negative connotation on green, neutral on yellow, and positive on pink. Each group writes its original word at the top of three columns drawn on a piece of chart paper or whiteboard, and then arranges the sticky notes into the appropriate categories.

The small-group discussion, as students choose similes and decide how to categorize them, will be valuable practice, as well as the large-group reflection afterward. Asking students to complete a class semantic gradient chart with the words usually sparks an interesting debate about how the words should actually be arranged according to nuances of meaning.

Another way to think about connotation and nuances of words is to invite students to create a word matrix on a wall chart with sticky notes. In a word matrix, students begin with a list of synonyms. Students draw a matrix that looks like a large plus sign. On one axis, they place words with negative connotations on the left and positive connotations on the right. On the other axis, they place the same words based on their levels of register from formal to informal. Students then discuss how to categorize each word and explain their thinking. The website ReadWriteThink provides an online tool that can be used to practice connotation and register using a manipulative word matrix. The word matrix can be found at http://www.readwritethink.org/classroom-resources/student-interactives/word-matrix-30071.html.

Verbal Analogies

When we hear the word *analogy*, what often comes to mind is a form of figurative language meant to clarify or to explain the relationship between two seemingly unrelated objects. For instance, when asked to describe radio, Albert Einstein famously answered using this analogy, "You see, wire telegraph is a kind of very, very long cat. You pull his tail in New York and his head is meowing in Los Angeles. Do you understand this? And a radio operates exactly the same way: you send signals here; they receive them there. The only difference is that there is no cat." In this sense, similes and metaphors can be a type of analogy as they describe unrelated objects or ideas in order to make language come to life and ideas comprehensible.

However, verbal analogies are based purely on logic. Verbal analogies are often found on standardized tests and college entrance exams because higher-level thinking involves the ability to use logical reasoning. For example, try this analogy:

Words are to vocabulary study as _____ is to _____.

What words come to your mind? Sand grains and a beach? Leaves and a tree? Students and a school? Most likely it was a pair of words where the first word is a small part of the second word. This type of "if-then" thinking about words is an example of a verbal analogy.

Exploring verbal analogies is a way to explore vocabulary. Analogies can at first seem like puzzles to kids. However, the reason to learn this type of thinking is not just for fun. It is also for brainpower. Understanding verbal analogies goes a step beyond basic word connections to deeper ways in which words relate to ideas as well as to other words. A verbal analogy is often written as a logic statement that has this basic structure:

_____ : _____ :: _____ : _____

The statement is read:

_____ is to _____ as _____ is to _____.

A simple analogy might be:

Red : apple :: smooth : silk (Red is to apple as smooth is to silk.)

In this analogy, the first word (*red, smooth*) describes a characteristic of the second word (*apple, silk*) in each. The two sets of words are not necessarily related to each other in meaning, but the thinking path is the same for both. A good introduction to analogical thinking, including an introductory video on analogies made for students and an analogies game, can be found at http://www.vocabulary.co.il/analogies/.

Teaching students to write verbal analogies as part of an instructional plan for vocabulary study helps them think about words and their relationships at a new level. Figure 5.8 includes examples of types of verbal analogies that are appropriate for middle grades students.

Tonie Weddle introduced verbal analogies to her seventh graders by first discussing how writers often use analogies to bring their writing to life. After sharing several models of analogies, she discussed the logical thinking that underlies word analogies—the _____ *is to* _____ *as* _____ *is to* _____ kind of thinking. She then invited students to work in pairs to complete a simple analogy generator graphic organizer she obtained online at http://printables .scholastic.com/printables/detail/?id=43538. As a result, Megan and Carlina came up with this synonym analogy:

segregation : apart :: separation : alone

After Weddle was certain that students understood the concept of a word analogy, she invited them to generate an analogy using synonyms or antonyms that were associated with their vocabulary words. Examples of some her students' analogies with other pairs of words include the following:

turbulent : violent :: calm : settled
promise : sure :: guarantee : certain
misgivings : doubt :: strong-minded : certain

Type of Analogy	What It Means	Example
Definition	The first word defines the second word. Probably the most common type of word analogy.	*usual : common :: unusual : uncommon*
Antonyms	Words that are opposite in meaning. Each of the word pairs are antonyms.	*disgust : delight :: unite : isolate*
Synonyms	Words that are similar in meaning. Each of the word pairs are synonyms (similar to definition analogies).	*combative : aggressive :: optimistic : hopeful*
Types	The first word is a member of the class the second word describes (or vice versa).	*hydrogen : gas :: ice : solid*
Degree	The first word is a lesser or greater degree of intensity than the first word. This type of analogy can be compared to semantic gradients.	*balmy : sultry :: angry : furious*
Part/Whole	The first word is part of the second word. The first word can also be the whole and the second word the part.	*Detroit : Michigan :: Sarasota : Florida*
Tool/Worker	The first word is a kind of tool and the second word is the worker who would use the tool, or the other way around.	*calculator : mathematician :: microscope : biologist*
Object/Action	The first word is an object and the second word is a verb that relates to the object.	*moon : revolve :: brain : think*
Item/Purpose	The first word is an item that is used for a specific purpose.	*claws : grasping :: teeth : chewing*
Source/Product	The first word is the source of the product.	*leather: shoe :: wool : coat*
Characteristic	One word is a characteristic of the other.	*vampire : immortal :: human : mortal*
Cause and Effect	One word stands for the reason and the other for the result.	*study : success :: drug : cure*

Figure 5.8 *Analogy types*

Writing verbal analogies is now one of the ways that students explore vocabulary in Weddle's class.

Another way to learn more about analogies is to download a free app for tablets and smartphones called *This Is to That—A Pop Culture Analogy Game* found at the iTunes app store. If projected on an electronic whiteboard, kids can play in teams to try to figure out the analogy. Having reference materials or Internet access close by will guarantee that students will do some double-checking on the meanings of words and phrases to understand the analogy. Requiring them to explain or provide evidence for their answers will help students do the kind of thinking behind verbal analogies. As with anything online, please review carefully before using with students.

Deeper Vocabulary Learning with Figurative Language

Sometimes, we make assumptions about kids' understanding. My grandmother, who grew up in Appalachia, often used to add "Don't be the cow's tail!" when she called us in to supper. As children, we knew she was really saying "Don't be the last one." We always thought it was funny and scurried to get into the house quickly.

One day I was finishing a lesson with eleven- and twelve-year-olds in my eastern Kentucky classroom. After giving the students instructions on what to do next, they began working on the activity. All except Daniel and Harry. As they slowly moved to get their materials together, I playfully said, "Come on, boys! Don't be the cow's tail!" After all, these kids lived in the mountains and many of them lived on family farms. Later, in one of those red-faced moments I still clearly remember, I was astonished to hear during a parent-teacher conference that Daniel thought I was literally calling him a "cow's tail." In fact, he had been upset to the point of tears that his teacher had called him such a horrible name. Needless to say, I had to backtrack and gently make sure that Daniel, as well as all my other students, understood that it was an old saying rather than an insult. To this day, I hope my explanation made a difference. As my grandmother would say, "no telling how many" other phrases I have innocently used over the years that some kids have misunderstood. Clearly, many kids need practice in how to interpret expressive and figurative language.

The English language is filled with phrases that don't seem to make sense, and creative authors often include unfamiliar expressions in their writing. Students in the middle grades are at various stages in moving from concrete to abstract thinking, and they are often especially perplexed by vague language. It takes a lot of background knowledge to be able to make a connection to phrases such as "burn a hole in one's pocket" or "be in a pickle" (or that one about the cow's tail) if a young adolescent has never heard them before. And English language learners have an even harder time.

Although middle grades students are becoming more independent readers and better equipped to delve deeper into word meanings, they often have a hard time initially understanding figurative language when they encounter it in text or speech. To comprehend challenging text, students need to be able to interpret these descriptive words and expressive phrases. Teaching students to recognize and interpret figurative language in reading, in listening, and in viewing, and to use figurative language in writing and creating multimedia presentations is considered to be part of vocabulary instruction.

Similes, Metaphors, and Allusions — Oh, My!

Figurative language is like that dab of whipped cream on a piece of pie—it adds richness to writing. We often teach students to use figurative language as part of writing instruction, but when you think about it, understanding and interpreting expressions is also an important part of reading competency. Writers use figurative language to help a reader envision a scene, an action, a procedure, or a character, and if students don't understand the figures of speech, they don't completely comprehend the text. Examples of figurative language are consistently found throughout literature, narrative essays, feature articles, and opinion pieces, such as editorials, where the writer wants to conjure an emotion or a feeling. Figurative language is also an aspect of vocabulary development, as figures of speech are often words or phrases that students need to add to their word banks. The names we give to figures of speech (*alliteration, simile, onomatopoeia*) are terms that are used to discuss, to analyze, or to critique the way a text is written; in other words, craft and structure. In this way, these terms can be considered content-area vocabulary in English language arts classes.

Some terms representing figures of speech or literary devices that students may need to know to discuss or write about text are presented below. Although these are not the only figures of speech, they are all related to vocabulary knowledge in some way.

>*Acronym.* An acronym is an abbreviation using the first letters of words. Some acronyms are words that can be pronounced but are actually made up of the first letters of words. These would include words such as RAM (random access memory) and NASA (National Aeronautics and Space Administration). Other are made up only of initials (which purists call "initialisms"). Examples of these would include FBI (Federal Bureau of Investigation) and DVD (digital video disk). Acronyms can interrupt students' comprehension if they don't have the necessary background knowledge to interpret them.
>
>*Alliteration.* Alliteration is repeating the beginning consonant sounds of words. Dr. Seuss books, such as *The Butter Battle Book* (Seuss 1984), provide excellent but fun examples of alliteration (while, in this case, also teaching a political science concept

about war). Alliteration is the main ingredient in a tongue twister but is used effectively by many more serious writers to add rhythm and mood to their poetry or prose.

Allusion. An allusion is referring to another text or famous person, place, or thing and assuming the reader will know who or what the author means. Allusions to the Bible or mythology are found throughout classic literature, essays, and speeches. Young adult literature, modern essays, editorials, and articles often contain references to pop or rock songs, historical events, stories, movies, or celebrities. For example, *The Book Thief* (Zusak 2006) alludes to literature (*Mein Kampf*), historical people (Adolf Hitler, Jessie Owens), places (Dachau), events (1936 Olympics), and music (Beethoven, Mozart).

I recently came across an allusion gone bad. Two middle grades girls had posted a video about figurative language they had created for a school project. They cleverly used sound clips of popular songs to illustrate different figures of speech. As I listened to the chorus of the Maroon 5 song "Moves Like Jagger," the girls earnestly explained the words that were written on the screen, which were "the person in the song moved like a guy named Mcjagger." Laughing, I told my husband this story. "Who's Maroon 5?" he asked. There is a lesson on allusion (and maybe irony) in there somewhere.

Assonance. Assonance is repeating vowel sounds in words that are close to each other, which also provides rhythm, rhyme, and lyrical language to poetry and prose. Many traditional poets made great use of assonance, from Edgar Allan Poe's "The Raven" to William Wordsworth's "Daffodils" to Robert Frost's "Fire and Ice." Dr. Seuss also provides examples of assonance, with the long *e* sound in this excerpt from his poem:

> *Upon an island hard to reach,*
> *the East Beast sits upon his beach.*
> *Upon the west beach sits the West Beast.*
> *Each beach beast thinks he's the best beast.*

Consonance. Consonance means repeating consonant sounds when the consonant is not necessarily the first letter in words, such as *pitter-patter*. Authors use consonance to establish rhythm, especially in poetry.

Eponyms. An eponym is a word that has been formed from the name of a famous person, place, or thing. Often, an eponym comes from a person in history. The word *sandwich* comes from the Earl of Sandwich, just as the word *pasteurize* came from Louis Pasteur. A number of words have been derived from mythology. *Atlas, Achilles' heel, herculean,* and *titanic* are examples of mythological eponyms.

Homographs. Homographs (*homo* means "alike" and *graph* means "writing") are two words that have the same spelling but have different meanings and sometimes pronunciations, depending on how it is used. Examples are *minute* (I'll be with you in a *minute*/the *minute* writing was hard to read) and *coordinates* (she *coordinates* the event/

coordinates on a map). When a student encounters a homograph in text, he or she needs to take a good look at context to determine the meaning and pronunciation.

Homophones. Homophones (*homo* means "alike" and *phon* means "sound") are words that sound the same but have different spellings and meanings. Examples of homophones are *their/they're/there* and *principle/principal*. For most students, homophones are an issue in writing but can also be a barrier to comprehension for struggling students or students learning English.

Hyperbole. Hyperbole is the best figure of speech ever! Actually, hyperbole is an exaggeration so extreme that no one would believe it. Hyperbole is often found in humorous writing and to make dialogue come alive. Tall tales make use of hyperbole, as in the beginning of the Paul Bunyan folktale "Babe the Blue Ox" (Schlosser 2014):

> Well now, one winter it was so cold that all the geese flew backward and all the fish moved south and even the snow turned blue. Late at night, it got so frigid that all spoken words froze solid afore they could be heard. People had to wait until sunup to find out what folks were talking about the night before.

Metonymy. A metonymy is a figure of speech that stands for a word closely related to it. Referring to people in the U.S. government as "the Oval Office" or using the term *corporate* to mean those who are people in charge of a company are examples of metonymy. If students do not have sufficient background knowledge, it is difficult to understand such terms.

Metaphor. A metaphor makes a hidden comparison between two apparently different objects or ideas without using the words *like* or *as*. An example of a metaphor from Shakespeare's *As You Like It* is "All the world's a stage, and all the men and women merely players." When students can create a metaphor for a vocabulary word, they have nailed it (see?). Choosing an image and explaining how the image is a metaphor for the term is an effective way for students to explore their thinking about vocabulary in all disciplines (Bloch 2013).

Onomatopoeia. Onomatopoeia is the use of a word that imitates the sound of the meaning, helping the reader hear the action as well as envision it. Comics about superheroes are filled with examples of onomatopoeia, such as *Wham*! *Zowie*! *Kerplunk*! Authors often use onomatopoeia to bring writing to life, as in Edgar Allan Poe's "The Bells." In this poem, he uses words such as *tinkle, tintinnabulation, jingling, clanging, screaming,* and *groaning* to describe the sounds of different kinds of bells.

Personification. Personification is giving human characteristics to nonhuman objects, ideas, or animals. A vivid example of personification can be found in *The Hunger Games*: *"We have to stand for a few minutes in the doorway of the train while the cameras gobble up our images, then we're allowed inside and the doors close mercifully behind us"* (Collins 2009).

Portmanteau. Lewis Carroll introduced a new word into the English language when *Through the Looking-Glass* was published (Carroll 1871). Alice in Wonderland asks Humpty Dumpty to explain some of the unusual words in the poem "Jabberwocky"—words such as *slithy* and *chortle*. In response, he explains that these words are like a portmanteau, which is a piece of luggage made up of two compartments—one to hang clothes and one to fold them (Kahane 2012). Slithy is a combination of *slimy* and *lithe*, whereas chortle is a blend of *chuckle* and *snort*. Portmanteau now means a word where two words are squeezed together and becomes a combination of both—*smoke* and *fog* make *smog*. When words such as *brunch* (breakfast and lunch), *blog* (web log), and *motel* (motor and hotel) become accepted parts of everyday language, they are not hard to understand. However, unfamiliar words or novel combinations can sometimes be stumbling blocks to comprehension.

Simile. A simile directly compares two seemingly different objects or ideas using the words *like* or *as*. Phrases such as "sing like an angel" or "as brave as a lion" are similes (old and tired, but similes nonetheless). Effective writers make exceptional use of fresh similes, as in Stephen Crane's *The Red Badge of Courage*: "In the eastern sky there was a yellow patch like a rug laid for the feet of the coming sun . . . "

Synecdoche. Synecdoche is a term given to a word that stands for a part of a whole. For example, the word *pigskin* represents football in the United States. Sometimes a synecdoche is a word that represents what an object is made of, as in *lead* for bullets or *plastic* for credit card. Sometimes a brand name becomes a word. For example, where I live, it is common to hear someone ask, "Are you thirsty? What kind of Coke do you want?" The word *Coke* has become synonymous with "soft drink," just as all kinds of facial tissue are called Kleenex, and all brands of adhesive bandages are called Band-Aids. These are also examples of synecdoche.

Verbal Irony. Irony can be dramatic, situational, or verbal. Verbal irony is saying one thing but meaning the opposite, such as "It is as clear as mud to me," when you really don't understand at all. When a little attitude is thrown in, verbal irony usually veers to sarcasm.

Idioms and Other Vague Phrases

Idioms are almost in a class by themselves. Idioms are groups of words where the meaning is not clear from the words in the phrase. Examples include "piece of cake" or "when pigs fly." According to Jag Bhalla, author of *I'm Not Hanging Noodles on Your Ears and Other Intriguing Idioms from Around the World* (2009), the origin of the word *idiom* comes from the Greek root *idios* (the same root as the word *idiosyncratic*) and means "personal, private, or of one's own." This makes sense; one has to be an insider in a language to know and understand its idioms. Idioms are especially puzzling for struggling readers and English learners.

Many idioms are steeped in historical or cultural tradition, and exploring the origins of such sayings can be fascinating. For instance, the phrase "Don't let the cat out of the bag" (meaning don't tell something you shouldn't) has a disputed historical explanation. One theory is that on ships, the dreaded whip known as the "cat-o'-nine-tails" was kept in a leather bag. Sailors who were being punished did not want to see the "cat" appear, and a sailor who told on another for a transgression was literally making the "cat come out of the bag." Another theory is that in the marketplace of the sixteenth century, piglets were often sold in bags ("a pig in a poke"). Unscrupulous tradesmen might slip a cat into the bag instead of the piglet if the customer was not paying close attention. Once the bag was opened it was too late because the cat was already out. Other sources dispute both these theories, asserting that the idiom is merely comparing the behavior of a cat in a bag to a secret—once they are both out, they can't be controlled. In any case, when students conduct short research projects to try to find the origins of idioms, they better remember the idioms as well as practice research and presenting skills.

There are quite a few expressive phrases in the English language that are hard to interpret without a good deal of background knowledge. Some originated with Aesop's fables or Greek and Roman myths. Others came from the King James's version of the Bible, translated in 1611. Animal-referenced expressions that come from this version of the Bible include "a bird in the hand is worth two in the bush," "a leopard can't change his spots," "the fly in the ointment," and "wolf in sheep's clothing." And, of course, the prolific William Shakespeare created numerous phrases that are still in everyday use, such as "out of house and home," "it's Greek to me," and "have your teeth set on edge."

Interpreting Figurative Language

Middle grades kids can explore the meanings of similes, metaphors, idioms, and other expressive phrases through art, drama, music, and technology. They can use art materials to illustrate and explain their interpretations of phrases, such as "blind as a bat" or "time is a thief." When they dramatize phrases such as "look for something with a fine-tooth comb" or "fly in the face of danger," students get the picture. When they craft lyrical summaries (McLaughlin and Allen 2009) by setting summaries to music or create technology projects about figures of speech they discover in movies, TV commercials, or popular songs, kids are more aware of the use and meaning of expressive phrases. And when they write their own descriptions using figurative language, we know students have made these phrases their own.

I often used popular song lyrics to teach my students to interpret figurative language, and I enjoyed these lessons as much as they did as we sang along together. I felt that it was a worthwhile activity. After all, a meaningful song is really a poem set to music, so when students learn to analyze songs they are also learning more about how to analyze traditional poetry. It was certainly motivating for my students, but now I know what I didn't know then—analyzing pieces of pop culture can actually help students improve critical-thinking skills (Evans 2004). It can also make examples of figurative language more prominent.

We may have to monitor the lyrics they are exploring in class, but students today still enjoy analyzing the words to songs. When New Zealand singer Lorde won the Grammy Award for Song of the Year ("Royals") and Best Pop Solo Performance in January 2014, students at Eastside Middle were fascinated to learn that the teenager writes her own songs and wrote many when she was their age. Lorde's songs often explore the emotional aspects of being a teenager in a confusing time. Seventh graders Carissa and Sean chose the Lorde song "Team" and created a poster to explore different aspects of the song, including examples of figurative language, rhythm, sound devices, sensory details, and overall meaning of the song. Part of their poster is depicted in Figure 5.9.

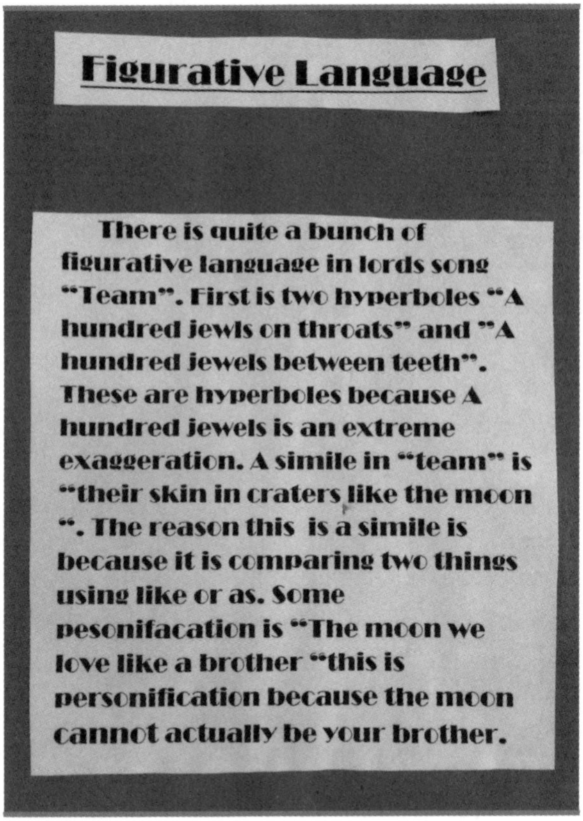

Figurative Language

There is quite a bunch of figurative language in lords song "Team". First is two hyperboles "A hundred jewls on throats" and "A hundred jewls between teeth". These are hyperboles because A hundred jewls is an extreme exaggeration. A simile in "team" is "their skin in craters like the moon ". The reason this is a simile is because it is comparing two things using like or as. Some pesonifacation is "The moon we love like a brother "this is personification because the moon cannot actually be your brother.

Figure 5.9 *Figurative language in the song "Team"*

Word Play

Hey, did you know that a chicken crossing the road is *poultry in motion*? I can hear the groans now! But seriously, folks, many middle grades kids will recognize that this is a joke yet not understand why it is supposed to be funny. Unless they know the meaning of *poultry* and have background knowledge of the phrase *poetry in motion*, not many will really get it. Playing with words in puns and riddles encourages students to think about multiple meanings and how word meanings relate. Teachers armed with this knowledge and a great sense of humor will share appropriate riddles, jokes, and puns to encourage word play to help kids develop word consciousness.

Puns

Puns have been called "the lowest form of humor . . . when you don't think of it first" (Oscar Levant). Others appreciate the clever play on words that puns provide. According to *Merriam-Webster*, a pun is "the usually humorous use of a word in such a way as to suggest two or more meanings or the meaning of another word similar in sound" (http://www. merriam-webster.com/dictionary/pun). Each year, the O. Henry Pun-off Contest is held in Austin, Texas, to find the best punster of the year. In London, small businesses compete for the punniest store name (it was fun to find out the winner for 2014 was "Junk and Disorderly," the name of a secondhand store).

Puns can be simple: "Why is a crossword puzzle like a quarrel? Because one word leads to another." However, even a short, simple pun takes background knowledge. To understand this pun, kids would have to know that the word *cross* is a synonym for "angry," and that the phrase *one word leads to another* means "a quarrel." Puns can also be long and complicated, like my favorite:

> *You know that he refused to wear shoes so his feet became hard and tough, right?*
> *You know that he went for long periods fasting and refused to eat meat, even when he wasn't fasting, right?*
> *And you know that both the fasting and his diet gave him extremely bad breath, right?*
> *And that he was of lean, slight build even into his later years?*
> *So he was a super callous fragile mystic plagued with halitosis.*

A boy triangle and a girl triangle are talking. "You're acute!" says the boy triangle. "You're all right yourself," replies the girl triangle. Okay, so it's not Shakespeare (although he certainly wrote his fair share of puns), but these examples can be funny in a math class. Kids can have fun with puns in all classes, and at the same time, become more highly aware of language. Find amusing puns to share in all content areas at websites such as *Pun of the Day* (www.punoftheday.com). Encouraging students to create their own puns will stretch their creative mind muscles as well as foster word consciousness.

Riddles

Fans of *The Hobbit* (Tolkien 1937) will know the answer to this famous riddle:

> *This thing all things devours:*
> *Birds, beasts, trees, flowers;*
> *Gnaws iron, bites steel;*
> *Grinds hard stones to meal;*
> *Slays king, ruins town,*
> *And beats high mountain down.*

When Gollum asks Bilbo Baggins this riddle, Bilbo answers "Time!" at the very last moment, right before possibly submitting to a dreadful fate. Several other riddles await in this classic story of adventure and fantasy creatures.

Riddles are fun, but they are often rich in figurative language such as metaphor, simile, and metonymy as well as vivid imagery. Introducing a riddle helps kids contemplate images based on the language used to describe the object. When students can write their own riddles, they practice this type of language. An excellent lesson by John Paul Walter on teaching middle school students to write riddles can be found at http://www.readwritethink.org/classroom-resources/lesson-plans/what-teaching-poetry-through-169.html.

Vocabulary Journals in the Middle Grades

When students explore words, they first record the selected words in a vocabulary journal or notebook. In *Word Nerds*, we used a consistent graphic organizer for students to explore words. The Frayer model (Frayer, Frederick, and Klausmeier 1969) has been successfully used with all ages of students for decades and helps students think about a word in several different ways. For elementary students, we shared it as shown in Figure 5.10.

This adapted Frayer model is a simple square box divided into fourths, with a concept word in the middle where the smaller boxes intersect. In the top left-hand box, students write a student-friendly definition of the concept word. Research shows that student-friendly definitions, rather than dictionary definitions, help students learn words. In the top right-hand box, students draw a sketch of the word to act as a logographic cue (Beers 2003). Creating a logograph, or picture that represents a concept, helps students internalize the meaning of the word within the context we have provided. The bottom left-hand box is where students list

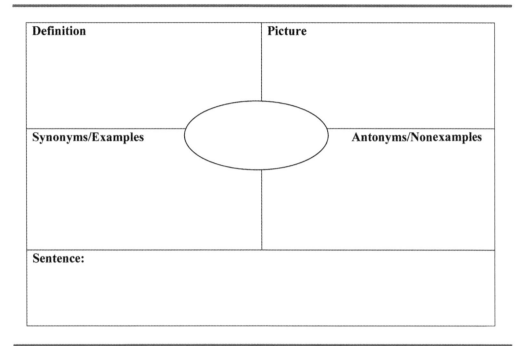

Figure 5.10 *Adapted Frayer model*

synonyms or examples of the word, and in the bottom right-hand box, they place antonyms or nonexamples. Generating synonyms and antonyms for words helps student connect words to a network (Stahl 1999), and research shows that higher-level thinking and word ownership are more likely to develop when students are required to think of an antonym or nonexample for a word (Powell 1986). We added a box at the bottom for students to write a 7-Up sentence, or a sentence with at least seven words. When students write more complex sentences, they must include adjectives, adverbs, or prepositional phrases, which are those very elements that constitute context clues. Our students completed this graphic organizer for each word as part of their vocabulary journals. The journal was then used as a reference for the rest of the school year. A blank adapted Frayer model can be found in Appendix D.

In the middle grades, teachers wanted to expand students' word knowledge, and so several went beyond the basic Frayer model to create a variety of graphic organizers for students to use to record the word and explore its aspects. For instance, Figure 5.11 shows the vocabulary journal organizer Tonie Weddle adapted from *Word Nerds* for her seventh-grade classes at Bullitt Lick so they could record all the vocabulary words for one vocabulary cycle on a single sheet of paper. The organizer includes sections where students write the word; the location of the word in a text; a student-friendly definition; a sentence of at least seven

Name: Megan   Text: More Perfect Union   Date: 5/6/14

Word	Definition	Sentence 7 or more words	Synonym(s) or Example	Antonym(s) or Example	Picture	Idioms, Analogies and/or Other Meanings
resolution pp. 263	the solution to a problem	To find the resolution to a conflict, you should see a therapist.	decision settlement	indecision timidity	"Tell me how you feel." Therapy	resolution: decision:: indecision: doubt
unity pp. 264	the state of being joined together as a whole	Sparta and Athens became a unity so they can beat the Persians.	agreement consensus	disagreement fighting	"Together"	unity: agreement:: disagreement: fighting
bankruptcy pp. 267	the state of being unable to pay debts	Most people go bankruptcy because of taxes.	loss overdraft	accomplishment achievement		bankruptcy: overdraft:: accomplishment: achievement
global pp. 266	affecting or involving the whole world	Pollution is global to the earth.	overall universal	local individual	Earth	global: universal:: local: individual
legacy 265	something handed down from one generation to another	when you die, you should leave some legacy behind.	tradition devise	non-tradition unusual		legacy: tradition:: non-tradition: advanced
stagnant pp. 266	inactive; not moving, growing or improving	when I first wake up, I am stagnant.	dormant stationary	spirited active		stagnant: stationary:: active: moving
strife pp.	a bitter conflict or struggle	My sister and I just had a strife about a movie.	clash emulation	concurrence peace	yelling!	strife: clash:: concurrence: unanimity
turbulent pp.	wild, violent, and conflict	An example of turbulent is a loose tiger.	fierce rough	settled calm	Cat	turbulent: fierce:: settled: calm
Extra Word Definitions						
_____ pp.						
_____ pp.						
_____ pp.						

Figure 5.11 *Vocabulary journal organizer*

words; synonyms, or examples; antonyms, or nonexamples; sketch a picture; and insert an analogy or other interesting aspect of the word. Weddle's blank one-page vocabulary journal organizer can be found in Appendix E.

Other teachers adapted the *Word Nerds* graphic organizer in various ways. Several of the English language arts teachers at Eastside worked together to create an organizer to introduce individual words. This organizer included a context-rich sentence related to or extracted from a text that students are reading in class so students could make predictions about the meaning after underlining context clues in the passage. After a brief class discussion, students explored words by completing boxes that required them to add a student-friendly definition, synonyms/examples, antonyms/nonexamples, other forms of the word, part of speech, connections to the word (how it is connected to the text), a 7-Up sentence, illustration, and analogy.

Exploring Vocabulary with a Goal in Mind

It's a radical thought: Word knowledge does not always equal vocabulary knowledge. For students to become vocabularians, they not only need to know words but also how they connect to other words. In this way, students can create networks of meaning and strategies to use to figure out the meanings of words they have never seen. Students who are vocabulary-rich appreciate language and the deeper meanings of words and phrases. They play with words, and enjoy learning new words for old concepts and new words as they learn new concepts.

Ultimately, the vocabulary goal is for students to be able to interpret unfamiliar words and phrases when they encounter them in text and to use expressive language when they write or speak. When students explore vocabulary words and their connections, they are on their way to knowing these words for life.

Chapter 6

CREATIVE PRACTICE FOR VOCABULARY PROWESS

For the things we have to learn before we can do them, we learn by doing them.

—Aristotle

Before a presentation at the Kentucky Council of Teachers of English/Language Arts Conference, I placed small packets of art materials on the tables. The first wave of teachers entered the room, ready to dutifully participate in a session about vocabulary instruction. "Hey! We have crayons!" exclaimed a high school English teacher, his face brightening. I immediately had an enthusiastic, ready-to-learn audience. We get the same reaction from students when we use creative methods to help them learn new words.

Student engagement is high when kids feel they will be participating in a pleasant experience. As Michael Opitz and Michael Ford (2014, 3) said, "Engaged students are more joyful in their learning pursuits." And as we said in *Word Nerds*, "In our classrooms, we want to see more of our students using new vocabulary confidently, but we also want them to feel joyful about their growing facility with words" (Overturf, Montgomery, and Smith 2013, 97).

One of the hallmarks of middle grades education (and really for all levels) is that students learn best when they engage in active learning. There is no doubt that physical activity and projects using the arts can be highly motivating to young adolescents who need to move frequently and enjoy social interaction. Integrated instruction using varied methods of teaching and learning seems to prompt willingness to learn and increase achievement (Guthrie and McCann 1997; Short, Kauffman, and Kahn 2000; Vega 2012). Active learning can also help meet the needs of students who learn best through multisensory instruction to develop visual, auditory, and kinesthetic-tactile pathways to language learning (International Dyslexia Association 2008).

Revisiting vocabulary words, synonyms, and antonyms and other word relationships provides practice with meanings that most students need. It is never enough to introduce a word, engage in a vocabulary exploration, and then forget about it until the test. Students also need to play with words and their definitions, creating experiences to make connections and help them remember.

The methods introduced in this chapter go beyond traditional paper-and-pencil vocabulary worksheets or flashcards. Here you will find strategies and activities that creative teachers have incorporated to encourage meaningful and motivating vocabulary practice.

Vocabulary Activities with an Art Focus

Hearts, flowers, superheroes, monsters, and doodles of all kinds cover notebooks and edges of assignment sheets in the middle grades. Most young adolescents love to draw or sketch, and art is a way that some students can best express their learning. We have found that vocabulary activities based on art are almost always greeted with enthusiasm and usually engage students in in-depth thinking about words.

However, as motivating as artwork is for middle grades kids, it is also considered an important academic tool. Demonstrating understanding through nonlinguistic representation is one of the ways that students best learn concepts (Marzano, Pickering, and Pollock 2001), and arts integration can increase achievement (Vega 2012). When students revisit the meanings of words through creative art expression, they must think deeply about definitions and the way words are used.

Word Colors

Word Colors is a quick, favorite activity, but it also requires students to think at high levels. Students choose a color to represent a word and justify their choice. It sounds pretty simple, but in reality, students engage in metaphorical thinking as they contemplate the meaning of a word, select a color to symbolize the word, and explain why they think the color represents the word. Thinking in metaphors can help students learn (Marzano, Pickering, and Pollock 2001).

Each student receives an index card and writes a selected vocabulary word in marker in manuscript letters on the unlined side. Then we ask them to choose a color to represent the meaning of the word. On the same side of the card, students use a crayon or colored pencil to lightly shade the background of the card in their chosen color. We ask them to use only one color (although they don't always listen!) because otherwise some students have a tendancy to be more concrete and draw a picture. There is no wrong color; the only stipulation is that students must justify their answers.

On the lined side of the card, they write an explanation of the color they chose to denote the word. This explanation must be in the form of a sentence that contains at least seven words to explain why the color represents the word. Using at least seven words ensures that students have to include adjectives, adverbs, prepositional phrases, or figures of speech—exactly the kind of details that make up context clues.

See Lexee's Word Color card from Bullitt Lick Middle. Her word *energy* is shown from both the front and back sides in Figures 6.1 and 6.2. The explanation she provided on the back of the card is, "The color green reminds me of the word <u>energy</u> because energy makes me think of nature's life cycle and a lot of nature is green.

 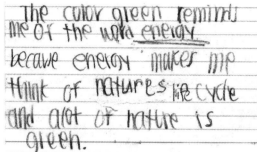

Figure 6.1 *Front side of Word Color card*   **Figure 6.2** *Back side of Word Color card*

Some Word Color explanations ooze with adolescent angst, such as "Pink is for <u>arrogant</u> because preppy girls think they are better than everyone else." Some choices may be fairly literal at first, but many show more in-depth thinking. Once they understand the concept, kids tend to get creative. Some examples of middle grades Word Color representations at Bullitt Lick and Eastside include the following:

> *I chose gray to represent <u>obscure</u>. This color represents obscure because if you can't see without glasses, you might see blurry gray.*
> *I chose red for <u>bias</u> because a biased person can also feel anger towards the idea, person (and etc) they are judgmental towards.*
> *I chose sky blue because <u>convey</u> is to explain and once you do, it's clear what it means like a blue sky is empty and clear.*
> *A <u>hyperbole </u>is an exaggeration and I chose tan, the color of a rubber band, because a rubber band stretches, and to exaggerate is to stretch the truth.*
> *The color "orchid" *cough* purple *cough* represents <u>exquisite</u> because when I hear the word I think of really high class women, and purple is kind of girly.*

Students love Word Colors, and it seems to help them attach a meaning with a word. As eighth grader Kerrigan explained at Eastside, "If you get to color and make something fun, then you make that memory. It is easier to remember the word because you have something that is in your brain that helps you connect with it." It seems easy and fun to kids, but in reality, students are using their minds to do some high-level thinking with their vocabulary words.

Christie Bolton, a special education teacher for a seventh-grade team at Eastside, has seen the same results with her students. As she explained, "A lot of my students can't write very well and have to have a scribe for testing, so this activity is great. When they choose a color and justify a reason they chose that color, they have to think hard about the definition. Writing a sentence with only seven words gets them to higher-level sentence structure, but it's not overwhelming. It's really awesome to see what they can do. They have a real connection to the word."

Illustrated Vocabulary (Word Illustrations)

In *Word Nerds*, we described an activity we called Word Illustrations, in which students write a vocabulary word in clear, dark manuscript writing. They then turn each letter into a representation of the definition of the word. The goal is to try to incorporate all the letters into an overall illustrated definition. Word Illustrations encourages kids to think deeply about the meaning of a word as it is used in a certain context.

For example, fifth grader David illustrated the word *nomadic*, a word from a social studies lesson. He turned the lowercase "n" into a Native American boy. The "o" became a basket. The "m," which he drew larger than the others, became mountains with arrows that indicated movement over them. The "a" became a buffalo, the "d" was transformed into a teepee, the "i" was a tree, and he made the "c" into another Native American. As he explained to me, "Some Native Americans were nomadic. They had to cross mountains to go to another village to find food."

When I introduced Word Illustrations to teachers of older students and showed them an example of a fifth grader's work, they were impressed. But before they introduced this practice to students, many wanted to try it for themselves. They also wanted to rename it Illustrated Vocabulary to make it a more sophisticated-sounding activity. Teachers immediately realized that Illustrated Vocabulary is a deep-thinking activity and much more challenging than it first seems.

"I thought it would be easy, but it took me a while to even begin to think of a way to turn my letters into a definition," a science teacher reported. But not the kids. Students who were normally creative began to see possibilities right away. For example, in Figure 6.3 Jared and Alexis worked together at Eastside to represent the word *contemptuous*. What appears to be separate illustrated letters is really hiding a story. When you know that these students were reading an excerpt from *Romeo and Juliet* in their English language arts class, you realize that the story is there: in the "c" representing something bad, the "t" with the heart and the arrows representing the star-crossed lovers, the "m" with a broken heart, and all the angry eyes glaring across space at one another—two contemptuous families.

Teachers were amazed to see that students who often struggle in school also quickly got to work and thought of original ways to illustrate words. Special

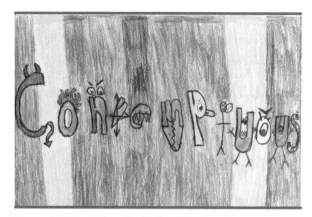

Figure 6.3 *Vocabulary illustration of* contemptuous

education teachers were especially thrilled to see how their students learned all definitions to a higher degree. "For the first time, I feel like my kids get it!" exclaimed Bolton, the special education teacher at Eastside. This held true for difficult and content-specific words. "They have to think so deeply about each letter, it helps cement the definition and the spelling, as well. I had never seen this activity before, but I really love it."

Content-area teachers have found that Illustrated Vocabulary works especially well with disciplinary terms. In science, Josh turned the word *speed* into a road, with a cheetah, a car with massive wheels, and a basketball player. Selena's *momentum* became basketballs, a bowling ball, trains on a track going over hills, a bow and arrow, a semitruck, a tree falling, a balloon filled with water, and baseballs, all bouncing down a set of steps. She included an explanation of *momentum* and how all these objects related to her picture and definition.

Illustrated Vocabulary helps kids explore depth of knowledge in word meanings and expand their thinking. As Ally, an eighth grader at Eastside, shared: "When we were doing the pictures where we had to draw each letter to represent a different picture, I tried to pick the most challenging word and find real-life elements that I could incorporate with it. We did the word *structure*, and at first everyone was trying to draw like bricks and building structures, but I tried to incorporate it with language arts and grammar. I tried to find ways to represent the letters in a way that the word actually had something to do with vocabulary."

Susan Carlisle, who teaches eighth grade at Eastside, ruefully shared a story for other middle-level teachers who might think this activity is so easy it doesn't need much teacher attention. "I tried Illustrated Vocabulary for the first time on a Monday morning and thought it was going to be a simple activity. I found that teachers really need to think about it themselves before setting the kids free. If you are trying to help students, and you haven't given this activity quite a bit of thought yourself (and if you are caught like I was before coffee), it can be a little disconcerting. It is so much more difficult than it looks, and I was caught off guard when students asked me questions about it." She chuckled at the memory. "Before these types of tasks, I just assigned words and gave kids a dictionary. I didn't have to do a lot of thinking and planning. But when I introduced Illustrated Vocabulary, I really had to back pedal because the kids needed a different kind of support to do more creative and challenging thinking. It's fun to do these types of activities, which require higher-level thinking on the part of the students and we have also jumped to higher-level words. But this also means higher-level thinking on the part of the teacher, too. It is not just coloring."

Definition Depiction

Another art activity that students find enjoyable is illustrating the definition of a word. The task seems simple, but students must add meticulous details that make the definition obvious and defend their drawing in writing or by presenting to the class, which makes it a higher-order thinking activity.

Several of Brandi Odom's students at Bowman illustrated the word *injustice* by drawing pictures depicting the civil rights movement. Their drawings included African Americans marching with picket signs that said things such as "Blacks deserve the right to vote." Theodore drew a picture a little closer to home, by showing two boys eating at a table. One of the boys had two pork chops on his plate, and the other only had one. "I think it is an injustice for my brother to have more than me," explained Theodore.

"When we do this activity and I ask for volunteers to share," reported Odom, "I get at least twenty hands waving in the air all wanting to talk about the vocabulary word. They really get into it, and it doesn't take much time. I think it is the most beneficial thing when they come up with their own definition and use it in a picture. They can see it. I could stand there all day with a worksheet and a list of definitions and they would never remember, but when they create illustrations of the word it really helps them retain it."

Definition Depictions can also be a useful tool in the content areas. For example, kids at Eastside depicted the Pythagorean theorem by creating mathematical drawings such as fire engines and ladders on graph paper and then supporting their thinking through a written explanation that included mathematical equations. The drawings were posted on a bulletin board in the hall, with this learning target attached: "I can demonstrate my knowledge of key vocabulary through illustrating words."

Vocabulary and Dramatic Expression

Integrating drama and movement into vocabulary instruction has often been recommended, especially for English language learners (Alber and Foil 2003; Rieg and Paquette

2009). Because students are learning more complex academic language and lower-frequency words through the activity, it is an especially appropriate activity for vocabulary practice in middle grades classrooms. Drama is second nature to most middle grades students, and they almost always appreciate a chance to be part of a performance (Wilhelm 1997, 2002). Creating a dramatic depiction of the definition of a word helps students internalize meanings and connect concepts.

Dramatizing Words

Robert Kuprenas, the seventh-grade math teacher at Bowman, makes liberal use of drama in his classes. He has found that when students can attach a story to a math term, they are more likely to remember it. Students in Kuprenas's classes pretended to walk up a mountain to demonstrate positive slope, walked back down to show negative slope, walked across flat ground for zero slope, and then pretended to fall off a vertical cliff for undefined slope. On another day, Kuprenas wanted to help students visualize *volume*. Trey volunteered to crawl into the recycling bin to demonstrate that volume is the amount of space inside a three-dimensional solid. The students were highly amused, and this dramatic interpretation cemented not only Trey's knowledge but the rest of the class's as well.

When Kuprenas's students were having trouble understanding the concept of *equation*, he drew a large equal sign on a piece of paper. He then had students stand in a line on each side of the equal sign and added and subtracted them, showing that an equation is a balancing act held together by the equal sign.

Drama is a clever way to motivate students to think about word meaning. Students in Don Hollandsworth's seventh-grade social studies class at Bowman learned the word *spiritual* as they worked on concepts relating to the Nat Turner slave rebellion. After he introduced the word, he drew a Frayer model graphic organizer on the whiteboard. The students came up with student-friendly definitions, drew a picture, added synonyms such as *hymn* and *prayer music* and antonyms such as *rap* and *rock*, and a sentence using at least seven words. They discussed the role of spirituals in the slave rebellion, how slave owners thought they were peaceful songs about Christianity, but how many actually contained hidden messages of uprising and directions to freedom. When it came time to practice vocabulary, the students were ready. Hollandsworth shared, "There was a copy of a spiritual in the book we read, so we all sang it together. One of my girls got up and sang the loudest spiritual I have ever heard anyone sing. Before we knew it, we were all into the spirit, singing and dancing together. Kids will never forget that word!"

Vocabulary Tableaux

Using tableaux is another way of dramatizing word meaning (Fontichiaro 2007; Wilhelm 2002, 2004). The word *tableau* (*tableaux* is plural) comes from the French phrase *tableau vivant*, which literally means, "living picture." A tableau is a group of people who silently act out a scene from a story or an event in history and "freeze" in the middle of the action. Tableaux were popular in the nineteenth century, when people would pay to come and see them. They were also a big hit as party games, where others had to guess what the frozen scene represented.

When kids create a vocabulary tableau, they work in small groups to think of a scene or an action that represents the definition of the word. The rest of the students make inferences about the group's tableau, guessing which vocabulary word the tableau portrays or discussing how the group decided to portray the word. Jeff Wilhelm (2002) shared how his students might "tap in" (tap one of the tableau members on the shoulder) so that the person could "come to life" and explain his or her part in the scene during comprehension instruction. In a vocabulary tableau, the person who is tapped explains his or her part in the definition.

A vocabulary tableau is an exciting strategy that is silent while it is being performed, but there is a lot of thinking going on behind the quiet. When students create a tableau, they are engaging in visualizing, an important comprehension skill.

Motor Imaging

Motor imagery is a popular technique in sports and dance. When an athlete practices, he or she sometimes performs a mental rehearsal to get the brain engaged and to help the muscles remember desired actions. In motor imaging of vocabulary, we do just the opposite—engage in a physical activity associated with a verbal action.

Motor imaging is another vocabulary strategy that sounds simple but actually takes some thinking. There is evidence that the act of creating a hand or body gesture for a word (a nice one; this is middle school) can help learners remember the information attached to it. Ula Casale (1985, 619) described college students creating hand gestures while they attempted to remember the definitions of words. Her research revealed that most people use subtle hand or body gestures when trying to retrieve a word from memory, what she described as a "psychomotor dimension of word learning."

Casale (1985, 620) taught younger students to create a "pantomime, or psychomotor meaning, as well as language meaning" for vocabulary words using a set routine. First, the teacher introduces a word and explains what it means. Then she asks students to create a simple pantomime by saying, "How could you show someone what this word means?"

Students perform their pantomime simultaneously. Amazingly, in Casale's research many of the gestures were the same, so they chose one to represent the word. Most students were also able to create gestures for more abstract words. Casale's speculation was that motor imaging is a "whole brain" learning strategy.

After *Word Nerds* was published, Leslie added motor imaging as one of her vocabulary practice activities in fifth grade. Students work in small groups to create gestures to represent vocabulary words they have explored and then show the gesture to the class, revealing remarkable depths of thinking in the process. It seems to help students recall words and definitions. In Figure 6.4, Dylan demonstrates the gesture he created for *inspiration*.

Figure 6.4 *Motor imaging of* inspiration

Vocabulary Activities Immersed in Music

As Duke Ellington said, "It don't mean a thing, if it ain't got that swing." Many kids who cannot remember algebraic formulas or figures of speech can often remember and sing the lyrics to an entire catalog of songs. Music and rhythm are great motivators—exciting emotion, generating enjoyment, and boosting brain cells. Research has shown that music can help memory and retention (Wallace 1994) and is effective with children with learning disabilities (Gfeller 1986) and with students learning new languages (Brown and Perry 1991). When we insert music into our vocabulary lessons, we help students remember words.

Vocabulary Rap

Vocabulary Rap is one method we have used to practice remembering synonyms and antonyms that correlate with vocabulary words (Overturf, Montgomery, and Smith 2013). Rap is a popular cultural phenomenon that resonates with all types of students. There is some speculation that a hip-hop beat can help us remember (Borgia and Owles, 2009/2010). The use of hip-hop and rap music to improve memory and retention can be found in some packaged vocabulary programs (for an example, see *Flocabulary* at www.flocabulary.com).

The elementary version of Vocabulary Rap was a "call and response" activity. Margot found free wordless beats on websites such as *World HipHop Beats* (www.worldhiphopbeats.com) or *Creative Commons* (www.creativecommons.org). We have found that instrumental beats with a rhythm of approximately eighty-four to ninety-four beats per minute is appropriate for Vocabulary Rap, which is fast enough to make it lively, but not so fast that kids can't keep up. Margot also prepared a handout for students with a number of phrases, such as "When I say DIVERSITY, you say DIFFERENT." Margot began the recorded beat, called out the phrase, and students followed along, reading aloud the ending word in rhythm. The first half of the rap included synonyms of vocabulary words, and the second required students to call out antonyms.

At the middle level, students can write and perform their own songs and raps that include vocabulary words, synonyms, and antonyms. In Tonie Weddle's class at Bullitt Lick, students had the option to write a rap with vocabulary words. Taylor and Destiny wrote the following rap with their teacher as the focus, giggling as they recited it, all in good fun:

> *When you see her comin'*
> *Yeah you'll start to quiver*
> *She's a new category of villain*
> *Comin' at you*
> *With her tremendous grammar...*
> *She's the Wicka-Wicka-Weddle*
> *Mwahahahahaha*

Weddle laughed as hard as everyone else, but there was a special delight as she saw how kids were using vocabulary words in context.

Lyric Definitions

In *Guided Comprehension: A Teaching Model for Grades 3–8* (2009), Maureen McLaughlin and Mary Beth Allen described a strategy called the Lyric Summary that uses music to help students think about text. In this strategy, students cleverly write a summary of a text by setting it to the tune of a familiar song. This activity is highly motivating to students, especially when they work in small groups and perform the summary for the class.

Students can also create new lyrics focused on word descriptions set to music. For vocabulary study, we might rename this activity Lyric Definitions. Students focus on a term and create new lyrics for a tune they already know. As they create the lyrics, they work the definition of the word or phrase into the rhythm and melody of the song. No one can write lyrics without singing them, so students repeat the information over and over as they prepare the songs.

Lyric Definitions can be an effective strategy in content areas as well. For example, seventh graders wrote Lyric Definitions about various aspects of their study on Greece and Rome in social studies, using terms they had learned and set to a tune they already knew. One small group created a Lyric Definition to define "Ancient Greek monarchy" set to the tune of Queen's "We Will Rock You." It began:

Ancient Greek monarchy
Ancient Greek monarchy
Monarchy is ruled by one person
And power is passed down to generation to generation
Ancient Greek monarchy
Ancient Greek monarchy

The Lyric Definition went on for several stanzas, describing the rule of Greek kings, laws, religious ceremonies, and the council of aristocrats. It ended:

Bye, bye, bye monarchy
Hello, hello, hello, oligarchy

Lyric Definitions can be a highly motivating way to revisit meanings of concept words and get kids moving.

Vocabulary Practice with Games

Thousands of years ago, Aristotle said, "Exercise in repeatedly recalling a thing strengthens the memory." A multitude of studies have shown that Aristotle might have been on target. Research suggests that testing memory, sometimes called *retrieval practice*, can actually aid in learning (Roediger and Butler 2011; Roediger and Karpicke 2006). In cognitive science, this phenomenon is called the *testing effect*. Retrieval practice is the idea behind activities such as using flashcards to practice word recollection, and vocabulary games are often based on repeatedly recalling words.

Games in pairs, small groups, or whole group can build community and become a fun way to revisit and think about words in ways that help students remember them (Marzano, Pickering, and Pollock 2001; Moen 2007). Evidence also suggests that sitting too much is bad for one's health (Saunders 2011), so we can use vocabulary practice as a time to get up and move!

The Hot Seat

"So to practice vocabulary today, we're going to play the Hot Seat," Weddle announced one day at Bullitt Lick Middle.

"Cool! I *love* the Hot Seat," exclaimed Jordon.

"I do, too!" Steven said. Seventh graders smiled and organized their desks in anticipation.

The Hot Seat is a game Weddle's students play to practice and review vocabulary words they have studied. One student sits in a captain's chair at the front of the room—the Hot Seat—in front of the electronic whiteboard. Weddle projects a vocabulary word on the screen so that it shows above the student's head. The student in the Hot Seat can't see the word, but the rest of the class can, as shown in Figure 6.5.

Figure 6.5 *The Hot Seat*

When playing the Hot Seat, students in the class provide clues to the person in the hot seat about the word. The clues go in this order: first letter, last letter, number of syllables, part of speech, synonym, antonym, definition, clues or other definitions, and comparisons.

Taylor was recently the person in the Hot Seat. Weddle first reminded the class of the guidelines for the game. "Call on someone for the first clue. Don't forget to look at the other side of the room, and remember to put your blinder up with your hand to block your peripheral vision. You don't want to inadvertently see the word." All eyes were then trained on Taylor as they waited for her to guess. She called on Maria to give her the first clue, which was "d." Taylor guessed, "Destruction."

"Great guess," Weddle said, "*Destruction* is good, but it's not the word."

Taylor called on John. "It ends with *n*." In the back, a girl named Katie looked like she was about to blurt out the answer, but Matthew, the boy next to her, stopped her just in time with a pointed look.

"Decision?" Taylor guessed next. Katie let out a deep breath.

John shook his head. "Nope."

Sylvia was the next to provide a clue. "It has five syllables . . . "

Taylor thought for a minute. I looked around. Every seventh grader in the class was on the edge of his or her seat, breathlessly waiting to hear what Taylor was going to say. "De...ter...min...a...tion..." Taylor said slowly, drawing out the word.

"Wow!" exclaimed Weddle, as the class clapped. "That's a great guess, but that's still not the word."

By the time she got to the synonym clue, Taylor knew the answer. When she guessed that the word was *discrimination*, the class cheered. Students waved their hands wildly to be the next one chosen for the Hot Seat.

The Hot Seat encourages students to think in categories, yet another way that students reach higher-level achievement (Marzano, Pickering, and Pollock 2001). For this game, it is important that students feel comfortable enough to guess in front of the class. We must work to establish an environment where it is okay to take risks.

Vocab Scattergories

If you remember the old board game Scattergories, where the object is to think of as many things beginning with a particular letter in a certain category, you understand the basic concept of Vocab Scattergories. This is a game that Jennifer Geddes adapted and that her Eastside students love to play. On the whiteboard, Geddes writes a category, such as "Something You Would Find in the Refrigerator" or "Things in My Room." Students then compare vocabulary words to random objects that fit into that particular category. Making comparisons is a way for kids to identify similarities and differences, which has been shown to increase achievement (Marzano, Pickering, and Pollock 2001).

Students have a time limit to try to think of how each of their vocabulary words fits with an object in the category. Then they share their Scattergory sentences, and students see how many different connections they have made. This not only enables students to share but also helps other kids envision the word in a new way. While playing Vocab Scattergories, sixth graders at Eastside created comparisons in the form of similes such as

> *Irony is like <u>my clothes</u> because it may look good at first glance, but when you put it on it may look horrible.*
> *<u>Determine</u> is like <u>Pepsi and Coke</u> because you usually just decide to have one. You don't usually have both (you're either a Coke or Pepsi person).*
> *<u>Conclusion</u> is like <u>my perfume</u> because conclusion is a decision or final thought, and I have to decide which perfume I'm going to spray on.*

"My kids think Vocab Scattergories is really fun," explained Geddes, "because it isn't an old school, regimented way of learning vocabulary." Students may be revisiting and practicing vocabulary, but they are looking at it with a new set of eyes. To them it is just a game.

Vocabulary Rock and Roll

Vocabulary Rock and Roll is another game that Weddle's students like to play. In Vocabulary Rock and Roll, students roll a die, look to see what number they have rolled, check a template for directions and do whatever the template says.

Weddle found several templates online but decided to adapt her own rock and roll sheet to better suit her students. She gave a copy of the template to each pair of students. It said:

1. Define the Word
2. Draw It
3. Make a List of Synonyms
4. What Does It Remind You Of?
5. Use the Word in a Sentence
6. Make a List of Antonyms

Figure 6.6 *Vocabulary Rock and Roll*

To keep the noise at a minimum and to add a bit of fun, she provided sets of colorful oversized spongy dice she bought at a teacher supply store (see Figure 6.6).

The students have a list of vocabulary words. The first player rolls the die and completes the action associated with the number rolled. Then it is the partner's turn. The kids love this kinesthetic practice with vocabulary words and their meanings.

Guess My Word

Guess My Word is a new take on the vocabulary lanyards that our elementary students wore for several activities described in *Word Nerds*. In Trish Priddy's seventh-grade class at Eastside, each student received a lanyard with an empty plastic pocket and a numbered index card cut to fit into the pocket. Each index card had a number written in a corner beginning with number one and progressing to the total number of students in the class. Students also received a list of vocabulary words with their correlating synonyms/examples and antonyms/nonexamples. Each student prepared a card by drawing a picture to represent one of the words and placing the drawing on the side of the card with the number showing. The student then placed the completed card with the picture displayed in the lanyard pocket.

To play Guess My Word, students put their lanyards around their necks but turned them backward so the pictures showed (see Figure 6.7). Students grouped and regrouped to study one another's drawings and to decide how the picture on each lanyard correlated with a word on the list.

After studying a card, students returned to their desks where they recorded which picture they would match with a specific word. The beauty of this game is that it required students to justify their guesses. Even when they were wrong and did not choose the word the student artist intended, they still had to justify their answers. More often than not, the justification made sense and involved deep thinking.

During one session, Devon carefully observed Treena's drawing of a creature that looked like a blue octopus next to a gray, undersea vessel. Tiny circles (obviously meant to be bubbles) filled the background of the card. A number one was in the right-hand corner of the card. After a moment, Devon went back to his seat and wrote (see Figure 6.8).

Figure 6.7 *Guess My Word*

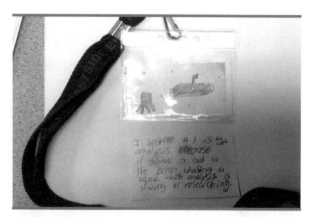

Figure 6.8 *Vocabulary lanyard. Devon wrote: "I believe #1 is the word* analysis *because it shows a sub in the ocean studying a squid. Which analysis is studying or researching."*

Correct or incorrect? It doesn't matter. The justification is where the learning and remembering take place. According to Priddy, "That's the type of deep thinking about words that wasn't happening in my class before. And they enjoy it because there is movement and art."

Word Widgets

When I was a child, a favorite recess activity was to make fortune-tellers. We carefully folded paper into sections and wrote numbers, colors, and the names of boys on the inside. The person whose fortune was being told had to pick a number. By manipulating the fortune-teller, you could "foretell" who your boyfriend would be. According to *Wikipedia*, in different parts of the country, these paper origami objects are called "fortune tellers," "cootie catchers," "chatterboxes," "salt cellars," or "whirlybirds." Tonie Weddle calls them Word Widgets and used them for her students to practice vocabulary at Bullitt Lick.

Weddle created a set of Word Widgets by folding the paper according to directions that were easily found online (for example, look for "paper fortune teller" on YouTube). She then used Bloom's taxonomy to come up with questions and tasks to help students think about selected vocabulary words at a higher level. A class set of eighteen Word Widgets allowed students to work in partners, and the widgets could be used repeatedly with different classes and varied sets of words. Figure 6.9 shows how a Word Widget is constructed.

To play, Partner 1 holds a numbered list of the vocabulary words. Partner 2 chooses the number of a vocabulary word on the list to spell. Partner 1 identifies the word on the list and manipulates the Word Widget as Partner 2 spells the word. Partner 2 picks a number, and Partner 1 manipulates the widget that number of times again. Partner 2 then picks the "fortune" that corresponds with that number.

The fortunes in the Word Widgets include different ways for students to think about the word they are practicing. Questions and tasks include

Figure 6.9 *Word Widget*

- Does the word imply a positive or negative connotation? How?
- Change the word by adding a prefix or a suffix. What does the new word mean?
- If this word was a color, what would it be and why?
- Which part of speech is the word?
- Use it in a sentence.
- What is the definition of the word?
- Identify a synonym for the word.
- What is an antonym for the word?

Students thoroughly enjoy using the Word Widgets to practice thinking about vocabulary. Teachers from other teams popped into Weddle's room to see what the kids were talking about and then made their own Word Widgets (Figure 6.10).

Figure 6.10 *Students practice vocabulary with Word Widgets.*

Chain Link/Word Links

As we described in *Word Nerds*, Leslie's fourth- and fifth-grade students became obsessed with the reading comprehension strategy of making connections, so much so that they would continue mentioning related ideas well beyond the literacy block. Leslie would try to get excited for them every time, but it didn't take long before the "connection craze" became a major distraction. To keep them focused, she asked the students to instead use a nonverbal cue, linking their fingers together like a chain whenever they made a connection to reading. This practice, reminiscent of Lori Oczkus's writing about interactive comprehension activities (2009), proved so successful that Leslie decided to extend it to vocabulary instruction. The Chain Link game was born (Overturf, Montgomery, and Smith 2013).

In Chain Link, students create a human concept map to show extensions of meaning. Students began by wearing their vocabulary words on lanyards around their necks. We asked one student to go to the front of the room, pronounce his or her word, and state its meaning. The rest of the class contemplated ways their own words can connect to the first word. From volunteers, we chose a student to explain the link. If the link made sense, the chosen student walked to the front of the room and linked elbows with the first student. Students must then think of ways to connect with either the first student's word or with the second. Our elementary students gave intricate explanations as they continued to think of links for words like *vast* and *satellite*, and they had to continually revise their thinking, as new words became the words to link. The kids just saw it as a game where the object was not to be the last student sitting.

Ruth Helen Yopp (2007) described a similar game to develop middle grades content vocabulary. She called it Word Links. Each student has a different word written on a large card or sheet of paper. The words should be terms that the kids have studied, such as *tissue* and *organ* or *eukaryotic* and *nucleus*. After students contemplate the meaning, they walk around the room to find someone whose word can link with theirs in some way. The pairs stand together and prepare an explanation about why their words link. The teacher then asks students to stand around the edge of the room and one by one explain their word links. When the explanations are complete, students then mingle to find a new partner and new word link. This means that students are engaged in deep processing of word meanings. Yopp (2007, 32) concluded that through this activity "students interact multiple times with words that have been previously taught, thus providing broad exposure to the words, and students are engaged in thinking about the language of the text."

Chain Link/Word Links fosters creative and abstract thinking because students must dive deeper into the context of words. Explaining their reasons for the word links cements the meanings for students.

Vocabulary Celebrations

At Eastside, Jennifer Geddes's students revisited words and reviewed for tests by playing a game called Vocabulary Celebration. This is an activity Jennifer devised after reading about vocabulary parties in *Word Nerds*.

Geddes assembled a box of simple props that she kept in a corner of her classroom. The props represented varied roles. When it was time to celebrate (review) vocabulary learning, she randomly passed out the props and assigned each student a role. For example, the student who received the cowboy hat became a cowboy. A superhero put on a cape and was ready to save the world.

Then the celebration (review) began. Geddes drew a student's name out of a jar on her desk, and a question out of another jar, such as, "What is a synonym for_____?" "What is an antonym for_____?" "What was your color for this word and why?" If the student got it right or provided an in-depth answer, the rest of the class celebrated by calling "Woohoo!" The kids who were playing roles celebrated in character. The cowboy stood up and called out "Yeehaw!" The superhero created a sound effect such as "Pow!" or "Dun-dun-dun!" If a student didn't get the answer right or couldn't think of a word, he or she was allowed to phone a friend. After a few rounds, students recycled costumes so classmates could have a chance to step into a role.

Geddes used a variety of review questions and encouraged creative movement to get kids excited about vocabulary and to show what they know. "They really enjoy little silly things that are different," she said. "You always have your little hams who want to get out of their seats and get that extra attention. It's a great change of pace and a great review before an assessment. For two weeks kids have been working on words, and this quickly celebrates their learning and helps them remember." When students write the questions for a review, they think about words in yet another way, and they become more invested in the celebration.

Vocabulary Activities with Poems, Puzzles, and Writing

Students enjoy writing with vocabulary words, if the writing task is something they find amusing. Kids enjoy creating their own puzzles, stories, poems, or raps with vocabulary. Writing is thinking. And thinking helps students learn words.

Student-Made Crossword Puzzles

Completing a crossword puzzle on a worksheet is a common vocabulary activity, but as a learning tool, it receives mixed reviews from researchers (Davis, Shepherd, and Zwiefelhofer

2009). When students complete a crossword puzzle, they have to think about the word that matches the clue. If they don't know the word, they are possibly prompted to do research and find out more. However, used too often and as a filler activity, a crossword puzzle can become rote and unimaginative like seatwork. I believe we can find more meaningful activities (don't get me started on "find the word" puzzles used for vocabulary instruction, which do not help students learn anything about meaning). The exception is letting students make their own crossword puzzles, which enables them to review vocabulary at a different level as they create a succinct, correlating definition.

At Bowman, Don Hollandsworth's social studies students often create crossword puzzles with terms they are learning in class. Students take a focus vocabulary word and then build the puzzle with synonyms, antonyms, and other related words they have studied. Sometimes students use a free online crossword puzzle maker. Other times, they draw the puzzles on graph paper. Hollandsworth found that this was a worthwhile activity as part of his vocabulary plan, which helped students contemplate words and their meanings. When Maria created a social studies crossword puzzle that included clues such as "people who opposed the Constitution" (*antifederalist*) or "a plan where the government would have three branches" (*Virginia Plan*), she not only had to think about the words and definitions in student-friendly language as she tried to put the clues together but also had to know how to spell so the letters would fit together correctly.

Acrostic Poems

Acrostic poems are usually written with the initial letters down the left side and then a word or a phrase that starts with each letter describing the overall word. For example, at Eastside sixth grader Michelle created an acrostic of the word *conclusion* (see Figure 6.11). Although not a strict interpretation of the acrostic rules, her back and forth way of thinking about the word *conclusion* certainly helped define it.

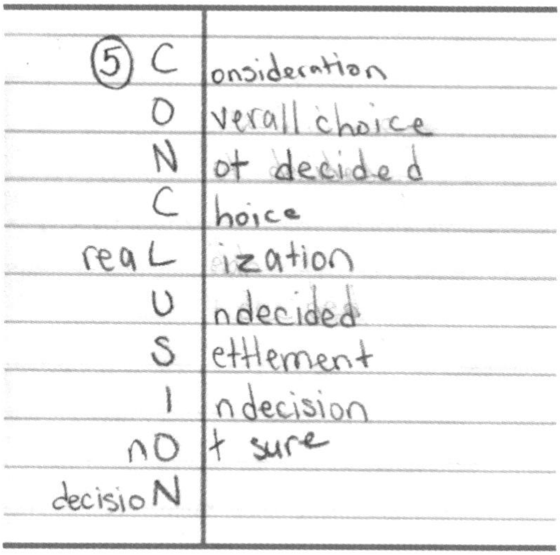

In social studies, Eastside's seventh graders were studying the Ancient Greeks. Chloe created an acrostic poster to explain the birth of democracy, written in an ancient-looking font and with plenty of clip art decorating the margins:

Figure 6.11 *Acrostic poem for* conclusion

Determined by citizens
Everyone has power
Men attended assemblies
Only men could vote
Crowd voted by show of hands
Red was marked on men by slaves
Assemblies held daily
Could be time-consuming
Young people couldn't vote.

Creating an acrostic for vocabulary in the disciplines is harder than it looks. Students need to contemplate content as they make connections with the letters and again as they explain their acrostic poems to others. For an additional experience, other students can ask questions about the acrostic information. The presenter then has to answer using a sentence containing the vocabulary word.

Vocabulary with Media and Technology

New games and apps are constantly being created for online platforms, but a note of caution about using online vocabulary activities. Most are little more than electronic worksheets, which require limited thinking. One exception is the tool Free Rice (www.freerice.com). This website is maintained by the United Nations World Food Programme. Students practice vocabulary, which is adjusted for ability as the student plays, and for each correct answer the World Food Programme donates ten grains of rice to help hungry people. This reward appeals to students' desire to help others, increasing empathy while also exposing them to many new words.

I have already mentioned two other games. This Is to That is a free analogy game app that includes different types of analogy structures and would be motivating as a team activity or in individual play (https://itunes.apple.com/us/app/this-is-to-that-pop-culture/id704690885?mt=8). The authors rate it for ages twelve and up due to mild references to smoking or alcohol, but when I played it for an hour (it can be addictive), I didn't see anything I wouldn't use with middle grades students. The What's the Word? game app requires players to review pictures and to think of words that sometimes have multiple meanings (https://itunes.apple.com/us/app/whats-word-new-quiz-pics-word/id573511269?mt=8). As we have seen, middle grades students were having a blast playing this deceptively simple game on their own time.

Another game I have not mentioned is an app called Vocabulary Practice: Greek and Latin Root Words Vocabulary Game by Always Ice Cream and Clever Dragons (https://itunes.apple.com/us/app/vocabulary-practice-greek/id667105899?mt=8). I discovered this one at a conference session about using technology in vocabulary study and think it is worth the time to play.

These apps are free, but all feature in-app purchases for more levels. However, they each offer enough free material that it would be easy to create a group game projected on an electronic whiteboard for occasional vocabulary thinking. As with anything online, please review carefully before using with your students.

Student Response Systems

In Tonie Weddle's class, the kids had been studying the elements and structure of short stories by reading "Harrison Bergeron." The science fiction story by Kurt Vonnegut (1961) features a dystopian society where it is a crime to be different in any way. Weddle decided to use Socrative, a computerized student response system, to combine the content terms she had introduced (*mood, tone*) with networks of Tier 2 vocabulary words students had been exploring.

Weddle projected the task onto the whiteboard: *Choose five words from the Smack Down Vocabulary that would contribute to the mood of the story "Harrison Bergeron."* Smack Down Vocabulary is what she called the vocabulary words from the purchased literacy program that she selected as appropriate for her particular students. When students saw the word in text, they smacked one hand on the word in recognition. The Smack Down words were kept on anchor charts on a wall of the classroom.

Bullitt Lick Middle School has a BYOD (bring your own device) policy, so many students use their own electronic devices to connect to the system. During one visit to the school, I saw every seventh grader in the class thoughtfully studying the Smack Down vocab-

ulary anchor charts and then earnestly programming their answers into tablets and smartphones (see Figure 6.12). They were obviously engaged with the activity and familiar with the online program.

To play, students enter their first names and then think about ways that seemingly unrelated words could connect to the mood of the story. They listed these in their devices. Within just a few minutes, students were finished and Weddle pushed the button to display

Figure 6.12 *Programming a vocabulary answer*

what students had chosen. The electronic board lit up with student answers. Cheyenne had chosen *strife, rage, protest, discrimination,* and *consequence.* Alex's words were *rage, pressure, outlook, random,* and *despair.* An anonymous "young man" (everyone knew who it really was) had listed sixteen words, including *turbulent, dramatic, curfew, strife,* and *global.*

Weddle asked students to review the lists and to see whether they agreed or disagreed with any answers. Students asked one another a few clarifying questions about certain choices. Then Weddle asked students to choose one word and provide a justification for that choice. "How does the word relate to the mood of 'Harrison Bergeron'? Why do you think so?" Students explained their answers to a partner, and then several students shared with the entire class.

Because students used electronic devices so often and had engaged with this type of student response system before, this activity took just fifteen minutes out of Weddle's class period. During that time, students had more deeply learned the concept of mood in narrative writing, reviewed previous vocabulary words, and thought about unusual connections. Every student in the class had participated and justified their thinking. Weddle was able to informally assess students' understanding of the term *mood,* as well as their understanding of Tier 2 vocabulary words and comprehension of the story. And they all enjoyed every minute!

Media Creations

As we all know, most young adolescents get a charge out of technology. Creating media presentations not only helps students learn life skills, such as how to pull a project together and work as teams, but also helps them learn vocabulary in a deeper way. Media also capture performances that might otherwise be lost.

Many schools have a daily broadcast. Student teams can create a vocabulary Word of the Day segment or students can perform a vocabulary tableau for others to guess across the school. Students can create podcasts about content-area vocabulary terms to be uploaded to the school or classroom website (Putman and Kingsley 2009).

Media presentations can provide a platform for exploring and sharing knowledge about words. PowerPoint Portrayals (Overturf, Montgomery, and Smith 2013) are another way that students can think about words and their meanings. By creating slides to show a word, a student-friendly definition, part of speech, origin of the word, a sentence, and an illustration (by selecting clip art or inserting a digital photo or a student illustration), students can share with others. The "record narration" feature allows students to explain their portrayals.

A Prezi (www.prezi.com) presentation could capture the same information in a flashier manner that could include video clips and music. In addition, Prezi's zoom-in, zoom-out feature allows students to focus on one portion of a presentation while retaining the bigger picture of how the entire presentation is connected. Exploring words by creating and sharing information through quick response (QR) codes to display an illustration, website, music, or video clip that connects to the word is exciting and motivating to students (see http://www.tangischools. org/Page/16589 for information on creative ways to use QR codes in the classroom).

Technology is also a useful tool in developing word consciousness. Making an electronic alphabet book about content-area vocabulary is a project that kids love, once they understand that ABC books exist for adults, as well as for younger children. In an electronic alphabet book, students create an illustration or image for words related to a topic from A to Z. This activity helps students think about content, choose twenty-six words or phrases that are related to a topic, and explore definitions for those words. Creating illustrations is a way of visualizing, a thinking strategy shown to increase achievement. For a description and sequenced lesson in how to use ABC bookmaking with middle grades students, see Laurie Henry's excellent lesson on *ReadWriteThink*, found at http://www.readwritethink.org/ classroom-resources/lesson-plans/bookmaking-builds-vocabulary-content-276.html.

Making Words Come Alive

It is no secret that students in the middle grades respond to classroom experiences that engage, excite, encourage, and enlighten as well as educate. As we shared in *Word Nerds*, "With activities that incorporate art, movement, technology, music, drama, public speaking, and more, vocabulary practice can not only motivate students to learn but also ensure that they remember" (Overturf, Montgomery, and Smith 2013, 86). Integrating multiple modes of learning and the arts into vocabulary instruction in all content areas helps students learn new words and make them their own. When interest in learning words becomes routine, students become vocabularians.

Chapter 7

ASSESSING VOCABULARY LEARNING

If you always do what you've always done, you will get what you've always got.

—Henry Ford

In *Hooray for Diffendoofer Day!*, Dr. Seuss (with some help from Jack Prelutsky and Lane Smith), tells the story of Diffendoofer School (1998). This school is a very different kind of place, where kids learn all sorts of interesting and mind-boggling things. But the big test is coming up and the principal, Mr. Lowe, is quite anxious that the kids aren't prepared. Miss Bonkers, one of the teachers, assures the students that they will do fine by saying:

> "We've taught you that the earth is round,
> That red and white make pink,
> And something else that matters more–
> We've taught you how to think."

Miss Bonkers has the right idea when it comes to vocabulary assessment as well. If kids learn to think strategically about vocabulary and have a toolbox of tactics for determining unfamiliar words and phrases, they will be ready for any assessment that measures vocabulary knowledge and use.

Contemplating Vocabulary Assessment

Did you ever have that common dream where you have to take a test on something you don't know? Now imagine that this item was on the test:

When teaching and assessing vocabulary, the best course of action is:
  a.   Assume that kids know every word in the dictionary.
  b.   Make sure that kids know every word in the dictionary.
  c.   Close your eyes and hope for the best.
  d.   Teach students what they need to do well on vocabulary assessments.

The answer, of course, is "d" (although if you chose "c," you are certainly not alone).

High-stakes tests are often called assessments, but in reality, assessment has a much broader role than fueling pressure in our academic lives. Every time we evaluate products or services, such as determining which apples look freshest at the supermarket (and, in this example, we really *are* comparing apples to apples), we are assessing. Every time we collect data and attempt to develop an explanation for what we see, we are analyzing. Every time we observe patterns and habits and change or respond to them, we are adapting our actions based on assessment.

Instruction would just be a collection of activities if we didn't pay close attention to what students are learning and adjust accordingly. Yes, we must prepare our students for high-stakes assessments that the outside world will use to judge the success of our work in the classroom, but we also want our students to realize that assessment is a natural part of learning. Research shows that teachers rarely assess vocabulary in a way that truly evaluates learning or use the results of such assessment to help them plan further instruction.

There are conflicting views and not much solid knowledge about what constitutes effective vocabulary assessment, sometimes even by those who create standardized tests (Pearson, Hiebert, and Kamil 2007). Historically, it has been difficult to assess vocabulary because it is so multifaceted (Stahl and Bravo 2010). Vocabulary knowledge is not just a definition of a word—it is knowledge of the word at numerous levels. It is also understanding how to use context and morphological awareness to determine the meanings of unfamiliar words in a passage, understanding that some words have multiple meanings, and knowing how to choose the correct definition for the context.

How do we plan for vocabulary assessment in ways that make sense? Rita Bean and Allison Swan Dagen (2006), researchers in the field of literacy, have outlined four general guidelines to follow when planning for vocabulary assessment at the classroom level. They urge teachers to think about the goals and purposes of the assessment, to use authentic measures of vocabulary progress, to plan for ways to assess depth of understanding, and to be aware of comprehension connections. That last point is particularly applicable to the middle grades. Often in the middle grades, students can decode and pronounce a word but are not sure of the meaning, even if it is a word they have heard before. Sometimes a student only knows one definition of a word and then has trouble comprehending when the same word is used in another context. And sometimes a student can comprehend everything in a passage except one word, but that word is the key that unlocks the meaning of the passage.

Test-taking is also considered a genre (Conrad et al. 2008; Greene and Melton 2007) and students need to know how to be test-savvy. As Bowman Assistant Principal Charles Williams said, "I talk with the kids about tests. I let them know I do very well on tests myself. It's not because I'm a genius. It's because I can read context clues. I might see a word I've never seen before, but I can figure out what it means because I can rip it apart and use the knowledge of those parts to get a pretty good understanding. That coupled with context clues—I can figure out most of what I read."

Many of our students don't know how to figure out unknown words with that same confidence, so we must help build their skills. However, just as it is difficult to find time for vocabulary instruction, it is also difficult to find time for vocabulary assessment. If students are going to learn the important vocabulary they need as well as strategies for determining the meanings of words they have never seen, we need to find a way to plan for vocabulary instruction and assessment for learning.

Focus on Formative Assessment

Formative assessment (sometimes called informal assessment, or assessment *for* learning) is a plan to gather day-to-day information about learners, what they are learning, and what they need to learn. The Council of Chief State School Officers (2008, 3) defines formative assessment as "a process used by teachers and students during instruction that provides feedback to adjust ongoing teaching and learning to improve students' achievement of intended outcomes." The International Literacy Association (2013, 2) has further defined it as "a purposeful process that provides teachers and students with descriptive feedback concerning students' literacy."

In urging teachers to focus more on assessment *for* learning rather than assessment *of* learning, Siobhan Leahy, Christine Lyon, Marnie Thompson, and Dylan Wiliam (2005, 19) wrote: "In a classroom that uses assessment to support learning, the divide between instruction and assessment blurs. Everything students do—such as conversing in groups, completing seatwork, answering and asking questions, working on projects, handing in homework and assignments, even sitting silently and looking confused—is a potential source of information about how much they understand." In their research, the authors have determined that five assessment strategies are effective for teachers at all grade levels:

1. Clarifying and sharing learning intentions and criteria for success,
2. Engineering effective classroom discussions, questions, and learning tasks,
3. Providing feedback that moves learners forward,
4. Activating students as the owners of their own learning, and
5. Activating students as instructional resources for one another. (Leahy et al. 2005, 20)

Clare Landrigan and Tammy Mulligan (2013, 23) showed the distinction between formative and summative assessment in their book *Assessment in Perspective*. Formative assessment strategies can appear in a variety of formats, such as quizzes, surveys, observations, self-assessments, and student work, but they take place "in the midst of instruction." Formative assessments provide information to help students learn at a higher level. Summative assessments can be high-stakes tests, standardized state exams, district or interim tests, midterms, and final exams, but they take place at the end of instruction. Summative assessments are used to check student mastery of a subject every few weeks or months and are measured against a standard or a benchmark. As we expressed in *Word Nerds* (Overturf, Montgomery, and Smith 2013, 121), "Formative vocabulary assessment is the glue that holds the pieces of our instruction together, and it helps us understand what our students actually know and can do. Summative assessment provides a record of progress that we can report to the public."

Formative Vocabulary Assessment

Robert Stakes, an education evaluation specialist, is credited with saying, "When the cook tastes the soup, that's formative; when the guests taste the soup, that's summative." To extend the metaphor, formative assessment tells us whether the soup needs more salt or whether we need to thicken the broth before we serve it in its final form. A classroom that infuses formative assessment often becomes a student-centered classroom as students take ownership for how they are progressing (Garrison 2009). And when teachers intentionally use formative assessment, they are more attuned to student learning. There are several ways to use informal classroom assessment to gauge understanding.

Observation

As Yogi Berra said, "You can observe a lot by watching." Circulate the room and "kid-watch" (Goodman 1978) carefully as students are engaged in activities, such as games, performances, or small group work. Do they use words easily? Are they struggling with meaning? Are they using complex sentences and challenging words in collaborative conversations? Are English language learners volunteering information or opinions using words they have learned in class? Listening to student discussion and observing facial expressions while they listen can tell us a lot about student understanding.

Most teachers of young adolescents have four or five classes to prepare daily, so remembering observations can be challenging. Keeping a list of names for each class and taking quick anecdotal notes while students are working is a good way to capture information that can be valuable in analyzing their vocabulary development.

Analyzing Student Work

Practice activities at the middle level often involve products to be reviewed. Through analyzing student work, whether through formal methods (Easton 2009) or more informally, we look for evidence of vocabulary learning while identifying misconceptions. For example, when students produce Word Colors, Lyric Definitions, or perhaps make a digital recording of a vocabulary skit or tableau, we can analyze their work to see how deeply they are thinking about words. Even though there is often no right or wrong answer in this type of student work, the connections students make tells us a great deal about the way they understand language.

When students explore words, they usually keep a vocabulary journal in the form of a chart or graphic organizer. These journal entries can also give us a great deal of information about what a student understands. In Tonie Weddle's class at Bullitt Lick, for each vocabulary word, students write a student-friendly definition, a 7-Up sentence, synonyms, antonyms, a picture, and an analogy or other language feature. Reviewing the information that her students include on their journal entries gives Weddle many clues about their language learning, from their understanding of the definition to misconceptions about how the word can be used in a sentence.

Teacher Questioning

Another way we use informal assessment to check for understanding is through teacher questioning. Peter Afflerbach (2012) describes the typical assessment questioning technique in most classrooms as the "initiate-respond-evaluate (IRE) discourse form." In the IRE form in many lessons, the teacher asks a student a question requiring a simple answer, and the student supplies the answer. The teacher then tells the student if the answer is correct or incorrect. Afflerbach gives this example that is focused on vocabulary:

Initiate (Teacher): What is a compass rose?
Respond (Student): It's the part of a map that shows directions.
Evaluate (Teacher): Yes, that's correct. (2012, 53)

As Afflerbach (2012, 61) points out, the IRE format is teacher directed and establishes "a teacher monopoly on assessment." Although we have all resorted to such simplistic questioning at one time or another, we should aim to ask questions that require students to explain and justify an answer, which reveals word knowledge as well as their thinking about language. Providing sufficient wait time after asking a question (Rowe 1986) can encourage more explanation and more positive student-to-student interaction.

Finding ways for all students to answer rather than one at a time can also help us know more about their knowledge and understanding. During vocabulary lessons and games, students can write answers on individual whiteboards, paper, or index cards and hold them up in the air. By walking around the room and doing a quick scan, teachers can easily see who has correct or incorrect answers. This helps us know when and what we need to reteach.

Student-Generated Questions

When students ask questions in class, they are also answering them. Student questioning has been considered a learning strategy for decades (Cornbleth 1975, 219), and "student questioning is also seen as a source of information about students' current knowledge, thought processes, and feelings." When students ask and answer questions, we listen for vocabulary knowledge in what they say.

Planning vocabulary experiences where student questioning is part of the lesson can also reveal vocabulary knowledge. For example, Leslie and Margot taught their fourth and fifth graders the difference between "thin" (literal level or memorization) questions and "thick" thoughtful questions that require inferential thinking (Lewin and Shoemaker 1998). After much modeling, students then wrote their own thick vocabulary questions for use in games and in classroom activities. We found that students were only able to ask thick questions about vocabulary words if they truly understand the word they are writing about, and so the questions they wrote became another form of assessment about their vocabulary learning.

Use of Rubrics

Many teachers already create and use rubrics to assess their students' work. When we carefully analyze our students' evidence of growing word knowledge and document it on a rubric as a team or department, we can better follow their progress over time. Figure 7.1 shows a vocabulary assessment rubric that can be used in formative assessment of vocabulary development in the middle grades.

Using rubrics as part of formative assessment creates a mind-set of success because there are no surprises. Adding a vocabulary category to existing student rubrics for content-area projects, performances, artwork, and other student work can emphasize the importance of using more extensive language as well as help teachers assess it.

Vocabulary Assessment Rubric

Name: Date:

Demonstrates...	Mastered	Almost Mastered	Not Yet Mastered
Appropriate use of vocabulary word in more complex sentences	Student can use vocabulary words in a way that makes sense in more complex sentences.	Student can use vocabulary words in a way that makes sense in sentences.	Student cannot consistently use vocabulary words in sentences in a way that makes sense.
Ability to determine meanings of vocabulary words in context	Student can determine meanings of vocabulary words in context in a sentence or passage of text by using context clues and logical thinking.	Student can identify and sometimes determine meanings of vocabulary words in context by using some context clues.	Student cannot identify or determine meanings of vocabulary words in context.
Ability to use affixes and roots as clues to meaning of a word	Student can use the meanings of both affixes and roots to determine the meaning of a multisyllabic word.	Student can use the meanings of a few affixes or roots to determine the meaning of a multisyllabic word.	Student cannot use the meanings of affixes or roots to determine the meaning of a multisyllabic word.
Ability to use reference materials	Student can use appropriate reference materials independently to find or verify the meanings of words and phrases.	Student can use appropriate reference materials to find the meanings of words.	Student is not able to use reference materials appropriately to find the meanings of words.
Ability to interpret figurative language (e.g., similes, metaphors, idioms)	Student can identify and interpret the meaning of figurative language in a sentence or passage.	Student can identify figurative language.	Student cannot identify or interpret figurative language.
Ability to determine word relationships (e.g., synonyms, antonyms)	Student can identify and correctly use synonyms/examples and antonyms/non-examples for vocabulary words.	Student can identify only synonym/ examples or antonyms/non-examples for vocabulary words.	Student cannot identify synonyms/ examples or antonyms/non-examples for vocabulary words.

Figure 7.1a *Vocabulary assessment rubric (part 1)*

Ability to determine word relationships (e.g., analogy)	Student can create a verbal analogy to demonstrate meaning of vocabulary word and shows understanding of novel verbal analogies.	Student can create a verbal analogy to demonstrate meaning of vocabulary word but may not understand novel verbal analogies.	Student cannot create a verbal analogy to demonstrate meaning of vocabulary word and cannot understand novel analogies.
Ability to determine nuances in word meaning (e.g., connotation, denotation)	Student can determine shades of meaning and connotation of words and phrases in text and use it in writing or speech.	Student can determine but not apply shades of meaning and connotation of words and phrases in text.	Student cannot determine shades of word meaning.
Higher–order thinking about vocabulary	Student can engage successfully in learning experiences that demonstrate higher–order thinking about vocabulary.	Student engages in learning experiences that show limited evidence of higher–order thinking about vocabulary.	Student displays only literal thinking in vocabulary learning experiences.
Application of vocabulary words outside of vocabulary instruction (in conversation or in other student work)	Student uses learned vocabulary appropriately and extensively outside of vocabulary instruction or assessment experiences.	Student uses learned vocabulary appropriately outside of vocabulary instruction or assessment experiences in a limited way.	Student does not use vocabulary except during vocabulary instruction or assessment experiences.

Figure 7.1b *Vocabulary assessment rubric (part 2)*

Summative Vocabulary Assessment

As teachers, we have all had the experience of taking a competitive standardized test, such as the SAT to be accepted to college or the GRE to enter a graduate program. These assessments often act as gatekeepers for the opportunities we will be afforded in the future. Many require complex vocabulary knowledge to score well, making the stakes of word learning very high indeed.

Standardized tests are extensively used by districts and states to gauge student knowledge and compare performance. When I first started teaching, we prepared students for a standardized test by saying, "The test is tomorrow. Get a good night's sleep, eat breakfast, and don't forget to bring two sharpened number two pencils." The kids would nod, go home, and then return for a morning or two of testing. Several weeks later, the results came back. As teachers, we would glance at the results (if they were shared with us) and they were never mentioned again. Whatever the tests could have told us about our students' learning or our own teaching was lost in the minutiae of paperwork stored in a filing cabinet somewhere.

Today, test-taking is taken quite seriously, and we are more likely to make certain students know how to approach the types of items they will encounter on the test. Almost every standardized assessment that students take includes vocabulary items, if not a separate vocabulary section. In the middle grades, vocabulary assessment is most often folded into tests of reading as a factor of comprehension. However, we don't always seem sure about how to prepare students for those types of questions. There are hundreds of words to know! How can we teach them all? The answer to that test question? We can't.

Author Charles Fuhrken (2012) has analyzed dozens of reading tests and has helped write hundreds of items for state tests in reading. In his book *What Every Middle School Teacher Needs to Know About Reading Tests*, he shares a common pattern among the vocabulary questions on most standardized tests.

These tests require students to do the following:

- Use context clues to derive the meaning of unfamiliar words
- Apply knowledge of word parts such as prefixes, suffixes, and derivational endings to recognize parts
- Use root words to determine word meaning
- Recognize which meaning of a multiple-meaning word applies to a word's use within a passage
- Identify the connotation of familiar words (Fuhrken 2012, 27)

This is the knowledge that students should have at their fingertips not only to do well on vocabulary assessments but also to be lifelong learners from text.

Examples from the two national consortia that have been charged with developing assessments for the Common Core standards demonstrate the importance of context ("evidence") in vocabulary questions included on the tests. In these assessments, students are required not only to choose the correct meaning of a word as it is used in a passage but also to identify the context clues that help them understand that particular meaning of the word. The Partnership for Assessment of Readiness for College and Careers (PARCC) can be found at www.parconline.org. As this book was written, the sample PARCC items for grades six to eight English Language Arts provided several passages with a number of questions aligned to the Common Core State Standards. The vocabulary items required students to answer a multiple choice question about the meaning of a word as it is used in a passage. For example, within an excerpt from a selection by author Gary Paulsen, students had to choose the correct meaning for the word *adversary* as it was used in the passage. As a second step, students had to choose the phrase from a multiple choice list that best clarified the meaning of *adversary* as it was used in the passage—clearly asking students to identify the context that helped them infer the meaning of the word. Teachers of grade five should know that this type of question can also be found on the ELA sample items for PARCC grades three to five.

The Smarter Balanced Assessment Consortium (SBAC) can be found at www.smarter-balanced.org. Sample items from SBAC also require the same skills for using context to determine the meanings of unfamiliar words and phrases. In each of these, a vocabulary word is pulled from a passage. Students are asked to "use the context of the sentence" to decide which of four phrases helps them understand the meaning of the word.

Students need sophisticated knowledge and more than a few strategies to be able to tackle vocabulary items on today's summative assessments. In addition to knowing a lot of words, they also must be able to use contextual analysis and cite evidence for their answers. It is clear that many middle grades students have difficulty using and indicating context clues and many have little knowledge of the meanings of word parts as a particular type of context clue. This kind of thinking can only come from experience with figuring out the meanings of words using these types of strategies.

Vocabulary Assessment Systems

A system of formative assessment is a path to prepare students for summative assessment. Doug Fisher and Nancy Frey (2014) advocate that schools should develop and implement formative assessment systems, which they describe as "an intentional system for collecting and analyzing evidence of learning, one that signals what needs to happen next." Fisher and Frey suggest that teachers begin with a learning target, which is a clear statement of what students should know and be able to do within the day's lesson, and then decide on a way to check for student understanding of the learning target. Once the teacher knows what the students know and can do, the next step is to plan to improve student understanding. This may mean reteaching, or it may mean taking instruction to a higher level. As Fisher and Frey (2014, 17) state, "If the learning targets are aligned with the standards and the data collection includes the various ways students are expected to demonstrate understanding, the summative assessments will take care of themselves."

In many schools that include students in the middle grades, teams or departments act as professional learning communities to plan, to develop, to implement, and to analyze student progress in content areas or literacy. Keeping track of student progress and analyzing patterns or errors help teachers understand what students need next (Greenstein 2013). Teachers in many schools are beginning to be familiar with formative assessment systems for mathematics, reading, writing, social studies, and science assessment. Yet we rarely talk about the same type of system for vocabulary development. What if we also prepared students for word knowledge, reading comprehension, and test-taking skills by keeping track of their vocabulary skill and helping them learn through formative assessment systems of vocabulary? I am the first to advocate that we do not need more tests. However, adding more depth of vocabulary knowledge to the tests we already have may help students think about words in a new way.

Integrated Vocabulary Quizzes: A Team Plan

At Bowman, interdisciplinary teams worked together to plan and teach vocabulary across the curriculum. Each two-week vocabulary cycle included five terms for each grade level, representing concepts under study: one word each for science, social studies, mathematics, and English language arts, with a Tier 2 word added across the entire school. Each teacher incorporated deeper assessment of the vocabulary word and its related terms related to his or her respective content areas on class assessments. For example, Michael Roccaforte, a math teacher at Bowman, expected students to be able to use accurate terms on classroom assessments. He explained, "On their math test, I usually have a writing section where the kids have to use the vocabulary word and show they know how terms work together."

However, the faculty also tested basic knowledge of the vocabulary cycle words by giving a quick team quiz at the end of each cycle. For this to work, a leader has to facilitate. Assistant Principal Charles Williams took the leadership on the vocabulary quiz at Bowman. On a half sheet of paper, he created a simple matching test of terms and definitions on one side and fill-in-the-blank sentences on the other (see Figures 7.2 and 7.3). Creating the matching test took just a few minutes, using the vocabulary words students had been exploring for the two weeks prior to the assessment.

The sentences were more challenging to write. Because content-area teachers had mainly worked on the words they had contributed from their own classes, Williams did not want to create cloze sentences that would inadvertently clue students to the subject area simply by associating a word with a particular teacher. Just as students do with vocabulary routines, Williams got better at the process as he practiced.

Teachers at Bowman administered the quiz with the class they had the last period, collected the assessments, and passed them on to Williams. He graded the quizzes and re-

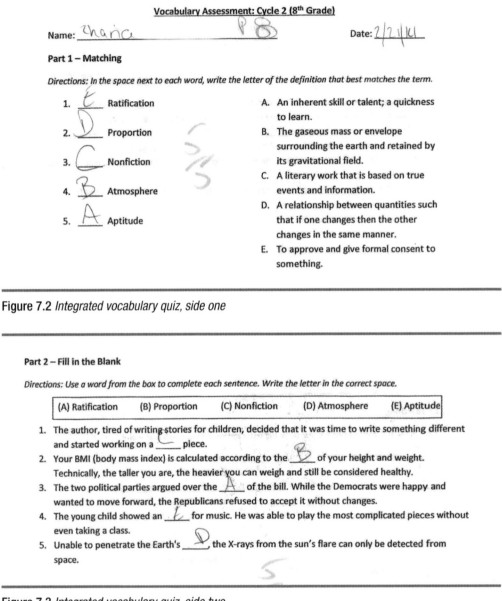

Figure 7.2 *Integrated vocabulary quiz, side one*

Figure 7.3 *Integrated vocabulary quiz, side two*

corded the results on a spreadsheet. Williams noted the grade level and how students scored on each vocabulary word and shared the results with the teachers. Later, at a team meeting, he facilitated a discussion about what the data revealed about vocabulary knowledge.

Figure 7.4 shows the results of the first vocabulary cycle during the 2013–14 school year.

Vocabulary Cycle 1						
Subject	7th Grade Words	Multiple Choice Percentage	Fill in the Blank Percentage	8th Grade Words	Multiple Choice Percentage	Fill in the Blank Percentage
ELA	Plot	97	91	Main idea	97	93
SS	Ethnocentrism	85	63	Confederation	72	78
SC	Nucleus	100	93	Solution	91	80
MA	Slope	97	93	Ratio	90	79
Tier 2 Word	Adversary	85	60	Adversary	70	65

Figure 7.4 *Vocabulary Cycle 1 percentage chart*

When teachers met and discussed the results of the first vocabulary cycle assessment, they were intrigued and a bit astonished at the information this quick little test revealed. For the most part, students did much better on the matching part of the test than on the fill-in-the-blank items, which required careful reading and the use of context. Students did not perform well with the schoolwide Tier 2 word *adversary*. Teachers were able to see how the results from their grade level and subject areas compared to the others, and they discussed similarities and differences in how they introduced words, allowed for word exploration, and incorporated practice activities. They agreed that some of their methods were working better than others. They also realized that few of them were concentrating on the schoolwide Tier 2 word.

"There's another thing," mused Stephen Currie. "When I looked over the tests, I noticed that some of our students picked the same word for two different choices. Like they would pick 'c' and then pick 'c' again. I asked a couple of kids about it. Their answer was that they panicked. The choices were so glaringly different I don't see how they could even get it wrong."

"Maybe they were just in a hurry," one of his teammates suggested.

"Maybe," Currie said, "but I don't think some of them are very confident."

After a brief discussion about the students and their word confidence, Williams looked thoughtful. "Well, we did give the assessment at the end of the day on Friday," he said. "The kids certainly didn't study; in fact, they probably didn't even remember they were supposed to have the quiz. Now that I think about it, they actually did surprisingly well. I doubt if we gave an assessment without notice on Friday afternoon in any other subject, they would do as well. Whether or not they know it, the words are sticking. But we need to ramp it up. I noticed that some kids really struggled with context clues on the sentences. Maybe we should add that somehow to help them become more confident with unfamiliar words."

The team continued to discuss the needs of particular students until it was time to return to class. Because of this quick quiz and its accompanying professional conversation, teachers understood better how to refine their approach to vocabulary instruction in their own classrooms and across the school. In future team meetings, they continued to talk about ways to refine teaching and assessment so it would best fit the needs of their learning community.

Before they left, Williams said, "One more second. I just want to tell this story. Yesterday I had to step into Mr. C's room because I heard a ruckus. I was sure there was a fight or something. But that wasn't it. What happened was that a student had done well on a vocabulary test. She was beyond ecstatic! The kids are like, wait a minute! I can do this?" The teachers left the meeting pleased that they knew more ways to help kids learn at higher levels.

Formative Vocabulary Assessment in a Professional Learning Community

At Eastside, teachers representing English language arts, special education, and library/media services worked together in a professional learning community with Tabi Echols, the district resource teacher assigned to the school, as the facilitator. As a group, they came to a decision about appropriate words for study at each grade and planned for vocabulary instruction as a department. To gauge vocabulary learning, these teachers decided to adapt the assessment we described in *Word Nerds*. This format included a cloze passage with blanks for the words on the front and multiple choice questions to assess word relationship knowledge on the back. They also decided to add a spelling test of the words to be given immediately before the vocabulary assessment.

Echols designed the assessment for each grade level, using the same basic format for each. The first page contained a word bank with eight words and a cloze passage. Students filled in the blanks with the vocabulary word from the word bank that best fit the passage context. Figure 7.5 shows the first page of an eighth-grade assessment passage with a combination of English language arts terms and Tier 2 words. Just a note, the term *iamb* was included as a Tier 3 word in preparation for an upcoming unit on Shakespeare.

On the second page of the assessment, each grade level included a multiple choice test on word relationships (see Figure 7.6). Each test contained at least one word the students had learned in a previous vocabulary cycle.

On this particular eighth-grade test, students had to choose the synonym or the antonym for the underlined word. Students were also required to choose a definition of a word they had not studied using context clues, and then to delineate the context clues that helped them understand the meaning.

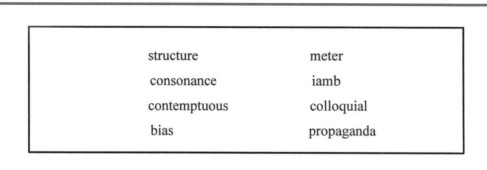

structure   meter

consonance   iamb

contemptuous   colloquial

bias   propaganda

William Shakespeare is revered as one of the greatest poets / playwrights of all time. At least that's what my teacher says. Last week she *gleefully* danced into the room and was all smiles before writing the words "Sonnet 18" on the board. Under these words, she added a name...William Shakespeare. She proceeded to tell us how much we were going to love this unit of study, but I feared that her words were full of (1)_____. I didn't know much about this Shakespeare fellow but I'll have to admit I already felt a bit (2)_____ toward him.

   I soon learned that Sonnet 18 was some sort of famous poem written by the notorious Shakespeare himself. I knew about poetry; *The Cat in the Hat* and *Green Eggs and Ham* were basically long poems and I had read both. How hard could this be? I would soon find out!

Apparently Dr. Seuss' poetic (3)_____ was a bit different from that of Mr. William Shakespeare! While Seuss used (4)_____ to form humor and rhyme, Shakespeare preferred to use the (5)_____, a metrical foot of stressed and unstressed syllables. I always thought that (6) _____ was just some sort of measurement used at track practice. But there was much more to it than that. It was a tool used by poets to actually create a rhythm in which the poem was to be read. Wow...it seemed like Shakespeare sure did put a lot of effort into his poetry writing!

The more I read and the more I learned, the more I began to understand the way in which Shakespeare wove words together to form a masterpiece. I also recognized the fact that, like Seuss, he was a pretty funny guy. His works were full of jokes and puns and catchy one-liners. Soon, I began to like old Shakespeare. I even read a few of his poems in my spare time.

Although I still have some personal (7)_____ towards the works of Dr. Seuss (*Horton Hears a Who* **IS** a classic), I'm beginning to appreciate the style and sophistication of Shakespeare. Though I prefer the (8)_____ language of my peers, I may even try to incorporate some poetic devices of my own into my speech. After all...it worked for Mr. Shakespeare!

Figure 7.5 *First page of eighth-grade vocabulary assessment*

After teachers analyzed the results and reflected about the kind of thinking that students might be asked to do on standardized assessments, they realized that thinking in analogies was an important skill they needed to include. The multiple choice questions began to include analogies, such as *big* is to *small* as *vocabulary word* is to *antonym*. For analogy questions, the Eastside teachers decided to concentrate on synonyms in the sixth

Choose a synonym / antonym for the underlined word in the sentence.   *Read carefully to determine whether a synonym or antonym is needed.*

8. I felt a bit <u>contemptuous</u> toward the villain in the book. *(synonym)*

A. hatred
B. polite
C. awkwardness
D. uncertain

9. The poet used <u>consonance</u> to create rhythm and rhyme. *(antonym)*
A. repetition
B. pattern
C. alliteration
D. dissonance

10. The architect designed the <u>structure</u> for town's new library. *(synonym)*

A. shape
B. strong
C. plans
D. legitimate

11. People from a certain region or area share a common <u>colloquial</u> language. *(antonym)*

A. formal
B. conversational
C. informal
D. regional

12. I have a certain <u>bias</u> towards the Kentucky Wildcats; I always think that they will win! *(synonym)*

A. attitude
B. idea
C. preference
D. impartiality

13. Based on the context clues in the first paragraph, what is the definition of *gleefully?*

a. to sing
b. happily
c. solemn
d. to dance

What context clues in the sentence helped you to define the word *gleefully?*

Figure 7.6 *Second page of eighth-grade vocabulary assessment*

grade, antonyms in the seventh grade, and mixed analogies in the eighth grade. As Echols explained, "It is a way tougher task to use both synonyms and antonyms in analogies."

The professional conversation around these assessments revealed some new understandings. Teachers realized that kids remember words when they explore and engage in experiences with the words. As Jennifer Geddes shared, "We found out, and so did the kids, that if they have really delved into the words during the two-week period, they don't have to study for a test at all. They already know the words."

Susan Carlisle chuckled as she said, "On the second assessment, when two words appeared that they had had before, they were astonished. They couldn't believe they were still responsible for them. They panicked at first, but then they realized that they still knew the words. I think the kind of instruction we have been using gives kids a chance to find a spot for the word in their brains—to find a connection and store it. They remember because it's meaningful."

Echols recorded the results of the assessments in a spreadsheet so that the students' vocabulary progress could be followed, and then students had a chance to review and analyze their own assessment. After each vocabulary cycle, she filed the word lists and assessment templates electronically to be revised the next year. In Kentucky, schools are required to keep a Kentucky Program Review portfolio as part of the state accountability system, which is a way to analyze an instructional program through various pieces of evidence. The Eastside PLC vocabulary work (student samples, photographs, and formative assessments) also became part of the school's electronic portfolio to demonstrate evidence of student learning. Teachers realized that this type of vocabulary assessment helps them find out if kids know words they have studied. In addition, the assessment gives teachers a better understanding of students' reading capabilities because they have to apply their knowledge of vocabulary strategies. As they saw it, vocabulary assessment can be a deep-thinking experience.

Formative Assessment of Vocabulary Learning Targets

As students entered Tonie Weddle's room at Bullitt Lick Middle School each day, they saw a small whiteboard posted on the wall that contained the learning targets for the class (see Figure 7.7). A learning target is a standard written in student-friendly language so that students understand what they are supposed to accomplish (Moss, Bookhart, and Long 2011). The learning targets for March 20 were as follows:

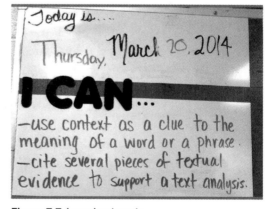

Figure 7.7 *Learning targets*

I can . . .
1.   use context as a clue to the meaning of a word or phrase.
2.   cite several pieces of textual evidence to support a text analysis.

Because vocabulary is such an integral part of comprehension, Weddle embedded vocabulary standards written as student learning targets as part of her literacy lessons. She identified a standard, included instruction on the concept of the standard, and assessed students' competence with that standard. In this way, she was able to analyze students' vocabulary progress.

The school where Weddle teaches receives federal Title I funds to support lower-income students. In addition to buying a published literacy program, the school used part of the funds to purchase an online progress monitoring system. Teachers also regularly create scrimmage tests that replicate the state assessment that their students will take in late spring. Students use a scan sheet to record their answers to twelve multiple choice questions. They then write answers to one short answer and one extended response question.

The scrimmage assessment Weddle created for reading comprehension was designed to look like a test for the core standards and was given to all the seventh graders in the school. She provided access to student copies of state scoring guides for short answer and extended response questions as the students worked on the assessment. The students read two different texts about the Greek myth of Pandora. One was a poem called "Pandora or Who Let the Plagues Out?" (Emmons 2006). Weddle found it online and adapted it for her students. The other text, "How Evil Came into the World," came from a reproducible social studies set (Edgar 2008). The directions asked students to read each text and answer the multiple choice questions that accompanied it.

On this particular assessment, the focus of the multiple choice questions was determining the meanings of words through context and citing textual evidence. The twelve multiple choice questions looked for the same type of vocabulary information as the national consortia standardized tests. Students had to decide the meaning of the bolded word based on the context of the passage. They then had to support their answer by choosing the phrase from the text that provided evidence for the meaning of the word (see Figure 7.8).

A short answer question asked students to write a paragraph that told how Pandora was described in both texts. A final extended response question required students to compare and contrast the character of Zeus in both texts and to explain which representation they believed was the most evil.

When Weddle scored the assessment for her students, the progress monitoring system allowed her to use the camera function on her iPad to quickly scan each bubbled answer sheet. Scores on the multiple choice section were then immediately calculated and stored electronically. A report was generated that pointed out what error each student had made and what instruction might be necessary. As Weddle viewed a printout of the class reports, she noted that the item analysis showed about half of the seventh-grade students missed a

After reading *How Evil Came Into the World,* **answer questions 1-6. Use the text to support your answers.**

1. What is the meaning of the word **bestow** as it is used in paragraph 1?

    A. To give
    B. To have
    C. To find
    D. To decide

2. Which phrase from paragraph 2 **best** helps clarify the meaning of **bestow**?

    A. "...could not take away any gift that another mortal had given."
    B. "...gift that might balance the account..."
    C. "a creature made up of all good things..."
    D. "The law of Olympus..."

3. What is the meaning of the word **industrious** as it is used in paragraph 2?

    A. a blacksmith
    B. hardworking
    C. a craftsman
    D. friendly

4. Which phrase from paragraph 2 **best** helps clarify the meaning of **industrious**?

    A. "a creature made up of all good things,"
    B. "...took a lump of clay and mixed it with a little bit of everything."
    C. "...a little bit of heaven and a great deal of earth."
    D. "...sweet things and bitter things and contradictory things:"

5. What is the meaning of the word **undisciplined** as it is used in paragraph 5?

    A. not thinking
    B. forgotten rules
    C. lacking self-control
    D. missing pieces

6. Which phrase from paragraph 5 best helps clarify the meaning of **undisciplined**?

    A. "...broke the seal and lifted the lid..."
    B. "Pandora was not a bad girl."
    C. "...better left alone."
    D. "just a little too curious..."

Figure 7.8 *Scrimmage assessment, including vocabulary*

particular question, leading her to wonder why. Overall, students chose the correct definition of the word but did not do well on the questions that asked them to determine the context clues from the text.

A few days later, Weddle and her students revisited the assessment. She had marked the errors in the multiple choice questions on their answer sheets so that students could analyze their own tests. She also provided blank copies of the test. After a class discussion about the answers, seventh graders Lizette, Dwight, and Sylvia sat together to review their answers and any errors they made on the scrimmage. Weddle observed that Lizette took this opportunity to engage in a little peer tutoring on using context clues.

Lizette:	Did anyone get number three wrong?
Dwight:	I did. For number three, I picked C.
Lizette:	So, why did you pick C?
Dwight:	Um . . . Because he's a craftsman?
Sylvia:	I got number three wrong, too.
Dwight:	Is number three A?
Lizette:	No, it's B because see right here, about *industrious*? It says he took "a little bit of everything." So if you were a god and you took a little bit of everything, don't you think that would be pretty hard?
Dwight:	What? So wait. The answer is "hardworking"? How?
Sylvia:	That's what we are trying to find out.
Lizette:	Because it says "the most industrious of all the gods took a lump of clay and mixed in a little bit of everything." And then it shows what all he mixed in. So if you were that god, how would you describe yourself and what you were just doing?
Dwight:	Well, if I was industrious I would be hardworking.
Lizette:	Well, that's the answer. It's hardworking. And now you have to look at the words that come before *industrious* and after *industrious* to help you understand why it means hardworking.
Dwight:	Wow. Hey, I picked the right answer the first time!
Sylvia:	I think it means hardworking because it says "a little bit of everything." You know?
Dwight:	Oh, yeah.
Lizette:	So, let's go to the next question.

Weddle noted Lizette's confidence in using context clues to determine word meaning and describing the process to others. Dwight was not as focused, and she wasn't sure about Sylvia's thinking. Along with assessment results, Weddle would continue to observe students to add to her knowledge about their abilities with context.

On the basis of assessment data, Weddle believed that the focus on vocabulary was working. Before she began teaching and assessing vocabulary, student scores on the literature and informational text reading sections of a computerized practice test aligned with the core standards were fairly low, and the vocabulary section was even lower. After she began focused vocabulary instruction, she saw an increase of students scoring in the top two categories, and the vocabulary scores evened with the other sections. Weddle hypothesized that an increased focus on vocabulary strategies helped her students raise their scores on the published program's tests and quizzes as well as the school's progress monitoring assessments.

Assessment: Thinking in Action

If we prepare students well, giving them multiple ways to explore and experience new vocabulary, they will reap the benefits of our strategic instruction. By the time they see a vocabulary word on an assessment, they will have thought about it in context, discussed its meaning and morphology, explored its connections using a graphic organizer, and perhaps committed it to memory using art, drama, games, and songs. As Jennifer Geddes at Eastside explained, "My kids didn't have to study. They had fun with words in class and that helped them remember. They did well on vocabulary quizzes because they had looked at word relationships and knew ways to use the word." She chuckled. "Not that they still always care. But like I tell the kids, it will come back to you and one day you'll need to use this word in a conversation with a teacher or employer or when you are doing some professional writing."

Eighth grader Kerrigan affirmed Geddes's statements when she explained to me, "We've been getting different words and I kind of know what they are but I don't fully understand them. So by the end of the two weeks and going through everything about them, I feel like I really have a good grasp on them now."

When the students at Diffendoofer School (Dr. Seuss, Prelutsky, and Smith 1998) took their assessment, they also felt that they had success within their grasp:

> *There were questions about other things*
> *We'd never seen or heard,*
> *And yet we somehow answered them,*
> *Enjoying every word.*

It is impossible for students to learn every word that they will ever encounter on a test. They must have strategies to help them figure out the meanings of unfamiliar words and phrases contained within passages.

Brandi Odom, the seventh-grade ELA teacher at Bowman, recently saw the results of teaching her students to use vocabulary strategies. Close to the end of the school year, she watched in amazement as her students used many of the strategies she had taught them while they were taking a test. Pointing in different directions in the air, they were obviously going through the motions associated with words they had learned or dividing them into word parts.

"Oh, my goodness! What are you doing?" Odom asked the kids.

A young man near the back grinned and replied, "Oh, sorry. I was just trying to remember. Actually, I'm thinking."

EPILOGUE

Poet Percy Bysshe Shelley once asked, "If winter comes, can spring be far behind?" Although Shelley was speaking metaphorically, his expression seemed appropriate when the exceptionally frigid winter of 2014 finally gave way to spring. A short, glorious summer passed much too quickly, and then it was the beginning of another school year.

As I finished this book, my mind whirled with my own wonder of learning about vocabulary instruction and assessment in the middle grades. When I began talking about vocabulary with teachers and administrators the previous fall, I had a loose plan to adapt *Word Nerds* to middle-level settings. As an experienced middle grades teacher, I knew the transition would not be simple, but I could not have imagined the powerful insights and transformations that came from working with educators in three very different organizational structures. Let me share a few examples here.

Vocabularians Have Super Powers!

Vocabulary is a powerful thing. We observed kids transferring words they had studied to academic conversations and writing. Math, science, social studies, and English language arts teachers were pleasantly surprised to hear students purposely using vocabulary terms in collaborative conversations. At times, they seemed to be testing their classmates with their knowledge.

Word consciousness was raised. "Kids notice words in reading," said one special education teacher, "and that has never happened before. One of my sixth graders was so excited when she saw the word *emerge* in her book for independent reading. What is really great is that it was a vocabulary word from several weeks ago, so she had retained it. Really cool!"

Students also asked more questions about vocabulary. "Kids are starting to say, 'I remember that word from a book back in fifth grade,' so they are starting to make connections," said

Tonie Weddle. "So often everything is so isolated for them and they think what they learned last year, they really don't need this year."

Just as younger students did in *Word Nerds*, we saw middle-level kids get excited when they encountered a word that another teacher had introduced. They often exclaimed in surprise, "Hey! I heard that word in science today!"

The emphasis on vocabulary helped students make stronger connections and deepen their work knowledge. For example, Weddle noticed the changes in Lisa, a student who struggled in her academic work. When her teacher introduced the Word of the Day, Lisa commented, "Oh! So that's what that word means!" With greater word confidence, Lisa also was more willing to try even if she guessed wrong.

Less Is More

Choosing a small number of high-utility words and helping students learn them in extensive ways is crucial. As Tabi Echols shared, "One of the biggest lessons we have learned is that the quantity of vocabulary words is not as important as the quality of the vocabulary instruction. Before working with *Word Nerds*, we were presenting students with a large number of vocabulary words, and we were focused on mastery of definitions. Now that we use a smaller, more intentionally chosen set of words, we focus more on the in-depth understanding of language. This helps students know more than just definitions; it enables students to use their knowledge of language to become better readers."

Everyone agreed that selecting a small number of words for in-depth study seems to be better for students. However, choosing which words to emphasize for vocabulary instruction in the middle grades still appears to be a daunting task for many teachers. I suspect that teachers are anxious about settling on a set of words in case they might be the wrong ones. Educators need to work together to think about words that represent concepts in their curricula or words that can become a model for skills that students need to develop. When students deeply understand a network of meaning for a smaller number of words, they deepen their knowledge of language.

The teachers at Eastside Middle School found that focusing on fewer words benefits struggling learners, in particular. For example, a small word list enabled special education students to work more closely with their peers in the mainstreamed classroom. Before, teachers had to modify and shorten vocabulary lists for some students, making collaborations awkward. Julie Cox, a sixth-grade teacher, reflected, "Having fewer words has really made a difference. It's probably one of the most important changes we have made. We have been able to do so much more with the words and the kids are retaining them more than they ever have in the past."

High-achieving students were also challenged to think deeply about smaller networks of words, allowing them to make more intricate connections. Because teachers flooded their classes with interesting words across the curriculum, students became more word conscious throughout the day.

Teacher Buy-In

Vocabulary development in the core disciplines can help students learn subject-area concepts in ways they won't forget, but it is sometimes difficult for teachers to get past thinking that vocabulary instruction is the English language arts teacher's job. As Charles Williams stated, a bit facetiously, "Not all teachers will share the same enthusiasm as the ELA teacher when it comes to vocabulary instruction." Having been an English language arts teacher himself, he knows that ELA teachers are often just as baffled about how to integrate vocabulary, sometimes more so. These teachers are also usually responsible for students meeting multiple sets of standards in the same amount of time.

Tonie Weddle realized that part of the problem was how she communicated with content-area colleagues. As she explained, "A big aha is that now when I talk about what I am doing, I don't say I focus on vocabulary. I say I focus on Reading Standard 4," a reference to the Common Core State Standards for literature, informational text, history/social studies, as well as science and technical subjects. In this standard, the expectation for all content areas is that students will be able to determine the meaning of unfamiliar words and phrases. "Reading Standard 4 embodies all that I am striving to teach when I teach vocabulary, and other English language arts teachers listen to this. Other content-area teachers also listen because they are also responsible for this standard in Kentucky." She completed her thought by saying, "My colleagues on my team saw the direct influence of vocabulary instruction and then were willing to support and supplement vocabulary instruction across the curriculum. I learned that when my whole cross-curricular team supports vocabulary development, student achievement increases exponentially."

As Williams added, "Like any program, consistent analysis and evaluation of the system's effectiveness is required. If something is not working, teachers need to be able to identify the problem and develop solutions. Likewise, if something is working well, teachers need to be made aware so that they may implement a similar strategy within their own classes."

Vocabulary Is Thinking

Before we began this project, I think many teachers and students would have said that vocabulary instruction meant memorizing definitions. A huge insight was the relationship between thinking and vocabulary knowledge.

Metaphorical Thinking

As we worked together, we became more aware of the importance of asking students to think about vocabulary metaphorically. We invited students to choose colors to represent words and justify the reason for their choices or to create illustrations or dramatize definitions. Any time we ask a student to choose an object or idea to represent a word, we are asking them to think in metaphors. Metaphorical thinking is critical thinking, and critical thinking plumbs depths of knowledge.

In Robert Marzano's research (2009) on vocabulary instruction, he found that asking students to create a picture, a pictograph, or a symbolic representation of a vocabulary term was a step in instruction that caused achievement to soar. Time and again, our middle grades students reported that they understood and remembered a word because they could associate it with something else.

The Productive Vocabulary Struggle

In addition to emphasizing metaphorical thinking, teachers must also plan activities that require students to occasionally stumble over new words. Weddle expressed it this way, "I learned that in order for my students to learn vocabulary they need to struggle with learning it. Through the struggle, my students wrestled with language. They learned how to analyze the vocabulary, and in the process learned how to unlock context clues, recognize multiple meanings, and so much more."

Vocabulary instruction doesn't need to be too hard, but it should be challenging and stimulating. Thinking about words should give the brain a good workout. That's how we absorb new knowledge and are able to apply it in novel situations. If we ask students to merely look up definitions and memorize them and then give an assessment that doesn't ask them to think deeply about vocabulary in context, we are depriving them of the struggle they need to own the words.

Providing opportunities for a productive struggle in vocabulary ensures that students will own strategies to determine the meanings of unfamiliar words they encounter in more challenging texts. They will then be better equipped to take on the demands of close reading lessons and disciplinary texts.

Time Bandits

So what about challenges? The major issue when implementing an integrated word study plan in the middle grades is clearly time—or lack of it. As Williams explained, "In our building a class is fifty minutes long. Teachers had a difficult time dedicating a portion of the class long enough for a deep, meaningful activity with vocabulary while still having enough time for the rest of the lesson." I daresay every teacher represented in these pages would express the same sentiment. Classes are still arranged in short blocks of time, and all teachers feel the pressure to teach everything that is required in the time they have.

In addition, teaching young adolescents is never easy, and many important strategies and skills don't get written into lesson plans. Students come to school with varied experiences and expertise so all teachers must be ready to respond to different aspects of student development besides the academic. Educators have to find ways to interest unmotivated, recalcitrant students who have learned ways to compensate for and hide what they don't know. Surging hormones also make kids say and do things that surprise both them and us. Most teachers are responsible for before- and after-school activities, such as bus duty, sports, clubs, and teams where kids must always be supervised, so time for meaningful professional learning and conversation is limited. When district and state paperwork and policy requirements are added to our lists, time becomes precious indeed.

What is less talked about are the social issues that plague many of today's kids, no matter their family income level. Divorce, illness, violence, mental health problems, and other traumas affect students indiscriminately. These troubles keep many students distracted, and sometimes their immaturity causes them to make bad decisions. Middle grades teachers often find themselves acting as informal counselors, and instead of being able to devote team meetings to instructional planning, they may need to spend those precious hours conferencing with parents or working with colleagues to address students' emotional issues.

All of these competing demands can make middle grades teachers feel as if they are barely keeping their heads above water. However, the need for vocabulary development is so critical for student success that we have to find a way to fit it into our classes. As Weddle observed, "My students need vocabulary all day, every day, whenever, however, it can be squeezed, pushed, shoved, or wrangled into the educational day."

Timing

There is a rhythm to every school year, and it was difficult to change that flow in midstream to begin learning how to plan and teach vocabulary systemically, especially during such an unpredictable winter. While I was visiting and working with the schools, I consistently heard, "This will be so great when we can start it at the beginning of the year!" For vocabulary to be a real part of the curriculum, it needs to be planned and implemented well. Even so, each school came up with a schedule for vocabulary instruction in its own particular setting, which the faculty members continue to refine (see Figure 1).

Vocabulary study also has to be seamlessly integrated into the curriculum and into individual classes in order for it to become an expected part of instruction. "We learned that vocabulary isn't an isolated skill but is a necessary component of a quality reading and writing program," Echols says. "If we teach vocabulary as an isolated skill it becomes just another thing to 'add to the list.' When the teaching of vocabulary is viewed as a natural part of instruction it no longer 'takes up time' but rather enhances the time spent teaching children to be fluent readers."

Williams advises, "If teachers have a set of 'go to' activities that they are familiar with and can easily implement within their lessons, they are more likely to devote a portion of the lessons to vocabulary instruction. These methods and strategies need to be addressed during professional learning sessions as well as the initial professional development at the beginning of the school year. If it isn't a natural part of the curriculum, it becomes too easy to revert to looking up words in a dictionary for homework."

Team Spirit

For middle grades teachers who want to begin a strategic integrated vocabulary plan, consider these steps to get started. First, have an honest conversation with your colleagues. English language arts teachers can incorporate some vocabulary instruction into their classes, but vocabulary development across the disciplines is the best way to expand students' word knowledge. Consider a schoolwide emphasis, with each team or department taking responsibility for creating a plan to select a small number of high-utility words, introducing the words in context, and engaging students in rich vocabulary explorations. Include practice activities that will give students multiple exposures to words and encourage metaphorical thinking and games that help them make connections. Assess vocabulary learning in ways that make sense for your students, and analyze the results together. No matter how solid your plan is, you will almost certainly want to revise it as you and your students learn more.

	Vocabulary Schedule	Selecting Words	Introducing Words	Word Exploration and Practice Activities	Assessment
Interdisciplinary Team	ELA, Math, Science, Social Studies teachers on each team. Facilitator was assistant principal.	Each teacher selected one word in an upcoming lesson and the facilitator selected one school-wide high utility word. Students worked on five networks of words for a two-week cycle.	Facilitator created a What's the Word? power point. Each teacher introduced words in a different way.	Embedded in content classes. Practice activities planned for last five minutes of each class.	Assistant principal designed a team-wide common quiz for each team. Teachers administered at the end of two weeks. Facilitator graded and shared the data with teachers. Discussed results as teams.
English Language Arts PLC	All ELA teachers in the building, plus special education and library/media specialist. Facilitator was a district resource teacher assigned to the school.	Teachers discussed and decided words that students needed to know in upcoming lessons. Students worked on five to eight networks of words total for two-week cycle.	Introduced one word a day in English language arts classes the first week of the vocabulary cycle.	A segment of the class period the second week of the vocabulary cycle.	Resource teacher designed common formative assessment. Each teacher administered in ELA. Teachers graded and discussed results in the PLC meeting.
Integrated within a Published Program	ELA teacher followed published unit plan but modified for student needs. Added enhanced vocabulary study. Shared ideas with other teachers.	Words were identified in the program before a new text. Students worked on seven to nine networks of words in ELA vocabulary study.	Introduced new words at the beginning of each unit in the published program.	Integrated into daily lessons.	Included brief quizzes and as part of reading scrimmage test for state assessment. Teacher graded and students analyzed assessment.

Figure 1 *Vocabulary schedules (variations)*

Here are recommendations of other resources that will help you refine your instruction and assessment:

- *Word Nerds: Teaching All Students to Learn and Love Vocabulary* by Brenda J. Overturf, Leslie Montgomery, and Margot Holmes Smith (2013). This is the book that started it all. Although it is focused on teaching elementary students, there are many transferable strategies and insights into student thinking.
- *Words, Words, Words: Teaching Vocabulary in Grades 4–12* by Janet Allen (1999). A widely used, to-the-point resource about word learning in middle school and high school. Author Janet Allen includes a range of research-based graphic organizers that are ideal for including in vocabulary study.
- *When Kids Can't Read: What Teachers Can Do* by Kylene Beers (2003). Chapter 9 on vocabulary instruction is a classic for middle school teachers and kids. In this book, Kylene Beers provides excellent suggestions for developing vocabulary with middle and high school students who are reading below grade level.
- *Teaching Academic Vocabulary K–8: Effective Practices Across the Curriculum* by Camille Blachowicz, Peter Fisher, Donna Ogle, and Susan Watts Taffe (2013). This book is a comprehensive resource for teaching vocabulary in the content areas. The authors describe effective vocabulary instruction connected to standards, making this book an outstanding choice for planning literacy development in every class.
- *Word Wise and Content Rich, Grades 7–12: Five Essential Steps for Teaching Academic Vocabulary* by Doug Fisher and Nancy Frey (2008). Doug and Nancy are researchers who also teach adolescents, so they have lots of suggestions about what works in their own schools and classrooms.
- *Bringing Words to Life: Robust Vocabulary Instruction* by Isabel Beck, Margaret McKeown, and Linda Kucan (2002). The ultimate source on vocabulary teaching and learning, based on the authors' research.
- A subscription to the International Literacy Association will bring with it access to *The Reading Teacher* and the *Journal for Adolescent & Adult Literacy*. These teacher-oriented journals include different research-based aspects of literacy, including vocabulary instruction and assessment. See www.reading.org.
- A subscription to the National Council of English/Language Arts entitles members to a subscription of *Voices from the Middle*, a teacher-friendly resource dedicated to literacy in the middle grades. See www.ncte.org.
- *ReadWriteThink*. This website is a collaborative effort by the International Literacy Association and the National Council of Teachers of English and includes dozens of excellent free lesson plans written by teachers. See readwritethink.org.

The Last Word

As this book comes to an end, teachers and administrators continue to think about vocabulary instruction and assessment, and how to refine vocabulary plans to more closely align with what they have learned. English language arts teachers are working with content-area teachers, connecting instruction for kids across disciplines. Middle grades educators are challenging students to grow as word learners.

I think back to my conversation with eighth grader Kerrigan that sunny day in June in the library at Eastside Middle. "I think studying vocabulary has been interesting because we do a lot of different projects," she said, breathlessly. "It used to be just tedious because we always did the same thing. Like we would just pick out a word and get the definition and then do boring things." Her eyes sparkled as she continued. "Then we started on projects like drawing pictures with the letters in it or finding colors that kind of go with the word, and it's like a really neat idea that somebody thought of to make it fun! And it helps me remember the words. I just feel like if you have something that can connect it to your mind easily and if you have a fun memory of making it feel like that, it really helps connect it rather than just reading it from a book."

I couldn't have said it better myself, Kerrigan! Make vocabulary fun and engaging for young adolescents while they are learning deeply, and words will come alive. This is how middle grades students become vocabularians.

Appendix A

Crystal Ball Words

Name _____

Date: _____

Crystal Ball Words

WORD:		
Prefix:	Root:	Suffix:
Prefix definition:	Root definition:	Suffix definition:
Other words with this prefix:	Other words with this root:	Other words with this suffix:

Look deep into a word to predict its meaning.

Appendix B

Concept of Definition Map

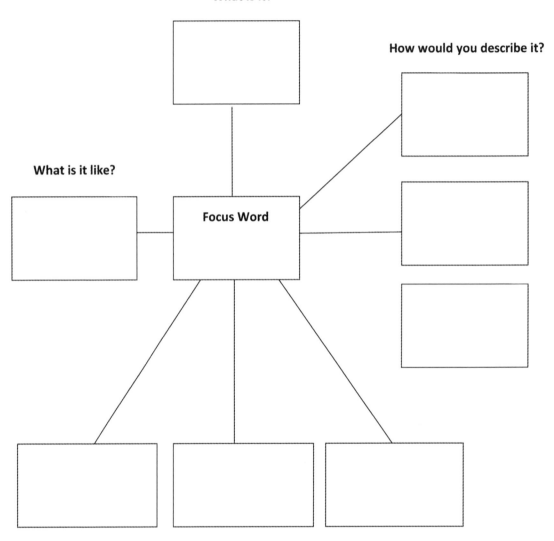

What is it?

How would you describe it?

What is it like?

Focus Word

What are some examples?

Summary

Vocabularians: Integrated Word Study in the Middle Grades by Brenda J. Overturf
with Leslie H. Montgomery and Margot Holmes Smith. ©2015. Stenhouse Publishers.

Appendix C

Semantic Feature Analysis

Words	Features					

Response Key: + = Yes   - = No   ? = Don't Know

Words	Features					

Response Key: + = Yes   - = No   ? = Don't Know

Appendix D

Adapted Frayer Model

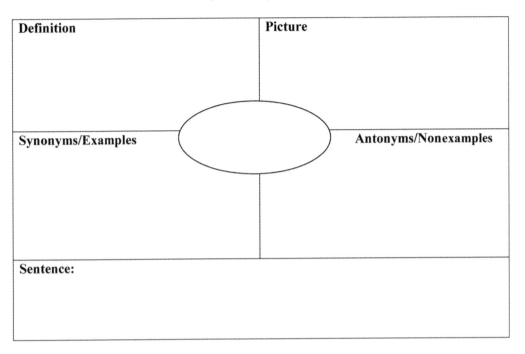

Appendix E

Vocabulary Journal Organizer (part 1)

Name: _____   Text: _____   Date: _____

Word	Definition	Sentence 7 or more words	Synonym(s) or Example	Antonym(s) or Example	Picture	Idioms, Analogies, and/or Other Meanings
_____ pp.____						
_____ pp.____						
_____ pp.____						
_____ pp.____						
_____ pp.____						
_____ pp.____						

Vocabulary Journal Organizer (part 2)

		Extra Word Definitions					
pp.	pp.		pp.	pp.	pp.	pp.	pp.

Vocabularians: Integrated Word Study in the Middle Grades by Brenda J. Overturf
with Leslie H. Montgomery and Margot Holmes Smith. ©2015. Stenhouse Publishers.

References

Student Literature and Resources

Bhalla, J. 2009. *I'm Not Hanging Noodles on Your Ears and Other Intriguing Idioms from Around the World.* Washington, DC: National Geographic.

Byrd, R. 2003. *Leonardo: Beautiful Dreamer.* New York: Dutton Children's Books.

Carroll, L. (1871) 1984. *Alice's Adventures in Wonderland and Through the Looking-Glass.* New York: Bantam Classics.

Collins, S. 2009. *The Hunger Games.* New York: Scholastic.

Coville, B. 1997. *William Shakespeare's Macbeth.* New York: Dial Books.

Crane, S. (1895) 1983. *The Red Badge of Courage.* New York: Bantam Classics.

Edgar, F. 2008. *Greek & Roman Mythology: Grades 6–12.* Greensboro, NC: Carson-Dellosa.

Emmons, S. 2006. *Word Chowder: A Little Collection of Light Verse.* Hallmark Licensing. Available online at http://www.wordchowder.com/Greek_Mythology.html.

Fleischman, P. 2002. *Weslandia.* Somerville, MA: Candlewick.

Kerley, B. 2010. *The Extraordinary Mark Twain (According to Susy).* New York: Scholastic.

Lee, H. (1960) 1998. *To Kill a Mockingbird.* New York: Grand Central.

Macintyre, B. 2001. "Zerplatzen on the Speelplaats." *New York Times Book Review.* May 20. Available at http://www.nytimes.com/books/01/05/20/reviews/010520.20macintt.html.

Neuschwander, C. 1997. *Sir Cumference and the First Round Table (A Math Adventure).* Watertown, MA: Charlesbridge.

Polacco, P. 1994. *Pink and Say.* New York: Philomel Books.

Schlosser, S. E. 2014. "Babe the Blue Ox." *American Folklore.* Available at http://americanfolklore.net/folklore/2010/07/babe_the_blue_ox.html.

Scieszka, J., and L. Smith. 1995. *Math Curse.* New York: Viking.

———. 2001. *Baloney (Henry P.).* New York: Viking.

———. 2004. *Science Verse.* New York: Viking.

Seuss, Dr. 1984. *The Butter Battle Book.* New York: Random House Books for Young Readers.

Seuss, Dr., J. Prelutsky, and L. Smith. 1998. *Hooray for Diffendoofer Day!* New York: Knopf Books for Young Readers.

Sis, P. 1996. *Starry Messenger: Galileo Galilei.* New York: Square Fish.

Tolkien, J. R. R. (1937) 2012. *The Hobbit, or There and Back Again.* Boston: Houghton Mifflin Harcourt.

Vonnegut, K. (1961) 2007. "Harrison Bergeron." *Welcome to the Monkey House.* New York: Random House.

Zusak, M. 2006. *The Book Thief.* New York: Knopf Books for Young Readers.

Professional Resources

Adams, M. J. 2010–2011. "Advancing Our Students' Language and Literacy: The Challenge of Complex Texts." *American Educator* (Winter): 3–11.

Addy S., W. Engelhardt, and C. Skinner. 2013. "Basic Facts About Low Income Children: Children Under 18 Years, 2011." National Center for Children in Poverty. Available at http://www.nccp.org/publications/pub_1074.html.

Afflerbach, P. 2012. *Understanding and Using Reading Assessment, K–12*. Newark, DE: International Literacy Association.

Alber, S. R., and C. R. Foil. 2003. "Drama Activities That Promote and Extend Your Students' Vocabulary Proficiency." *Intervention in School & Clinic* 39 (1):22–29.

Albright, L. 2002. "Bringing the Ice Maiden to Life: Engaging Adolescents in Learning Through Picture Book Read-Alouds in Content Areas." *Journal of Adolescent & Adult Literacy* 45 (5):418–428.

Albright, L. K., and M. Ariail. 2005. "Tapping the Potential of Teacher Read-Alouds in Middle Schools." *Journal of Adolescent & Adult Literacy* 48 (7):582–591.

Allen, J. 1999. *Words, Words, Words: Teaching Vocabulary in Grades 4–12*. York, ME: Stenhouse.

Anders, P. L., and C. S. Bos. 1986. "Semantic Feature Analysis: An Interactive Strategy for Vocabulary Development and Text Comprehension." *Journal of Reading* 29 (7):610–616. Available at www.jstor.org.

Anderson, R. C. 1990. *Teachers and Independent Reading*. Champaign, IL: Center for the Study of Reading.

Anderson, R. C., and W. E. Nagy. 1991. "Word Meanings." In *Handbook of Reading Research*. Vol. 2, ed. R. Barr, M. L. Kamil, P. B. Mosenthal, and P. D. Pearson. New York: Longman.

Association for Middle Level Education. 2010. *This We Believe: Keys to Educating Young Adolescents*. Westerville, OH: Association for Middle Level Education.

Atwell, N. 1987. *In the Middle: Writing, Reading, and Learning with Adolescents*. Portsmouth, NH: Heinemann.

Barton, M. L., C. Heidma, and D. Jordan. 2002. "Teaching Reading in Mathematics and Science." *Educational Leadership* 60 (3):24–28.

Baumann, J. F., E. C. Edwards, E. Boland, and G. Font. 2012. "Teaching Word-Learning Strategies." In *Vocabulary Instruction: Research to Practice*. 2nd ed., ed. E. J. Kame'enui and J. F. Baumann. New York: Guilford.

Baumann, J. F., and M. F. Graves. 2010. "What Is Academic Vocabulary?" *Journal of Adolescent & Adult Literacy* 54 (1):4–12.

Baumann, J. F., D. Ware, and E. C. Edwards. 2007. "'Bumping into Spicy, Tasty Words That Catch Your Tongue': A Formative Experiment on Vocabulary Instruction." *Reading Teacher* 61 (2):108–122.

Bean, R. M., and A. Swan Dagen. 2006. "Vocabulary Assessment: A Key to Planning Vocabulary Instruction." In *Vocabulary-Enriched Classroom: Practices for Improving the Reading Performance of All Students in Grades 3 and Up*, ed. J. Mangieri and C. Collins Block. New York: Scholastic.

Bear, D. R., M. Invernizzi, S. R. Templeton, and F. R. Johnston. 2008. *Words Their Way: Word Study for Phonics, Vocabulary, and Spelling Instruction.* 4th ed. Upper Saddle River, NJ: Prentice Hall.

Beck, I. L., and M. McKeown. 2001. "Text Talk: Capturing the Benefits of Read-Aloud Experiences for Young Children." *Reading Teacher* 55 (1):10–20.

Beck, I. L., M. G. McKeown, and L. Kucan. 2002. *Bringing Words to Life: Robust Vocabulary Instruction.* New York: Guilford.

Beers, K. 2003. *When Kids Can't Read: What Teachers Can Do.* Portsmouth, NH: Heinemann.

Berger, W. 2014. "5 Ways to Help Your Students Become Better Questioners." *Edutopia.* August 18. Available at http://www.edutopia.org/blog/help-students-become-better-questioners-warren-berger.

Bitz, M. 2010. *When Commas Meet Kryptonite: Lessons from the Comic Book Project.* New York: Teachers College.

Blachowicz, C., and P. Fisher. 2010. *Teaching Vocabulary in All Classrooms.* 4th ed. Boston: Allyn & Bacon.

Blachowicz, C., P. Fisher, D. Ogle, and S. Watts Taffe. 2013. *Teaching Academic Vocabulary K–8: Effective Practices Across the Curriculum.* New York: Guilford.

Blachowicz, C. L. Z., P. J. Fisher, and S. Watts Taffe. 2005. *Integrated Vocabulary Instruction: Meeting the Needs of Diverse Learners in Grades K–5.* Naperville, IL: Learning Point Associates.

Bloch, T. 2013. "Learning Vocabulary with Metaphors." *Sweat to Inspire.* August 17. Available at http://sweattoinspire.com/2013/04/17/learning-vocabulary-with-metaphors/.

Block, M. 2009. "An Enchanting Tour Through a World of Idioms." *National Public Radio.* July 3. Available at http://www.npr.org.

Block, M., and R. Siegel. 2014. "Tell Your Bestie: The OED Has New Words." *National Public Radio.* March 14. Available at http:www.npr.org.

Borgia, L., and C. Owles. (2009) 2010. "Using Pop Culture to Aid Literacy Instruction." *Illinois Reading Council Journal* 38 (1):47–51.

Brabham, E., C. Buskist, S. C. Henderson, T. Paleologos, and N. Baugh. 2012. "Flooding Vocabulary Gaps to Accelerate Word Learning." *Reading Teacher* 65 (8):523–533.

Braisby, N., J. E. Dockrell, and R. Best. 2001. "Children's Acquisition of Science Terms: Does Fast Mapping Work?" In *Research on Child Language Acquisition: Proceedings of the 8th Conference of the International Association for the Study of Child Language*, ed. M. Almgren, A. Barreña, M. Ezeizabarrena, I. Idiazabal, and B. MacWhinney, 1066–1087. Somerville, MA: Cascadilla. Available at http://oro.open.ac.uk/3641/1/IASCL_Paper_II.pdf.

Bransford, J. D., and M. K. Johnson. 1972. "Contextual Prerequisites for Understanding: Some Investigations of Comprehension and Recall." *Journal of Verbal Learning and Verbal Behavior* 11:717–726.

Bravo, M. A., and G. N. Cervetti, 2008. "Teaching Vocabulary Through Text and Experience in Content Areas." In *What Research Has to Say About Vocabulary Instruction*, ed. A. E. Farstrup and S. J. Samuels, 130–149. Newark, DE: International Literacy Association.

Bromley, K. 2007. "Nine Things Every Teacher Should Know About Words and Vocabulary Instruction." *Journal of Adolescent & Adult Literacy* 50 (7):528–537.

———. 2012. *The Next Step in Vocabulary Instruction: Practical Strategies and Engaging Activities That Help All Learners Build Vocabulary and Deepen Comprehension*. New York: Scholastic.

Brown, P. L., and J. P. Concannon. 2014. "Investigating Student Perceptions of Vocabulary and Learning in Middle School Science." *Advances in Social Sciences Research Journal* 1 (3):196–206.

Brown, T., and F. Perry. 1991. "A Comparison of Three Learning Strategies for ESL Vocabulary Acquisition." *TESOL Quarterly* 25:655–670.

Buehl, D. 2011. *Developing Readers in the Academic Disciplines*. Newark, DE: International Literacy Association.

Cairney, T. 2014. "Why Older Kids and Adults Need Picture Books and Graphic Novels." *Literacy, Families and Learning*. September 6. Available at http://trevorcairney.blogspot.com /2014/09/why-older-kids-adults-need-picture.html?utm_source=22853205&utm_ medium=Email&utm_campaign=High+Road.

Carlisle, J. F. 2010. "Effects of Instruction in Morphological Awareness on Literacy Achievement: An Integrative Review." *Reading Research Quarterly* 45 (4):464–487.

Carey, S., and E. J. Bartlett. 1978. "Acquiring a Single Word." *Papers and Reports on Child Language Development* [Stanford University] 15:17–29.

Carter, J. B., and E. Evensen. 2013. *Super-Powered Word Study: Teaching Words and Word Parts Through Comics*. Gainesville, FL: Maupin House.

Cary, S. 2004. *Going Graphic: Comics at Work in the Multilingual Classroom*. Portsmouth, NH: Heinemann.

Casale, U. P. 1985. "Motor Imaging: A Reading-Vocabulary Strategy." *Journal of Reading* 28 (7):619–621. Available at www.jstor.org.

Center for Research on Education, Diversity, and Excellence (CREDE). 2014. "Instructional Conversation." Available at http://manoa.hawaii.edu/coe/credenational/instructional-conversation/.

Conrad, L. L., M. Matthews, C. Zimmerman, and P. A. Allen. 2008. *Put Thinking to the Test*. Portland, ME: Stenhouse.

Cornbleth, C. 1975. "Student Questioning as a Learning Strategy." *Educational Leadership* 33:219–222.

Council of Chief State School Officers. 2008. *Attributes of Effective Formative Assessment*. Available at http://www.ccsso.org/Resources/Programs/Formative_Assessment_for_Students_and_Teachers_(FAST).html.

Cowan, K., and P. Albers. 2006. "Semiotic Representations: Building Complex Literacy Practices Through the Arts." *Reading Teacher* 60 (2):124–137.

———. 2007. "Mediating the Matthew Effect in Reading: Fostering Word Consciousness." *Voices from the Middle* 15 (1):34–43.

Cunningham, A. E., and K. E. Stanovich. 1997. "Early Reading Acquisition and Its Relationship to Reading Experience and Ability Ten Years Later." *Developmental Psychology* 33:934–945.

Davey, B. 1983. "Think-Aloud: Modeling the Cognitive Processes of Reading Comprehension." *Journal of Reading* 27:44–47.

Davis, T. M., B. Shepherd, and T. Zwiefelhofer. 2009. "Reviewing for Exams: Do Crossword Puzzles Help in the Success of Student Learning?" *Journal of Effective Teaching* 9 (3):4–10. Available at http://uncw.edu/cte/et/articles/vol9_3/davis.pdf.

Easton, L. B. 2009. "Chapter 3. Protocols for Examining Student Work." *ASCD*. Available at http://www.ascd.org/publications/books/109037/chapters/Protocols-for-Examining-Student-Work.aspx.

Evans, J. 2004. "From Sheryl Crow to Homer Simpson: Literature and Composition Through Pop Culture." *English Journal* 93 (3):34–38.

Fisher, D., and N. Frey. 2008. *Word Wise and Content Rich, Grades 7–12: Five Essential Steps to Teaching Academic Vocabulary.* Portsmouth, NH: Heinemann.

———. 2014. "Formative Assessment: Designing and Implementing a Viable System." *Reading Today.* July/August.

Fisher, D., N. Frey, and C. Rothenberg. 2008. *Content-Area Conversations: How to Plan Discussion-Based Lessons for Diverse Language Learners.* Alexandria, VA: Association for Supervision and Curriculum Development.

Fisher, D., C. Rothenberg, and N. Frey. 2007. *Language Learners in the English Classroom.* Urbana, IL: National Council of Teachers of English.

Fisher, P., and C. Blachowicz. 2007. "Teaching How to Think About Words." *Voices from the Middle* 15 (1):6–12.

Flanigan, K. 2013. "Seeing the 'Big Picture': Using Academic Language as a Lens for Reading and Thinking About History." Paper presented at the Literacy Research Association Conference, December 4–7, Dallas, TX.

Flanigan, K., and S. C. Greenwood. 2007. "Effective Content Vocabulary Instruction in the Middle: Matching Students, Purposes, Words, and Strategies." *Journal of Adolescent & Adult Literacy* 51 (3):226–238.

Flynt, E. S., and W. G. Brozo. 2008. "Developing Academic Language: Got Words?" *Reading Teacher* 61 (6):500–502.

Fontichiaro, K. 2007. *Active Learning Through Drama, Podcasting, and Puppetry.* Santa Barbara, CA: Libraries Unlimited.

Frayer, D., W. C. Frederick, and H. J. Klausmeier. 1969. *A Schema for Testing the Level of Cognitive Mastery.* Madison: Wisconsin Center for Education Research.

Frey, N., and D. Fisher, eds. 2008. *Teaching Visual Literacy: Using Comic Books, Graphic Novels, Anime, Cartoons, and More to Develop Comprehension and Thinking Skills.* Thousand Oaks, CA: Corwin.

———. 2010. "Structuring the Talk: Ensuring Academic Conversations Matter." *Clearing House: A Journal of Educational Strategies, Issues, and Ideas* 84 (1):15–20.

Fuhrken, C. 2012. *What Every Middle School Teacher Needs to Know About Reading Tests (From Someone Who Has Written Them)*. Portland, ME: Stenhouse.

Garrison, C. 2009. "Formative Assessment: Debunking the Myths" (podcast). *Today's Middle Level Educator*. June 4. Westerville, OH: National Middle School Association. Available at http://www.amle.org/Publications/TodaysMiddleLevelEducator/tabid/1409/Default.aspx.

Gfeller, K. E. 1986. "Musical Mnemonics for Learning Disabled Children." *Teaching Exceptional Children* (Fall):28–30.

Goldenberg, C. 1991. *Instructional Conversations and Their Classroom Application*. Educational Practice Report 2. Santa Cruz, CA: National Center for Research on Cultural Diversity and Second Language Learning.

Goodman, Y. M. 1978. "Kid-Watching: An Alternative to Testing." *National Elementary Principal* 57 (4):41–45.

Goodwin, A., M. Lipsky, and S. Ahn. 2012. "Word Detectives: Using Units of Meaning to Support Literacy." *Reading Teacher* 65 (7):461–470.

Goodwin, A. P., J. K. Gilbert, and S. Cho. 2013. "Morphological Contributions to Adolescent Word Reading: An Item Response Approach." *Reading Research Quarterly* 48 (1):39–60.

Graves, M. 2006. *The Vocabulary Book*. New York: Teachers College.

———. 2007. "Vocabulary Instruction in the Middle Grades." *Voices in the Middle* 15 (1):13–19.

———. 2009. *Essential Readings on Vocabulary Instruction*. Newark, DE: International Literacy Association.

Graves, M., and R. Silverman. 2011. "Interventions to Enhance Vocabulary Development." In *Handbook of Research in Reading Disabilities*, ed. R. Allington and A. McGill-Franzen. New York: Routledge.

Graves, M. F., J. F. Baumann, C. L. Z. Blachowicz, P. Manyak, A. Bates, C. Cieply, J. R. Davis, and H. Von Gunten. 2013. "Words, Words Everywhere, but Which Ones Do We Teach?" *Reading Teacher* 67 (5):333–346.

Graves, M. F., and S. Watts Taffe. 2002. "The Place of Word Consciousness in a Research-Based Vocabulary Program." In *What Research Has to Say About Reading Instruction*. 3rd ed., ed. A. E. Farstrup and S. J. Samuels, 140–165. Newark, DE: International Literacy Association.

Greene, A. H., and G. D. Melton. 2007. *Test Talk: Integrating Test Preparation into Reading Workshop*. Portland, ME: Stenhouse.

Greenstein, L. 2013. "Formative Assessment and the Common Core: Blending the Best in Assessment." *Voices from the Middle* 21 (2):36–42.

Groves, F. H. 1995. "Science Vocabulary Load of Selected Secondary Science Textbooks." *School Science and Mathematics* 95 (5):231–235.

Guthrie, J. T., and A. D. McCann. 1997. "Characteristics of Classrooms That Promote Motivations and Strategies for Learning." In *Reading Engagement: Motivating Readers Through Integrated Instruction*, ed. J. T. Guthrie and A. Wigfield. Newark, DE: International Literacy Association.

Harmon, J. M., and W. B. Hedrick. 2005. "Research on Vocabulary Instruction in the Content Areas: Implications for Struggling Readers." *Reading & Writing Quarterly* 21:261–280.

Harmon, J. M., K. D. Wood, K. D., and K. Kiser. 2009. "Promoting Vocabulary Learning with the Interactive Word Wall." *Middle School Journal* 40 (3):58–63.

Harris, S. J. 1961. "You Need an Ear for Words to Write." *Last Things First*. Boston: Houghton Mifflin.

Hart, B., and T. Risley. 1995. *Meaningful Differences in the Everyday Experiences of Young American Children*. Baltimore: Paul H. Brookes.

Hayes, D. P., and M. G. Ahrens. 1988. "Vocabulary Simplification for Children: A Special Case of 'Motherese'?" *Journal of Child Language* 15 (2):395–410.

Helman, L. 2013. "Language as a Tool or a Trap: Supporting Students' Academic Language and Concept Development in Mathematics." Paper presented at the Literacy Research Association Conference, December 4–7, Dallas, TX.

Henry, L. 2014. "ABC Bookmaking Builds Vocabulary in the Content Areas." *ReadWrite-Think*. Available at http://www.readwritethink.org/classroom-resources/lesson-plans/bookmaking-builds-vocabulary-content-276.html?tab=4#tabs.

Hughes-Hassel, S., and P. Rodge. 2007. "The Leisure Reading Habits of Urban Adolescents." *Journal of Adolescent & Adult Literacy* 51 (1):22–33.

International Dyslexia Association. 2008. *Multisensory Structured Language Teaching*. Available at http://www.interdys.org/EWEBEDITPRO5/UPLOAD/MULTISENSORY_STRUCTURED_LANGUAGE_TEACHING_FACT_SHEET_11-03-08.PDF.

International Literacy Association. 2013. *Formative Assessment: A Position Statement of the International Reading Association*. Newark, DE: International Literacy Association.

Ivey, G., and K. Broaddus. 2001. "'Just Plain Reading': A Survey of What Makes Students Want to Read in Middle School Classrooms." *Reading Research Quarterly* 36:350–377.

Jenkins, J., M. Stein, and K. Wysocki. 1984. "Learning Vocabulary Through Reading." *American Educational Research Journal* 21:767–788.

Johnson, D. D., and P. D. Pearson. 1984. *Teaching Reading Vocabulary*. 2nd ed. New York: Holt, Rinehart & Winston.

Johnson, D. D., S. D. Pittelman, and J. E. Heimlich. 1986. "The Reading-Writing-Thinking Connection." *Reading Teacher* 39 (8):778–783.

Kahane, K. 2012. "Mimsy, Chortle, and Galumph: Alice in Wonderland and the Portmanteau." *Oxford Dictionary: Language Matters*. July 6. Available at http://blog.oxforddictionaries.com/2012/07/mimsy-chortle-and-galumph-alice-in-wonderland-and-the-portmanteau/.

Kelley, J. G., N. K. Lesaux, M. J. Kieffer, and S. E. Faller. 2010. "Effective Academic Vocabulary Instruction in the Urban Middle School." *Reading Teacher* 64 (1):5–14.

Kieffer, M. J., and N. K. Lesaux. 2007. "Breaking Down Words to Build Meaning: Morphology, Vocabulary, and Reading Comprehension in the Urban Classroom." *Reading Teacher* 61 (2):134–144.

———. 2010. "Morphing into Adolescents: Active Word Learning for English-Language Learners and Their Classmates in Middle School." *Journal of Adolescent & Adult Literacy* 54 (1):47–56.

Krashen, S. 2004a. *The Power of Reading: Insights from the Research*. 2nd ed. Westport, CT: Libraries Unlimited.

———. 2004b. "The Route to Academic Language Proficiency." Available at http://www.conntesol.net/documents/Krashen%20CONNTESOL2012%20route%20to%20academic%20language.pdf.

Kucan, L., W. R. Trathen, W. J. Straits, D. Harsh, D. Link, L. Miller, and L. Pasley. 2007. "A Professional Development Initiative for Developing Approaches to Vocabulary Instruction with Secondary Mathematics, Art, Science, and English Teachers." *Reading Research and Instruction* 46 (2):175–195.

Landrigan, C., and T. Mulligan. 2013. *Assessment in Perspective: Focusing on the Reader Behind the Numbers*. Portland, ME: Stenhouse.

Lane, H. B., and S. A. Allen. 2010. "The Vocabulary-Rich Classroom: Modeling Sophisticated Word Use to Promote Word Consciousness and Vocabulary Growth." *The Reading Teaacher* 63 (5):362–370.

Leahy, S., C. Lyon, M. Thompson, and D. Wiliam. 2005. "Classroom Assessment: Minute by Minute, Day by Day." *Educational Leadership* 63 (3):19–24.

Lesaux, N. K., J. R. Harris, and P. Sloane. 2012. "Adolescents' Motivation in the Context of an Academic Vocabulary Intervention in Urban Middle School Classrooms." *Journal of Adolescent & Adult Literacy* 56 (3):231–240.

Lewin, L., and B. J. Shoemaker. 1998. *Great Performances: Creating Classroom-Based Assessment Tasks*. Alexandria, VA: Association for Supervision and Curriculum Development.

Lightsey, G. E., C. B. Orliff, and C. Cain. 2006. "Using Crossover Picture Books with Adolescent Learners." *Florida Literacy and Reading Excellence Professional Paper*. Orlando, FL: FLaRE.

Manzo, A. V., U. C. Manzo, and M. M. Thomas. 2006. "Rationale for Systematic Vocabulary Development: Antidote for State Mandates." *Journal of Adolescent & Adult Literacy* 49 (7):610–619.

Margosin, C. M., E. T. Pascarella, and S. W. Pflaum. 1982. "The Effects of Instruction Using Semantic Mapping on Vocabulary and Comprehension." *Journal of Early Adolescence* 2:185–194.

Marzano, R. J. 2004. *Building Background Knowledge for Academic Achievement: Research on What Works in Schools*. Alexandria, VA: Association for Supervision and Curriculum Development.

———. 2009. "The Art and Science of Teaching/Six Steps to Better Vocabulary Instruction." *Educational Leadership* 67 (1):83–84. Available at http://www.ascd.org/publications/educational-leadership/sept09/vol67/num01/Six-Steps-to-Better-Vocabulary-Instruction.aspx.

Marzano, R. J., D. Pickering, and J. E. Pollock. 2001. *Classroom Instruction That Works: Research-Based Strategies for Increasing Student Achievement*. Alexandria, VA: Association for Supervision and Curriculum Development.

Marzano, R. J., and J. A. Simms. 2013. *Vocabulary for the Common Core*. Denver, CO: Marzano Research Laboratory.

McKeown, M. G. 1993. "Creating Effective Definitions for Young Word Learners." *Reading Research Quarterly* 28:16–31.

McKeown, M. G., and I. L. Beck. 2004. "Direct and Rich Vocabulary Instruction." In *Vocabulary Instruction*, ed. J. F. Baumann and E. J. Kame'enui. New York: Guilford.

McKeown, M. G., I. L. Beck, R. C. Ormanson, and M. T. Pople. 1985. "Some Effects of the Nature and Frequency of Vocabulary Instruction on the Knowledge and Use of Words." *Reading Research Quarterly* 20:522–535.

McLauglin, M. 2015. *Inside the Common Core Classroom: Practical ELA Strategies, Grades 6–8*. Boston: Pearson.

McLaughlin, M., and M. B. Allen. 2009. *Guided Comprehension in Grades 3–8*. Newark, DE: International Literacy Association.

McLaughlin, M., and B. J. Overturf. 2013. *The Common Core: Teaching Students in Grades 6–12 to Meet the Reading Standards*. Newark, DE: International Literacy Association.

Miller, G., and P. Gildea. 1985. "How to Misread a Dictionary." *AILA Bulletin:*13–26.

Moats, L. C. 1999. *Teaching Reading Is Rocket Science: What Expert Teachers of Reading Should Know and Be Able to Do.* Washington, DC: American Federation of Teachers.

———. 2000. *From Speech to Print: Language Essentials for Teachers.* Baltimore: Paul H. Brookes.

Moen, C. B. 2007. "Bringing Words to Life and into the Lives of Middle School Students." *Voices from the Middle* 15 (1):20–26.

Moje, E. B., D. Stockdill, K. Kim, and H. Kim. 2011. "The Role of Text in Disciplinary Learning." In *Handbook of Reading Research, Vol. 4,* ed. M. L. Kamil, P. D. Pearson, E. B. Moje, and P. P. Afflerbach. New York: Routledge.

Moss, C. M., S. M. Brookhart, and B. A. Long. 2011. "Knowing Your Learning Target." *Educational Leadership* 68 (6):66–69.

Mountain, L. 2002. "Flip-a-Chip to Build Vocabulary." *Journal of Adolescent & Adult Literacy* 46 (1):62–68.

———. 2005. "ROOTing Out Meaning: More Morphemic Analysis for Primary Pupils." *The Reading Teacher* 58:742–749.

———. 2007. "Synonym Success—Thanks to the Thesaurus." *Journal of Adolescent & Adult Literacy* 51 (4):318–324.

Nagy, W., and D. Townsend. 2012. "Words as Tools: Learning Academic Vocabulary as Language Acquisition." *Reading Research Quarterly* 47 (1):91–108.

Nagy, W. E., and R. C. Anderson. 1984. "How Many Words Are There in Printed School English?" *Reading Research Quarterly* 19 (3):304–330.

Nagy, W. E., R. C. Anderson, and P. A. Herman. 1987. "Learning Word Meanings from Context During Normal Reading." *American Educational Research Journal* 24:237–270.

Nagy, W. E., and P. A. Herman. 1987. "Breadth and Depth of Vocabulary Knowledge: Implications for Acquisition and Instruction." In *The Nature of Vocabulary Acquisition*, ed. M. G. McKeown and M. E. Curtis, 19–55. Hillsdale, NJ: Erlbaum.

Nagy, W. E., and J. A. Scott. 1989. *Word Schemas: What Do People Know About Words They Don't Know?* Technical Report No. 456. Champaign: Center for the Study of Reading, University of Illinois at Urbana-Champaign.

———. 1990. "Word Schemas: Expectations About the Form and Meaning of New Words." *Cognition & Instruction* 7 (2):105–127.

———. 2000. "Vocabulary Processes." In *Handbook of Reading Research*, ed. M. L. Kamil et al. Mahwah, NJ: Erlbaum.

National Center for Education Statistics. 2012. *The Nation's Report Card: Vocabulary Results from the 2009 and 2011 NAEP Reading Assessments* (NCES 2013-452). Washington, DC: Institute of Education Sciences, U.S. Department of Education.

National Governors Association Center for Best Practices & Council of Chief State School Officers (NGA/CCSSO). 2010. *Common Core State Standards: English Language Arts and Literacy in History/Social Studies, Science, and Technical Subjects.* Washington, DC: National Governors Association Center for Best Practices & Council of Chief State School Officers. Available at http://www.corestandards.org/assets/CCSSI_ELA%20Standards.pdf.

National Institute of Child Health and Human Development. 2000. *Teaching Children to Read: An Evidence-Based Assessment of the Scientific Research Literature on Reading and Its Implications for Reading Instruction.* Report of the National Reading Panel. Washington, DC: National Institute of Child Health and Human Development. Available at http://www.nichd.nih.gov/publications/nrp/smallbook.cfm.

Nobori, M. 2012. "How the Arts Unlock the Door to Learning." *Edutopia.* August 29. Available at http://www.edutopia.org/stw-arts-integration-reform-overview.

Oczkus, L. 2009. *Interactive Think-Aloud Lessons: 25 Surefire Ways to Engage Students and Improve Comprehension.* New York: Scholastic.

Opitz, M. F., and M. P. Ford. 2014. "Engage Students (and Entertain Them a Little, Too!)." *Reading Today Online.* May 8.

Overturf, B. J. 2013. "Multiple Ways to Learn Words: The Keys to Vocabulary Development in the ELA Standards." *Reading Today* 31(2):14.

Overturf, B. J., L. H. Montgomery, and M. H. Smith. 2013. *Word Nerds: Teaching All Students to Learn and Love Vocabulary.* Portland, ME: Stenhouse.

Pearson, P. D., E. H. Hiebert, and M. L. Kamil. 2007. "Vocabulary Assessment: What We Know and What We Need to Learn." *Reading Research Quarterly* 42 (2):282–296.

Powell, W. R. 1986. "Teaching Vocabulary Through Opposition." *Journal of Reading* 29:617–621.

Pressley, M. 2008. "What the Future of Reading Research Could Be." In *Comprehension Instruction: Research-Based Best Practices.* 2nd ed., ed. C. C. Block and S. R. Parris. New York: Guilford Press.

Putman, S. M., and T. Kingsley. 2009. "The Atoms Family: Using Podcasts to Enhance the Development of Science Vocabulary." *Reading Teacher* 63 (2):100–108.

Rasinski, T. V., N. Padak, J. Newton, and E. Newton. 2011. "The Latin-Greek Connection: Building Vocabulary Through Morphological Study." *Reading Teacher* 65 (2):133–141.

Reinhart, J., and R. Martinez. 1996. "Teaching Mainstreamed Dyslexic Students." In *How to Become a Better Reading Teacher,* ed. L. Putnam. Englewood, NJ: Merrill.

Rieg, S. A., and K. R. Paquette. 2009. "Using Drama and Movement to Enhance English Language Learners' Literacy Development." *Journal of Instructional Psychology* 36 (2):148–154.

Roediger, H. L., and A. C. Butler. 2011. "The Critical Role of Retrieval Practice in Long-Term Retention." *Trends in Cognitive Sciences* 15 (1):20–27.

Roediger, H. L., and J. D. Karpicke. 2006. "The Power of Testing Memory: Basic Research and Implications for Educational Practice." *Perspectives on Psychological Science* 1:181–210.

Rowe, M. B. 1986. "Wait Time: Slowing Down May Be a Way of Speeding Up!" *Journal of Teacher Education* 37:43–50.

Ruddell, M. R., and B. A. Shearer. 2002. "'Extraordinary,' 'Tremendous,' 'Exhilarating,' 'Magnificent': Middle School At-Risk Students Become Avid Word Learners with the Vocabulary Self-Collection Strategy (VSS)." *Journal of Adolescent & Adult Literacy* 45:352–363.

Saunders, T. 2011. "Can Sitting Too Much Kill You?" *Scientific American*. January 6. Available at http://blogs.scientificamerican.comguest-blog/2011/01/06/can-sitting-too-much-kill-you/.

Schwartz, R. M., and T. E. Raphael. 1985. "Concept of Definition: A Key to Improving Students' Vocabulary." *Reading Teacher* 39 (2):198–205.

Scott, J. A., D. Jamieson-Noel, and M. Asselin. 2003. "Vocabulary Instruction Throughout the Day in Twenty-Three Canadian Upper-Elementary Classrooms." *Elementary School Journal* 103 (3):269–286.

Shanahan, T., and C. Shanahan. 2008. "Teaching Disciplinary Literacy to Adolescents: Rethinking Content-Area Literacy." *Harvard Educational Review* 78 (1):40–59.

Shanklin, N. 2007. "What This New Emphasis on Vocabulary All About?" *Voices from the Middle* 15 (1):52–53.

Short, K., G. Kauffman, and L. Kahn. 2000. "I Just *Need* to Draw: Responding to Literature Across Multiple Sign Systems." *Reading Teacher* 54 (2):160–171.

Snow, C. E., and P. Uccelli. 2009. "The Challenge of Academic Vocabulary." In *The Cambridge Handbook of Literacy*, ed. D. R. Olson and N. Torrance. New York: Cambridge University Press.

Stahl, K. A. D., and M. A. Bravo. 2010. "Contemporary Classroom Vocabulary Assessment for Content Areas." *Reading Teacher* 63 (7):566–578.

Stahl, S. A. 1999. *Vocabulary Development*. Cambridge, MA: Brookline Books.

———. 2003. "Words Are Leaned Incrementally Over Multiple Exposures." *American Educator* 27 (1): 18–19.

———. 2005. "Four Problems with Teaching Word Meanings (and What to Do to Make Vocabulary an Integral Part of Instruction)." In *Teaching and Learning Vocabulary: Bringing Research to Practice,* ed. E. H. Hiebert and M. L. Kamil. Mahwah, NJ: Erlbaum.

Stahl, S. A., and M. M. Fairbanks. 1986. "The Effects of Vocabulary Instruction: A Model-Based Meta-analysis." *Review of Educational Research* 56 (1):72–110.

Stahl, S. A. and W. E. Nagy. 2006. *Teaching Word Meanings*. Mahwah, NJ: Erlbaum.

Stahl, S. A., and S. J. Vancil. 1986. "Discussion Is What Makes Semantic Maps Work in Vocabulary Instruction." *Reading Teacher* 40 (1):62–67.

Stanovich, K. 1986. "Matthew Effects in Reading: Some Consequences of Individual Differences in the Acquisition of Literacy." *Reading Research Quarterly* 21:360–401.

Steinburgh, J. 1999. "Mastering Metaphor Through Poetry." *Language Arts* 76 (4):324–331.

Sternberg, R. J. 1987. "Most Vocabulary Is Learned from Context." In *The Nature of Vocabulary Acquisition*, ed. M. G. McKeown and M. E. Curtis, 89–105. Hillsdale, NJ: Erlbaum.

Swanborn, M. S. L., and K. de Glopper. 1999. "Incidental Word Learning While Reading: A Meta-analysis." *Review of Educational Research* 56:72–110.

Templeton, S., D. R. Bear, M. Invernizzi, and F. Johnson. 2010. *Vocabulary Their Way: Word Study with Middle and Secondary Students*. Boston: Pearson.

Tharp, R. G., and R. Gallimore. 1988. "Rousing Schools to Life." *American Educator* 13 (2):20–25, 46–52.

———. 1991. *The Instructional Conversation: Teaching and Learning in Social Activity*. Research Report 2. Santa Cruz, CA: National Center for Research on Cultural Diversity and Second Language Learning.

Thompson, T. 2008. *Adventures in Graphica: Using Comics and Graphic Novels to Teach Comprehension, Grades 2–6*. Portland, ME: Stenhouse.

Vega, V. 2012. "A Research-Based Approach to Arts Integration." *Edutopia*. August 20. Available at http://www.edutopia.org/stw-arts-integration-research.

Wadlington, E. 2000. "Effective Language Arts Instruction for Students with Dyslexia." *Preventing School Failure* 44 (2):61–65.

Wallace, W. 1994. "Memory for Music: Effect of Melody on Recall of Text." *Journal of Experimental Psychology: Learning, Memory, and Cognition* 20 (6):1471–1485.

Watts, S. M. 1995. "Vocabulary Instruction During Reading Lessons in Six Classrooms." *Journal of Reading Behavior* 27 (3):399–424.

Wilhelm, J. 1997. *"You Gotta BE the Book": Teaching Engaged and Reflective Reading with Adolescents.* New York: Teachers College Press.

———. 2002. *Action Strategies for Deepening Comprehension: Role Plays, Text-Structure Tableaux, Talking Statues, and Other Enactment Techniques That Engage Students with Text.* New York: Scholastic.

———. 2004. *Reading IS Seeing: Learning to Visualize Scenes, Characters, Ideas, and Text Worlds to Improve Comprehension and Reflective Reading.* New York: Scholastic.

Winters, R. 2009. "Interactive Frames for Vocabulary Growth and Word Consciousness." *Reading Teacher* 62 (8):682–690.

Wood, K. D., and N. Robinson. 1983. "Vocabulary, Language, and Prediction: A Prereading Strategy." *Reading Teacher* 36 (4):392–495.

Yates, P. H., K. Cuthrell, and M. Rose. 2011. "Out of the Room and into the Hall: Making Content Word Walls Work." *Clearing House: A Journal of Educational Strategies, Issues, and Ideas* 84:31–36.

Yopp, R. H. 2007. "Word Links: A Strategy for Developing Word Knowledge." *Voices from the Middle* 15 (1):27–33.

Zwiers, J., and M. Crawford. 2011. *Academic Conversations: Classroom Talk That Fosters Critical Thinking and Content Understandings.* Portland, ME: Stenhouse.

INDEX

A

academic conversations, 39–40, 91. *See also* conversations

academic vocabulary

Common Core State Standards (CCSS) and, 28–29

English language arts, 25–26

math, 22–23

overview, 21

science, 22, 23–24

selecting words to teach and, 36

social studies, 22, 24–25

acronyms, 105

acrostic poems, 135–136, 135*f*

active learning. *See also* learning

middle grades and, 32

mini-lessons and, 43

overview, 117

adapted Frayer model

Dramatizing Words activity and, 123

form for, 176

overview, 112–113, 113*f*

Afflerbach, Peter, 145

Allen, Mary Beth, 92, 126

alliteration, 105–106

allusion, 106

analogies

overview, 101–104, 103*f*

types of, 103*f*

vocabulary assessment rubric, 147*f*–148*f*

analyzing student work, 145

Anders, Patricia, 94

Anderson, Richard, 34

antonyms

adding to word networks, 95–96

as a context clue, 60

formative assessments, 155–157, 155*f*, 156*f*

overview, 38

reference material and, 96–97, 97*f*

semantic gradients and, 98–99, 98*f*, 99*f*

vocabulary assessment rubric, 147*f*–148*f*

vocabulary journals and, 113, 113*f*, 114*f*, 115

word learning and, 16

art focus, 118–122, 119*f*, 121*f*

assessment

context and, 55, 58–59

formative assessments, 33, 143–146, 147*f*–148*f*

integrated vocabulary quizzes, 151–154, 152*f*, 153*f*

middle grades and, 31–33

overview, 13, 141–143, 161–162, 169*f*

professional learning communities (PLCs), 154–157, 155*f*, 156*f*

resources for, 170

summative assessment, 55, 58–59, 144, 148–150
vocabulary assessment systems, 150–161, 152f, 153f, 155f, 156f, 157f, 159f
Assessment in Perspective (Landrigan and Mulligan), 144
Association for Middle Level Education (AMLE), 31–33
assonance, 106
Atwell, Nancie, 42

B

Baader-Meinhof phenomenon, 7
background knowledge
academic vocabulary and, 22
instructional conversations and, 18
word learning and, 16
Baloney (Henry P.) (Scieszka and Smith), 61–62
Barton, Mary Lee, 23
Bean, Rita, 142
Beck, Isabel, 24–25, 56, 90
Be the Bard activity, 87
Bhalla, Jag, 108–109
Blachowicz, Camille, 16, 23, 24–25, 95
Bolton, Christie, 120
Bos, Candace, 94
Bowman Academy. *See* Thea Bowman Leadership Academy
Bransford, John, 53
Brenston, Gabrielle, 25–26
Bringing Words to Life (Beck, McKeown, and Kucan), 13, 56, 170
Buehl, Doug, 23, 24
Bullitt Lick Middle School, 49–50, 50f

C

Calipari, John, 99
Callahan, Mary, 76
Carlisle, Susan, 66–67, 97, 121–122, 157

Casale, Ula, 124–125
Center for Research on Education, Diversity, and Excellence (CREDE), 17–18
Chain Link game, 133
Cho, Sun-Joo, 74
Circles of Knowledge, 56–58
close reading, 81–82
cloze sentences
formative assessments, 151, 154
integrated vocabulary quizzes and, 151
introducing new words for a deep study and, 62–63, 68, 68f
code switching, 20–21
cognitive strategies, 73
Colbert, Stephen, 99
comic books, 42
Common Core State Standards (CCSS)
context and, 54–55
morphological awareness and, 74
summative assessment and, 149–150
vocabulary development and, 26–29
word parts, 78
communication, 39–40. *See also* conversations; discussion
complexity of text, 56
comprehension
academic vocabulary and, 21, 25–26
Common Core State Standards (CCSS) and, 28–29
formative assessments and, 158
morphological awareness and, 81–84, 82f
wide reading and, 42
concept development, 20–22
concept of definition map, 16, 92–94, 93f, 174
concepts, 90–95, 91f, 92f, 93f, 95f
concept word walls, 38–39
confidence of students
Circles of Knowledge and, 57

morphological awareness and, 87–88
connections
    fast mapping and, 39
    morphological awareness and, 78, 81
    overview, 19–20
    rich conversations and, 17–18
connotation, 99–101, 149
consonance, 106
content-area instruction. *See also*
    instructional practices
    academic vocabulary and, 21–22
    buy-in from teachers, 165
    concept word walls and, 38–39
    English language arts, 25–26
    Illustrated Vocabulary activity, 121
    integrated vocabulary quizzes, 151–154,
        152*f*, 153*f*
    integrated vocabulary study, 50–51
    math, 22–23
    overview, 168, 169*f*
    science, 22, 23–24
    social studies, 22, 24–25
    team-based vocabulary approach and,
        46–47
    at Thea Bowman Leadership Academy,
        46–47
context
    Baloney (Henry P.) (Scieszka and Smith)
        and, 61–62
    Circles of Knowledge, 56–58
    Common Core State Standards (CCSS)
        and, 54–55
    importance of, 55–56
    introducing new words, 12, 62–69, 64*f*,
        65*f*, 68*f*
    levels of words, 14
    overview, 53–54, 69
    patterns and networks of meaning and,
        16
    practicing with a picture book, 61–62

strategic vocabulary instruction model
    and, 12
summative assessment and, 149
types of context clues, 58–61
use of to infer meaning, 26, 27
vocabulary assessment rubric, 147*f*–148*f*
contextual analysis, 58–61
contrast, 60
conversational scaffold, 38–39. *See also*
    scaffolding
conversations. *See also* discussion
    academic conversations, 39–40
    connecting word learning to students'
        lives, 19–20
    word learning and, 17–18
Cox, Julie, 164–165
Crawford, Marie, 39
critical thinking, 166–167
crossword puzzles, 134–135
Crystal Ball Words graphic organizer,
    84–85, 85*f*, 173
Culver, Maurice, 24
curriculum. *See also* content-area
    instruction
    introducing words within, 67–69, 68*f*
    middle grades and, 31–33
    morphological awareness and, 78, 81
    overview, 169*f*
    using an ELA published program,
        49–50, 50*f*
Currie, Stephen, 24, 64–65, 83–84, 153–
    154

D

Dagen, Allison Swan, 142
decoding, 57
deep study
    context and, 56
    introducing new words for, 62–69, 64*f*,
        65*f*, 68*f*

multisyllabic words and, 13
selecting words to teach, 34–37
Definition Depictions activity, 122
definitions
concept of, 16, 92–94, 93*f*
connotation and denotation and, 100
as a context clue, 59
ineffectiveness of in learning new words, 14–15
overview, 89–90
word maps and, 91–92, 91*f*, 92*f*
denotation, 99–101
derivational endings, 77, 149. *See also* suffixes; word parts
dictionary use, 14–15
direct instruction, 16–17. *See also* instructional practices
discussion. *See also* conversations
academic conversations, 39–40
formative assessments and, 160
word learning and, 17
domain-specific vocabulary. *See* academic vocabulary
dramatic expression, 122–125, 125*f*
Dramatizing Words activity, 123

E

Eastside Middle School, 47–48
Echols, Tabi, 3, 48, 154, 156, 157, 164
Einstein, Albert, 101
Ellery, Valerie, 81
emotional expression, 32
English language arts. *See also* content-area instruction
Common Core State Standards (CCSS), 26–29
introducing new words for a deep study and, 66–67
overview, 169*f*
selecting words to teach and, 36

using an ELA published program, 49–50, 50*f*
vocabulary development and, 47–48
vocabulary development in, 22, 25–26
eponyms, 106
etymology, 78, 81
examples, 59
Explore-a-Root activity, 81
exposures to new words, 14. *See also* introducing new words
extended mapping, 39
Extraordinary Mark Twain, The (According to Susy) (Kerley), 41

F

Fairbanks, Marilyn M., 16
fast mapping, 39
figurative language
Common Core State Standards (CCSS) and, 28
deeper vocabulary learning with, 104–105
interpreting, 109–110, 110*f*
overview, 105–108
vocabulary assessment rubric, 147*f*–148*f*
Fisher, Doug, 40, 95, 150
Fisher, Peter, 16
Flanigan, Kevin, 24–25, 39
Flip-a-Chip activity, 86–87
Ford, Michael, 117
formative assessments. *See also* assessment
integrated vocabulary quizzes, 151–154, 152*f*, 153*f*
middle grades and, 33
overview, 143–146, 147*f*–148*f*
professional learning communities (PLCs), 154–157, 155*f*, 156*f*
vocabulary assessment systems, 150–161, 152*f*, 153*f*, 156*f*, 157*f*, 159*f*
Frayer model, adapted

Dramatizing Words activity and, 123
form for, 176
overview, 112–113, 113*f*
Free Rice website, 136
frequency illusion, 7
Frey, Nancy, 40, 150
Fuhrken, Charles, 149

G

games, 127–134, 128*f*, 130*f*, 131*f*, 132*f*
Geddes, Jennifer, 56, 67, 129, 134, 157, 161
general academic vocabulary. *See* academic vocabulary
Gilbert, Jennifer, 74
Goodwin, Amanda, 74
grammar, 60–61
graphic novels, 42
graphic organizers, 112–115, 113*f*, 114*f*
Graves, Michael, 11–12, 11*f*, 21, 26–27, 55–56, 58
Greek roots, 74, 78, 87. *See also* root words
Greenwood, Scott, 39
Guess My Word game, 130–131, 131*f*

H

Harris, Sydney J., 90
Hart, Betty, 10
Heidema, Clare, 23
Helman, Lori, 23
history. *See* social studies
history of the English language, 73–74
Hollandsworth, Don, 89–90, 123, 135
home environment/situation, 167
homographs, 106–107
homophones, 107
Hooray for Diffendoofer Day! (Seuss), 141
Hot Seat game, 128–129, 128*f*
hyperbole, 107

I

idioms, 108–109, 147*f*–148*f*
Illustrated Vocabulary activity, 120–122, 121*f*
illustrations, 59
individual word instruction, 11–12, 11*f*. *See also* instructional practices
inference
  connotation and, 100
  context and, 53, 56, 60
inflectional suffixes, 76–77. *See also* suffixes
informal assessment. *See* assessment; formative assessments
initiate-respond-evaluate (IRE) discourse form, 145
instructional conversation, 18
instructional practices. *See also* content-area instruction; vocabulary instruction; word learning
  art focus, 118–122, 119*f*, 121*f*
  challenges and, 167
  dramatic expression, 122–125, 125*f*
  games and, 127–134, 128*f*, 130*f*, 131*f*, 132*f*
  integrated vocabulary study, 50–51
  with media and technology, 136–139, 137*f*
  middle grades and, 31–33
  morphological awareness and, 73
  music activities, 125–127
  with poems, puzzles, and writing, 134–136, 135*f*
  resources for, 170
  thinking processes and, 166–167
integrated vocabulary quizzes, 151–154, 152*f*, 153*f*
integrated vocabulary study, 50–51, 117, 168, 169*f*
intentional word play, 44–45
interdisciplinary team. *See also* content-area instruction

integrated vocabulary quizzes, 151–154, 152*f*, 153*f*
introducing new words for a deep study and, 63–66, 64*f*, 65*f*
overview, 168, 169*f*
at Thea Bowman Leadership Academy, 46–47
vocabulary development across, 45–46
International Literacy Association, 170
interpreting, 147*f*–148*f*
introducing new words. *See also*
  instructional practices; words to teach
  connecting word learning to students' lives, 19–20
  context and, 62–69, 64*f*, 65*f*, 68*f*
  within an existing literacy curriculum, 67–69, 68*f*
  levels of words, 13–14, 35–37
  overview, 12–13, 169*f*
  repeated exposures and, 14
irony, 107

J

"Jabberwocky" (Carroll), 60–61, 107
Johnson, Marcia, 53
Jordan, Deborah, 23
journals
  form for, 177–178
  overview, 112–115, 113*f*, 114*f*
  vocabulary exploration and, 13
"just right" words, 37. *See also* selecting words to teach

K

Kelley, Joan, 34
Kieffer, Michael, 72–73
Krashen, Stephen, 42
Kucan, Linda, 56, 90
Kuprenas, Robert, 39, 42–43, 94, 123

L

Landrigan, Clare, 144
language arts. *See* English language arts
language experiences, 11–12, 11*f*
language heritage, 73–74
Latin roots, 74, 78, 87. *See also* root words
Leahy, Siobhan, 143
learning, 32
Leonardo (Byrd), 41
Lesaux, Nonie, 72–73
levels of words, 13–14, 35–37
Lyon, Christine, 143
Lyric Definitions activity, 126–127

M

Macintyre, Ben, 62
manga, 42
Marshall, Alfred, 69
Marzano, Robert, 16–17, 19, 36, 166
math, 22–23. *See also* content-area instruction
Math Curse (Scieszka and Smith), 41
Matthew effect, 9
McIntyre, Dr. Ellen, 53
McKeown, Margaret, 24–25, 56, 90
McLaughlin, Maureen, 92, 126
media use, 136–139, 137*f*. *See also* technology
metacognitive understanding, 16
metaphor, 107, 147*f*–148*f*, 166
metonymy, 107
middle grades
  overview, 3–7, 31–34, 117–118
  strategic vocabulary instruction model and, 12–13
  vocabulary development and, 10–11
mini-lessons, 42–43, 43*f*
Moats, Louisa, 76–77, 95
Moje, Elizabeth, 23
Montgomery, Leslie, 2–3, 33, 71, 133, 146

morphemes, 75. *See also* morphological awareness

Morpheme Triangles activity, 85–86

morphemic analysis, 75, 84–87, 85*f. See also* morphological awareness

morphological awareness. *See also* word parts
- developing, 75
- history of the English language and, 73–74
- making connections and, 78, 81
- overview, 71–73, 87–88
- prefixes, 75–76
- scaffolding, 81–84, 82*f*
- suffixes, 76–78, 77*f*
- teaching, 13, 84–87, 85*f*
- word-learning strategies, 18–19

motor imagery technique, 124–125, 125*f*

Muench, Karen, 19–20

Mulligan, Tammy, 144

multiple meanings of a word
- reference material and, 96–97, 97*f*
- selecting words to teach and, 35

multisyllabic words
- morphological awareness and, 13, 75
- root words and, 78
- use of word parts to infer meaning, 26–27
- word-learning strategies, 19

music activities, 125–127

N

Nagy, William, 15–16, 34, 95

National Assessment of Educational Progress (NAEP), 9–10, 55

National Center for Education Statistics (NCES), 9–10, 55

National Council of English/Language Arts, 170

networks of meaning, 15–16

O

observation in formative assessments, 144

Oczkus, Lori, 133

Odom, Brandi, 39–40, 56–58, 66, 122, 161–162

onomatopoeia, 107

Opitz, Michael, 117

organizational approaches, 45–47, 48

P

pantomime, 124–125, 125*f*

Partnership for Assessment of Readiness for College and Careers (PARCC), 149–150

patterns, 15–16

Paulsen, Gary, 150

peer assessment, 33. *See also* assessment

personification, 107

phrases, 104–105, 108–109

picture books, 40–41, 61–62

Pink and Say (Polacco), 41

poems, 134–136, 135*f*

portmanteau, 107

practice opportunities
- art focus, 118–122, 119*f*, 121*f*
- dramatic expression, 122–125, 125*f*
- games and, 127–134, 128*f*, 130*f*, 131*f*, 132*f*
- music activities, 125–127
- overview, 13, 117–118, 169*f*

prefixes. *See also* morphological awareness; word parts
- context and, 54
- list of common prefixes, 79*f*
- overview, 72, 75–76
- summative assessment and, 149
- teaching morphemic analysis, 84–87, 85*f*
- vocabulary assessment rubric, 147*f*–148*f*
- word learning and, 16

prereading, 94–95, 95*f*

presentations, 138–139. *See also* technology

Prezi presentation, 138–139
Priddy, Trish, 58, 66, 96, 98–99, 130–131
productive-oral vocabulary, 21
productive vocabulary, 21
productive-written vocabulary, 21
professional learning communities (PLCs)
    formative assessments and, 154–157,
      155f, 156f
    introducing new words for a deep study
      and, 66–67
    overview, 3, 48
punctuation, 60–61
puns, 111
purposeful learning, 32. *See also* learning
puzzles, 134–136, 135f

Q

QR codes, 139
quantity of vocabulary words, 164–165.
    See also words to teach

R

Raphael, Taffy, 92
Rasinski, Tim, 74
read-alouds, 40–41
ReadWriteThink website, 26, 76, 81, 170
receptive vocabulary, 21
reference material
    use of, 27–28, 96–97, 97f
    verbal analogies and, 104
    vocabulary assessment rubric, 147f–148f
repeated exposures to new words, 14
resources, 170
restatement, 59–60
retrieval practice, 127. *See also* practice
    opportunities
"Richard Cory" (Robinson), 100
rich conversations, 17–18. *See also*
    conversations
riddles, 112

Risley, Todd, 10
Roccaforte, Michael, 22–23, 91–92, 151
root words. *See also* morphological
    awareness; word parts
    context and, 54
    history of the English language and, 74
    list of common root words, 79f–80f
    overview, 72, 78
    summative assessment and, 149
    teaching morphemic analysis, 84–87,
      85f
    vocabulary assessment rubric, 147f–148f
    word learning and, 16
Rosenbloom, Jennifer, 81
routine, 33
rubrics, 146, 147f–148f

S

scaffolding
    concept word walls and, 38–39
    morphological awareness, 81–84, 82f
Scattergories game, 129
schema, word
    context and, 56
    overview, 15–16
    Word Schema (CCSS Language
      Standard 5), 28
Schwartz, Robert, 92
science, 22, 23–24. *See also* content-area
    instruction
Science Verse (Scieszka and Smith), 41
Scott, Judith, 15–16
selecting words to teach
    at Bullitt Lick Middle School, 49–50
    deep study and, 34–37
    at Eastside Middle School, 48
    levels of words, 13–14, 35–37
    overview, 12–13
    quantity of vocabulary words to teach,
      164–165

at Thea Bowman Leadership Academy, 47
self-assessment, 33. *See also* assessment
semantic feature analysis, 94–95, 95*f*, 175
semantic gradients, 98–99, 98*f*, 99*f*
semantic mapping, 90–91, 91–92, 91*f*, 92*f*
Shakespeare, William, 87
simile, 107, 147*f*–148*f*
Simms, Julia, 36
Sir Cumference and the First Round Table (Neuschwander), 41
Smack Down words, 50, 137–138, 137*f*
small-group work, 100–101
Smarter Balanced Assessment Consortium (SBAC), 150
Smith, Margo Holmes, 2–3, 33, 125–126, 146
social studies, 22, 24–25. *See also* content-area instruction
Stahl, Steven, 7, 16, 34, 90, 95
Stakes, Robert, 144
standardized assessment, 55, 58–59, 148–150. *See also* assessment
Starry Messenger (Sis), 41
strategic vocabulary instruction model, 11–13, 11*f*. *See also* vocabulary instruction
structural analysis, 75. *See also* morphological awareness
student-generated questions, 146
student-made crossword puzzles, 134–135
student response systems, 137–138, 137*f*
students, 6–7, 57, 87–88, 166–167
student work, 145
suffixes. *See also* morphological awareness; word parts
context and, 54
list of common suffixes, 80*f*
overview, 72, 76–78, 77*f*
summative assessment and, 149
teaching morphemic analysis, 84–87, 85*f*

vocabulary assessment rubric, 147*f*–148*f*
word learning and, 16
Suffix Web, 77–78
summative assessment, 55, 58–59, 144, 148–150. *See also* assessment
synecdoche, 107
synonyms
adding to word networks, 95–96
as a context clue, 59–60
formative assessments, 155–157, 155*f*, 156*f*
overview, 38
reference material and, 96–97, 97*f*
semantic gradients and, 98–99, 98*f*, 99*f*
vocabulary assessment rubric, 147*f*–148*f*
vocabulary journals and, 113, 113*f*, 114*f*, 115
word learning and, 16
syntax knowledge, 16

T

tableaux, 124
Taffe, Susan Watts, 95
teacher questioning, 145–146
teachers
buy-in from, 165
middle grades and, 31–33
selecting words to teach and, 34–35
team-based vocabulary approach and, 46–47
Teaching Academic Vocabulary K–8 (Blachowicz, Fisher, Ogle, and Taffe), 170
Teaching Children to Read (National Institute of Child Health and Human Development), 10–11
team-based vocabulary approach. *See also* content-area instruction; interdisciplinary team
integrated vocabulary quizzes, 151–154, 152*f*, 153*f*

overview, 168, 169f

at Thea Bowman Leadership Academy, 46–47

technology

formative assessments and, 158, 160

overview, 137f

reference material and, 96–97, 97f

Templeton, Shane, 81

testing effect, 127

test-taking skills, 143, 149–150. *See also* assessment

text analysis, 81–82

text complexity, 56

Thea Bowman Leadership Academy, 45–46, 46–47

thick vocabulary instruction, 20

think-alouds, 73

thinking processes, 166–167

This Is to That—A Pop Culture Analogy Game app, 104, 136

Thompson, Kim, 69, 96

Thompson, Marnie, 143

Tier 1 words, 13–14, 35–36

Tier 2 words

Eastside Middle School and, 48

"just right" words and, 37

overview, 13–14

selecting words to teach and, 36

Thea Bowman Leadership Academy and, 47

Tier 3 words

"just right" words and, 37

overview, 13–14

selecting words to teach and, 36

Thea Bowman Leadership Academy and, 47

TP-CASTT (title, paraphrase, connotation, attitude/tone, shifts, title revisited, and theme) template, 26

V

verbal analogies, 101–104, 103f. *See also* analogies

verbal irony, 107

visual representations, 90–95, 91f, 92f, 93f, 95f

Vocab Scattergories game, 129

vocabulary assessment rubric, 146, 147f–148f

Vocabulary Celebrations game, 134

vocabulary development

Common Core State Standards (CCSS), 26–29

as concept development, 20–22

English language arts, 25–26

within an English language arts department, 47–48

math, 22–23

in the middle grades, 3–7, 10–11

organizational approaches, 45–47

overview, 9–10, 29, 163–164

science, 22, 23–24

social studies, 22, 24–25

using an ELA published program, 49–50, 50f

vocabulary explorations

overview, 13, 169f

visual representations of words and concepts, 90–95, 91f, 92f, 93f, 95f

vocabulary instruction. *See also* instructional practices; strategic vocabulary instruction model; word learning

English language arts, 25–26

framework for, 11f

importance of, 20

math and, 22–23

middle grades and, 12–13

science, 23–24

social studies, 24–25

vocabulary journals. *See* journals
vocabulary learning targets, 157–161, 157*f*, 159*f*
vocabulary plan, 2–3
Vocabulary Practice: Greek and Latin Root Words Vocabulary Game app, 137
Vocabulary Rap activity, 125–126
Vocabulary Rock and Roll game, 130, 130*f*
vocabulary tableaux activity, 124
Vocabulary Their Way (Templeton et al.), 78, 86

W

Weddle, Tonie, 3–4, 19–20, 29, 44, 49–50, 67–69, 76, 81–83, 102, 104, 113–114, 126, 128–129, 130, 132, 137–138, 145, 157–158, 160–161, 163–164, 165
Weslandia (Fleischman), 40–41
What Every Middle School Teacher Needs to Know About Reading Tests (Fuhrken), 149
"What's the Word?" game, 63–66, 64*f*, 65*f*, 136
When Kids Can't Read (Beers), 170
wide reading, 17, 41–42, 56
Wilhelm, Jeff, 124
Wiliam, Dylan, 143
Williams, Charles, 46, 47, 58, 63–64, 151–154, 165, 167
William Shakespeare's Macbeth (Coville), 41
word building, 86–87
Word Colors activity, 118–120, 119*f*
word consciousness
    developing, 18
    overview, 37–45, 163–164
    strategic vocabulary instruction model and, 11–12, 11*f*
Word Illustrations activity, 120–122, 121*f*
word knowledge, 13–14
word learning. *See also* vocabulary instruction

connecting to students' lives, 19–20
developing word consciousness and, 18
direct instruction and, 16–17
patterns and networks of meaning and, 15–16
rich conversations, 17–18
strategic vocabulary instruction model and, 11–12, 11*f*
teaching students to use, 18–19
wide reading, 17
Word-Learning Strategies (CCSS Language Standard 4), 26–28
Word Links game, 133
word maps, 91–92, 91*f*, 92*f*
word meanings, 28
Word Nerds (Overturf, Montgomery, and Smith), 2–4, 16, 33, 38, 46, 62, 66, 84–85, 85*f*, 96, 112, 113, 115, 117, 120, 125, 130, 133, 144, 154, 164, 170
word networks, 95–96
"Word of the Day," 44, 44*f*
word parts. *See also* morphological awareness; prefixes; root words; suffixes
    as a context clue, 61
    overview, 71–72, 87–88
    scaffolding, 81–84, 82*f*
    summative assessment and, 149
    teaching morphemic analysis, 84–87, 85*f*
    use of to infer meaning, 26–27
word play, 44–45, 110–112, 169*f*
word relationships, 28, 147*f*–148*f*
words
    connotation and denotation, 99–101
    figurative language, 104–110, 110*f*
    idioms, 108–109
    overview, 89–90, 115
    reference material and, 96–97, 97*f*
    semantic gradients and, 98–99, 98*f*, 99*f*
    vague phrases, 108–109
    verbal analogies, 101–104, 103*f*

visual representations of, 90–95, 91*f*,
  92*f*, 93*f*, 95*f*
  vocabulary assessment rubric, 147*f*–148*f*
  vocabulary journals and, 112–115, 113*f*,
  114*f*
Words, Words, Words (Allen), 170
word schema, 15–16
Word Schema (CCSS Language Standard
  5), 28
Words Their Way (Bear et al.), 86
words to teach
  at Bullitt Lick Middle School, 49–50
  deep study and, 34–37
  at Eastside Middle School, 48
  levels of words, 13–14
  overview, 12–13
  quantity of vocabulary words to teach,
    164–165
  at Thea Bowman Leadership Academy,
    47
Words to Teach (CCSS Language Standard
  6), 28–29
word study cycle, 2–3, 168, 169*f*
word walls, 38–39
Word Widgets game, 131–132, 132*f*
Word Wise and Content Rich, Grades 7–12
  (Fisher and Frey), 170
writing-based vocabulary activities, 134–
  136, 135*f*

Y

Yopp, Ruth Helen, 133

Z

Zwiers, Jeff, 39